TRAUMA, FEAR
AND LOVE

Green Balloon Publishing

Professor Dr Franz Ruppert is Professor of Psychology at the University of Applied Sciences in Munich, Germany. He gained his PhD in Work and Organisational Psychology at the Technical University of Munich in 1985.

Since 1995 he has specialised in psychotherapeutic work, with a particular focus on the aetiology of severe mental disorders. This has led him to an in depth study of attachment processes and the impact of traumatisation on these early issues. Through this exploration Ruppert developed his theory of Multi-Generational Psycho-Traumatology.

Along with this Professor Ruppert has developed the methodology of the Constellation of the Intention as an effective means of working towards resolving traumatic experiences.

His publications include: *Verwirrte Seelen* (2002, Kösel, Munich), (*Confused Souls*, not available in English), followed by three books translated from German into English: *Trauma, Bonding & Family Constellations: Understanding and Healing Injuries of the Soul* (2008), *Splits in the Soul: Integrating Traumatic Experiences* (2011), *Symbiosis & Autonomy: Symbiotic Trauma and Love Beyond Entanglements* (2012), all published in English by Green Balloon Publishing, UK.

Ruppert facilitates workshops in Germany and many other countries including Brazil, Canada, Britain, Ireland, Italy, Russia, Netherlands, Poland, Portugal, Romania, Turkey and Spain, furthering his insights into the deeper transgenerational effects of trauma in different cultures, and researching the methodology of constellations as a means of better understanding the effects and healing of trauma.

About this Book

This, the fourth book by Professor Franz Ruppert to be translated into English, continues his exploration of the impact of trauma on humans. Following on from the previous three books, and building on his previous developments, this book explores three important aspects of trauma: the first part of the book explores the psychosomatic system, the mind and body, its basic functioning, purpose and structure, how our psyche, senses and perceptions develop, and how our experiences as we grow up affect how we perceive our world, in some circumstances such as traumatisation, distorting our perception. Ruppert looks at the 'healthy' psyche as a means to understanding these disorders and distortions.

The second aspect of this book builds on Ruppert's previous ideas about traumatisation as the underlying cause of disturbance and disorder to the functioning of the psyche, in particular delving into the complex dynamics of victimisation, the perpetrator/victim dynamics.

The third focus of this book is the methodology of the Constellation of the Intention, the means by which psychotherapists and clients can work to resolve traumatic experiences, which is followed by many intriguing and illuminating case examples using the Constellation of the Intention.

In the final section, Ruppert looks at the issue of how we can interrupt the processes of traumatisation, and become psychologically healthy, what this means and how best we can secure healthy relationships for ourselves and our society.

Other books by the author published in English by Green Balloon Publishing:
Trauma, Bonding and Family Constellations: Understanding and Healing Injuries of the Soul (2008)
Splits in the Soul: Integrating Traumatic Experiences (2011)
Symbiosis and Autonomy: Symbiotic Trauma and Love Beyond Entanglements (2012)
(Above titles originally published in German by Klett-Cotta, Stuttgart www.klett-cotta.de)

TRAUMA, FEAR
AND LOVE

How the Constellation of the
Intention Supports Healthy Autonomy

Franz Ruppert

Translated by Julia Stuebs
with the assistance of Rick Hosburn

Edited by Vivian Broughton

Green Balloon Publishing

First published in the United Kingdom in 2014
by Green Balloon Publishing

German edition first published under the title *Trauma Angst und Liebe*
by Kösel-Verlag, Verlagsgruppe Random House

Green Balloon Publishing
Steyning, West Sussex BN44 3GF
www.greenballoonbooks.co.uk

ISBN 978-0-9559683-6-5

Book production by The Choir Press, Gloucester
Set in Times

Contents

Preface

For the proposed fifth edition of my book *Confused Souls* (Verwirrte Seelen) the publishers kindly gave me the opportunity to rewrite the text. However, after several attempts I realised that this was not possible. There had been too many changes in my theoretical approach, and in my practical work in the ten or more years since the first edition of this book in 2002.

The most obvious course of action was, rather than trying to improve *Confused Souls* by making additions and corrections, to allow the book instead to take its rightful place in the history of how my work has developed in general. *Confused Souls* expresses my insights as well as my errors between 1994 and 2002. This book is still of use, however, in pointing out that even the most severe psychological illnesses such as the diagnoses of 'psychosis' or 'schizophrenia', can be explained consistently with the concept of a psychotraumatology across generations, and can be treated effectively with therapy. Multi-Generational Psychotraumatology is an alternative theoretical explanation and a new psychotherapeutic method of treatment for psychological illnesses. Within the psychiatric field, it takes a clear stand against therapies based purely on medication.

This current book, therefore, follows on from many insights that I first published in *Confused Souls*. It compresses them, but also corrects them where necessary. It illustrates the present context of my experience and understanding. My

premise is still that trauma is the main cause of human psychological and physical health problems. My practical work has
also allowed me to recognise clearly how the energy and
content of traumas are passed from one generation to another
through the mother-child bonding. A child's psyche literally
soaks up the traumas of previous generations.

The theoretical concept that attempts to define these
circumstances is *'symbiotic trauma'*. Arising from symbiotic
trauma are the various forms of *'symbiotic entanglement,'*
which in turn give rise to the whole spectrum of psychological
abnormalities and 'illnesses'.

I have now started to replace the word 'soul', which can
cause confusion – particularly in English-speaking countries
through its religious/spiritual connotations – with the less
ambiguous definition of 'psyche' as psychological processes.
The concept of 'psyche' represented here is also helpful in
more precisely defining the term psychological trauma. A
trauma is an event which causes the psyche to block unbearable
reality from consciousness, instead of maintaining connection
to the reality. Furthermore, when defining the concept of
trauma, I now also focus on the phenomenon of the splitting of
the personality into three distinct parts after the trauma.

With the theory of symbiotic trauma, multi-generational
psychotraumatology touches a deep social taboo. *Mothers'
traumas* are seen as one of the main causes of psychological
disorders in their children. From this viewpoint, therapeutic
work with patients and clients has taken on a clear focus: it is
not about the resolution of entanglements within a family, or
finding some reconciliation with the parents, but about the
practical and psychological detachment from the traumatised
parents, and a withdrawal from symbiotic entanglements within
a familial system. It is about the integration of the parts of the
individual's personality that have been split off by a symbiotic
trauma, and all the other traumas connected with it. The basic
aim of the therapy is to support the healthy part of the individual, thereby supporting his ability to exercise autonomy and
self-responsibility in his life. In order to achieve such

autonomy, it is essential for the individual to leave behind him the world of symbiotic illusions and all other survival strategies that have been employed. These strategies prevent contact with the reality of the trauma, and interfere with the individual's ability to access his feelings of compassion towards himself, thereby blocking his connection to himself and his environment. Externally and internally, a person should be neither victim nor perpetrator, but should aim to return to the calm waters of healthy psychological development.

This new understanding of psyche and trauma allows a different therapeutic approach. On this basis, I have developed a new psychotherapeutic concept that, with the use of human representatives to make the person's internal psychological state externally visible, initiates processes of change in a logical way. This I call the 'constellation of the intention'.

When using the method of the 'constellation of the intention', work is done systematically according to the intention of the client in each given situation. On the one hand, this avoids futile therapeutic efforts if a client is unable or unwilling to put forward an intention to instigate change; on the other, it guards against the danger of overtaxing the client during the work, and of thereby causing a re-traumatisation.

If we find our way out of our entanglements, if we are able to integrate our splits, and let our feelings flow freely with the current of life, then we are wholly alive, close to reality and close to ourselves. We can also be close to other people if that is our wish, and alone if we need peace and distance. Then we will experience a constructive symbiotic bond at the same time as autonomy.

Franz Ruppert
Munich 2013

Preface to the English edition and Acknowledgements

To practice efficiently we need clear theoretical concepts. Whatever is unclear in our thoughts and words will be also unclear in how we see our clients and how we act as psychotherapists in our work. Theory has to do with logical understanding, and our psyche, when properly understood, is logical, although it sometimes seems as if our psychological processes don't follow any rational principles. But this only shows our lack of understanding about what is really going on in our perceptions, feelings, thoughts and our memory.

In this book I have tried to be as clear as possible in defining what the 'psyche' is and in making this concept a sensible basis for a therapy of the 'psyche'. As our psyche only needs therapy if trauma is involved, I call what I offer and practice 'psychotraumatherapy'.

Another major topic of this book is a deeper understanding of the victim/perpetrator dynamic, and how the fact of being a victim or being a perpetrator leads to numerous surviving strategies that I have called 'victim attitudes' and 'perpetrator attitudes' respectively. To find ways that can really lead out of victim/perpetrator dynamics seems to me one of the biggest challenges for psychotraumatherapy.

What is also new in this book is the way I have developed of working with the constellation method. This new approach I call the 'Constellation of the Intention' (CoI), and it has turned out to be a very efficient and creative way of working with clients.

Again, as with my three previous books, Vivian Broughton has invested a lot of work in editing 'Trauma, Fear and Love' in English. I am very thankful from my heart to her. I also thank Julia Stuebs for her clear and fluent translation, and John Mitchell of Green Balloon Publishing for co-ordinating the publishing of the book.

Munich, November 2014   Franz Ruppert

Editor's Foreword

My task as editor of the English version of *Trauma Angst und Liebe*, the book you hold, was made immeasurably easier by the meticulous work of Julia Stuebs, the translator. The job of translation of such a book is demanding, as some of the ideas require considerable thought before it is possible to make a good transition from one language to another; I have enjoyed working with her.

I would also like to acknowledge Miles Bailey and his colleagues of Choir Press for handling the production of this book; John McClean for his work as our primary proof-reader, and John Mitchell of Green Balloon Publishing for his co-ordination and management of the project.

A word about quotations: where possible quotations from German versions of English books are given in this book in their original English version.

1

What are the root causes of psychological problems?

Reasons for seeking psychotherapy

I am a university professor and a practising psychotherapist. Why do people come to me looking for psychotherapeutic help? In my experience it is usually for one of the following reasons:

- A relationship with a partner has failed
- The person's relationship with his or her children is increasingly stressful
- Some people are lonely, have no partner and long for a permanent relationship
- Others feel isolated within groups and communities
- Many suffer from fear and depression, and some occasionally from psychosis
- Some are afflicted with physical symptoms, perhaps a severe chronic illness, or even cancer
- Sometimes it is a work conflict that the person cannot cope with on his own

Seeking psychotherapeutic help is not a sign of weakness, but of self-confidence. The desire to detach oneself from dependency, and step into one's own power takes over. Almost 80% of those who come to individual or group therapy, hoping for an improvement in their situation by exploring themselves, are women. They want to understand themselves better, and grow as individuals. Women seem to manage their feelings and talk about their relationships more easily and openly than men. They want to assume an increasing amount of responsibility for their lives and to improve their relationships with their partners and their children.

If men seek support in therapy it is usually because their partner/wife has left them, or because they have difficulties and conflicts at work, or a forced break in their career. I am happy if men come straight out with their psychological difficulties, and seek help to understand the cause of their problems with their relationships and their lives.

The following request, for example, came from a man: "I should like to have individual therapy with you. In situations of stress I lose control: my heart races, my breathing is laboured, I can't think properly and I sometimes become aggressive, insulting others and saying things that I regret later. It's worrying me increasingly. I'm sure my father is the cause. He was an alcoholic and extremely quick-tempered, and as a child I was often terrified of him. This terror still reappears today in stress situations. Even though I understand it intellectually, I'm still at its mercy. I'd like you to help me resolve this block so that my life can start to move again!"

This sincere and considered request demonstrates a mature psychological capacity. When working with this client, the small boy within him, who had been split off internally, appeared, and he was then able to have access to him. This small boy then was no longer a 'block' for him, but instead became a source of vitality and energy.

After 25 years of psychotherapeutic work, I am convinced that everyone, male or female, can experience psychological recovery if they take this path and pursue this goal. The person has to devote time, patience and courage, with the willingness to transcend his own inner resistance to overcoming the obstacles on the path to his psychological healing.

My experience over the past 20 years and more as a psychotherapist has continually shown me that the problems we have at any one time, with which we are unable to cope on our own, refer back to unresolved psychological conflicts from our past. These problems draw our attention to the fact that old conflicts within us are not over. In my work, then, it is not uncommon to go all the way back to the beginning of childhood, to birth and sometimes even to conception.

Case study 1

Finding a man who suits me (Laura)

In a group seminar Laura sat next to me so that she could do a constellation. She is a middle-aged woman, seems likeable, pleasant and attractive. She tells me that she hasn't had a proper relationship with a man since her divorce twelve years before. Any brief love affairs she has had have been long-distance relationships, or relationships with married men. The explanation she gives herself is: "I think I'm afraid they'll leave me, and of course there's no risk of that with married men – they have already left."

I ask Laura about her childhood. She tells me that she was given to her aunt when she was 16 months old, because her mother had to go into hospital for a while. A year later she returned to her mother. She has always had a difficult relationship with her mother.

I ask Laura about her mother's life. Her mother was the fifth of eight children. Before her mother was born, one of her brothers died very young. Then it occurred to Laura that before her own birth her mother had given birth to a stillborn baby – a girl who had died in the womb in the final month of pregnancy. For the time being, that is enough information for me and I ask Laura what her intention is for her constellation.

Laura says that her intention for the constellation is to see how she could find a lasting relationship "with a man who suits me". I suggest she choose someone from the group to represent her intention and position them in the room, and that she then stay in the constellation with her 'intention'.

The woman Laura chooses to represent her intention is very sympathetic towards Laura and thinks that her intention is fine. She says that she notices that Laura's eyes look sad. Laura herself starts to feel anxious. She says she feels she would like to run away (Figure 1).

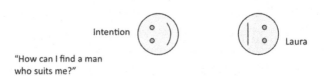

Figure 1: Laura and her intention

I suggest that Laura choose another person to represent the part of her that would like to run away. She chooses someone. The representative for this part says she does not feel any inclination to run away; on the contrary, she feels completely calm and would like to stay there. Laura and the representative of her intention have been standing facing each other; they now turn to face the other representative, standing next to each other. Laura does not feel any further anxiety; instead she feels more at ease (Figure 2). The representative for the inclination to run away wants to come closer. To begin with Laura does not want that, but after a while she agrees that the representative can take two small steps towards her.

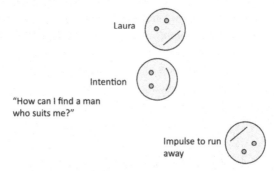

Figure 2: The inclination to run away

I now recommend that Laura choose two further representatives: one for her mother and one for herself as a baby of 16 months. She does this and the representatives of mother and baby immediately hug each other. The 'baby' cries and rests her head on the 'mother's' shoulder (Figure 3). Curiously enough, the 'mother' says that she loves Laura, but cannot be there for her.

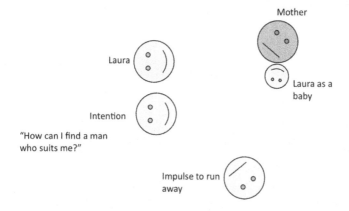

Figure 3: Laura, her intention, her mother and Laura as a baby

Then I ask Laura to select a representative for the stillborn child her mother gave birth to before she was born. After she has done that, the representative for her mother becomes more and more uneasy. She says: "You can't do that!" She turns away from the 'baby' resting on her shoulder and moves away. As the representative for the baby loses the support of the 'mother' she flops to the ground, doubling over into a foetal position and starts crying violently, screaming for her mother. The 'mother' does not return to the 'baby' (Figure 4).

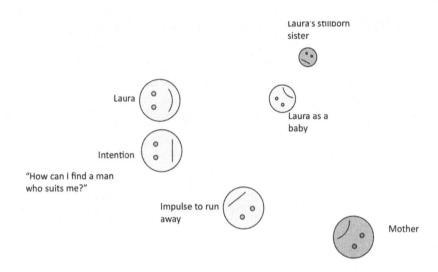

Figure 4: Laura's mother leaves the baby

Laura is very affected by the despair expressed by the representative for the baby part of her. After a while she and her 'intention' go over to the 'baby'; she starts to stroke and comfort the 'baby' and to embrace her. The 'baby' still calls for the 'mother', and Laura tries to explain to her that Mummy has gone, but that she (Laura) is now there, as an adult part. The 'baby' cannot understand this. She continues crying, and Laura tries in vain to comfort her (Figure 5).

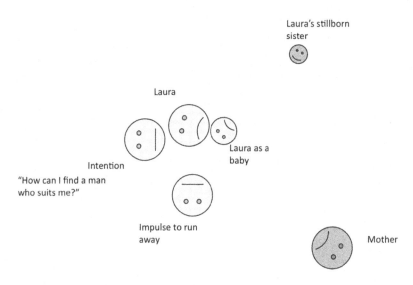

Figure 5: Laura tries to comfort the baby

After a while, the representative for the baby says to Laura: "You have to tell me that we belong together!" Laura does so, and also starts crying, and then both lie on the floor and embrace each other. In doing so, it is important to Laura that her 'intention' behind her is keeping in physical contact with her. After a while the 'baby' suggests standing up. Laura and the 'intention' help the 'baby' to stand. It seems as if the 'baby' is trying to stand on her own, on very wobbly legs, and take her first steps. With help from Laura and her 'intention' she succeeds and is happy and proud. She soon begins to laugh heartily and this hilarity also affects Laura. She is very happy with the contact she has established with the representative for the baby.

The three of them stand next to each other: Laura, her 'intention' and the 'baby'. The representative of the 'inclination to run away' moves to face Laura. She asks Laura whether she can come another step closer. Laura tells her she can, but that she does not want her to come right up to her. Laura's 'mother' is now watching what is happening from a distance and says she is now very proud of Laura. We end the constellation with this picture (Figure 6).

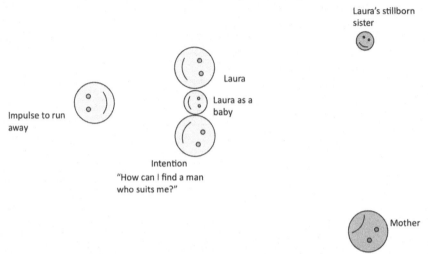

Figure 6: Laura establishes contact with herself

Two days after the seminar, Laura wrote to me, saying "The weekend was quite exhausting for me, but at the same time really good and enjoyable. I feel really well and happy."

What conclusions can we draw from this constellation, the original intention, the process as it developed and the result?

- Laura's intention seems on the one hand to be clear, expressing an understandable need for a stable relationship with a man. On the other hand, she has already expressed her ambivalence during the preliminary talk: she realises that she tends to look specifically for men with whom a permanent relationship is out of the question (men who are either married or who live a long way away from her). So the phrase 'a man who suits me' is strangely ambiguous: is it the fault of the men, or Laura's fault, that she is unable to find a suitable partner? She wishes for intimacy, and at the same time she is afraid of it and avoids closeness. It was therefore important for the constellation to show more clearly what causes this ambiguity.

- The constellation indicates that there is a part of Laura that finds it difficult to tolerate intimacy. The reason seems to be the separation from her mother when she was a baby, which continues to have an effect: when she was only 16 months old, her mother suddenly disappeared for more than a year. A baby is unable to understand this and will cry and scream for its mother, and if a baby continues like this for a while, it is likely to expend all its energy doing so, which can become life-threatening. A psychological protective mechanism has to be put in place to enable the child to go on living, even if her mother is no longer there. The part of the child that continues to look for the mother has to be suppressed to make way for a part that is prepared to accept the new situation and a substitute mother. A psychological split occurs in the baby. In Laura's case, her bonding problem was intensified by the fact that her mother reclaimed her after a year, when the part that was responsible for her survival had become used to having her aunt as a substitute mother.

- The reason for Laura's mother leaving her alone for so long was a physical illness, which meant that the mother had to have medical treatment. According to the constellation, however, the deeper reason seemed to be the mother's trauma at having given birth to a stillborn baby before Laura was conceived. This must have been so terrible for Laura's mother that she had to suppress and split off the painful experience, and she then seemed to have avoided contact with the new baby by becoming ill.

- During the constellation, when Laura emotionally turned towards that part of herself that had been split off as a baby, she was able to help it detach itself from its situation, become more autonomous and able to connect with its intended development.

- By doing this, Laura was able to come closer to herself. Her original survival mechanism, which caused her to run away from her anxiety when she became involved in an intimate relationship lost its urgency. She became able to tolerate coming closer to herself. Her fear of being abandoned no longer automatically precipitated an internal flight and psychological splitting in intimate situations. Instead she was able to distance herself and say 'stop' if things became too intimate when she didn't want them to.
- As long as Laura avoids contact with herself, there can never be anyone who 'suits her'; only those partners who cannot provide her with a stable relationship will 'suit her'. In other words, Laura will only be able to find a suitable man when she has found herself again, and to do this she has to re-integrate the traumatised and split off baby into her psyche.

In general terms the result of this constellation can be summarised as follows: If we have a psychological split within us as a result of traumatic experiences in our childhood, we are unable to develop a good relationship with ourselves. We re-enact the original problem repeatedly in our current relationships. As a result of having no confidence in ourselves and being unable to cope with our fears, as well as our anger and pain, we are unable to develop confidence in people who are close to us or who could be close to us. A good relationship with oneself is the basis of good relationships with others. To develop this, we have to find our way out of our splits, reversing anachronistic behavioural patterns or reactions that have become habitual, and no longer fit the current reality of our life.

The 'constellation of the intention'

The therapeutic method I mainly use, and I employed in the example above, I call 'the constellation of the intention'. I developed this method gradually from my experience with the 'family constellations' method. I first came into contact with 'family constellations' in 1994 when attending some seminars given by Bert Hellinger. I tried out the family constellations method myself and worked with it intensively in my therapy practice. The pros and cons of this method became very clear to me. The method I developed and use now is quite different from the original philosophy and method of 'family constellations'. I therefore use the term 'trauma constellations' to refer to my way of working with constellations.

I am fascinated by the constellations method, the phenomenon of 'representation by proxy'. How is it possible that people chosen to be representatives in a constellation seem able to understand the emotional life of another person intuitively, even if they have never met that person? Based on my experience of almost 20 years of working in this way I can say that I believe this method to be valid. I regularly experience patients who feel that the representatives in a constellation have understood and mirrored their inner emotional life correctly. If at some point this is not the case, the person will usually say so, and there is always a specific reason for it. After a constellation there is frequently an extraordinary confirmation of facts that have come to light during the constellation, and which could not have been known by the representatives beforehand.

I call the particular constellation format I have been working with therapeutically since 2010, 'the constellation of the intention'. It is based on my theory of psychological trauma across several generations and is therefore not just a technique, but is the methodical implementation of a psychotherapeutic concept (Ruppert 2008, 2010, 2013). In this current book I will use many case studies to show how this method can be usefully employed.

Some of my former questions concerning the constellations method that were there some years ago have now been answered to my satisfaction, and many uncertainties have been resolved. All the same I feel that even after years of intensive therapeutic work, the journey of discovery is not yet finished; the observations I have made still require further systematisation and clarification. The many new insights that are currently being revealed at a rapid pace by attachment research, trauma theories, and research into the workings of the brain need to be integrated into the whole concept.

The effective steps that enable psychological healing can only be determined in regular therapeutic work. People frequently come to me after having tried out a variety of different therapies. Some have helped, but some of the problems have remained untouched. For me this is proof that psychotherapy as a whole still has to develop further. There is much that we still do not understand, or are only just beginning to understand, about the dynamics of the psyche, but our efforts to establish psychological health will remain unsuccessful or get stuck midway if we do not completely understand the human psyche. Otherwise such efforts may even cause more harm than good.

Based on the insights I have described in my previous books, this book focuses mainly on the following questions:

- How can the human 'psyche' as the main point of reference of psychotherapy be more clearly defined?
- What, then, would be an appropriate definition of 'psychological health'?
- What, then, would be the logical steps necessary for the human psyche to recover health?
- How can these steps be best implemented by use of the constellations method?
- What makes the use of constellations such a valid psychotherapeutic technique?
- What conclusions can be drawn from such insights in order to prevent the development of further psychological illness?

2
What does 'psyche' mean?

Physical body and psyche

Every human is made up of a body; this means that we humans have the characteristics of matter and substance. It is a recognised fact of modern physics that matter consists of solid particles, but also of electromagnetic waves. Humans therefore consist of solid matter and systems of energy in various forms.

The word 'psyche' comes from the Greek meaning 'breath'. It is also translated as 'breath of life' or 'life force'. Early civilisations did not understand the emotional life of people. They pictured all sorts of things in order to explain the mysterious happenings within themselves that we now know as feelings and emotions. Emotions remained a profound mystery to even the most intelligent people right up to modern times.

In ancient Greece, it was the philosophers and poets who wrote eloquently about people's experiences, life and death, passion and fate. In one of these dramas of Greek mythology a woman named Psyche became the lover of Eros, the god of love, and countless adventures and challenges had to be overcome before Psyche and Eros could finally be reconciled as lovers. Through such dramas the people of that time projected their own experiences into the domain of the gods of Mount Olympus.

Because it is hard for us to grasp the concept of 'psyche', the psyche is frequently seen as something intangible and detached, separate from matter. 'Psyche' then appears to be an external entity, separate from the human body. This leads to the idea that psyche and body are independent of one another, and this dualistic perspective is present in most human cultures.

I am going to stay with the term psyche because it has become the standard in the scientific context since the academic subject of psychology emerged. I believe that the psyche is the interaction of matter, energy and information, in the same way as the body, as stated above. How else could one think of a living heart, since the heart is matter as well as the energy that keeps it beating, and information that regulates the frequency and intensity of this heartbeat? The dualistic separation of the physical and the psychological may have had advantages for theoretical reasons, but it is not tenable from a practical viewpoint. If we regard our own body and psyche as separate from one another we split ourselves, and if we treat other people from this perspective, we split them. When we think in this way we separate something that is actually a single entity into two parts, and in doing so we are likely to cause harm.

Psychosomatic network

Human development begins with the growth of body cells, and the simultaneous development within the cells of more and more psychological characteristics. After the fusion of egg and sperm the energy, information and action programs held in the genes ensure the systematic development of a new human being through cell-to-cell communication. There are genetically coded information programs to facilitate cell splitting and cell building. These programs allot each cell its place and its particular function in the whole of the developing organism.

The system of hormones and neurotransmitters is a further important part of the regulation of a living organism. Hormones are the substances that activate the organism to its full power or send it into a deep sleep. They can direct the organism's attention, increase its activities or obstruct them. Neurotransmitters determine the level of stimulation of the organism in precise doses, and launch a multitude of electromagnetic currents and oscillations.

The organism would not be able to survive without a highly intelligent immune system to protect it from constant external attack. Antigens, phagocytes and killer cells combine with a phenomenal ability to memorise the blueprint of antibodies, forming the basis of a highly efficient immune system that has to win the continual battle against new damaging influences that threaten the organism.

The psyche itself is formed of countless interconnected nerve pathways that form the larger units of the brain. It is able to condense an immense amount of information from outside the body and re-form it within the living organism every second, consolidating it into appropriate units.

Genetic information, the system of hormones in the blood, the immune system and the psyche with its countless nerve branches, are the most important parts of a 'psychosomatic network' (Faulstich, 2010) interwoven through the living organism. They are in constant communication, and pervade the living organism from the moment of conception until its death (Figure 7). My understanding is that the psyche is a fundamental element of all living organisms. The more complex the organism, the more developed the psyche has become in the course of evolution, and in the case of human beings, this development is still in a process of evolutionary development.

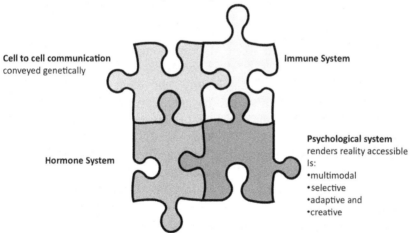

Figure 7: The psychosomatic network and its sub-systems

Characteristics of the psyche

In a general sense the psyche allows the organism access to external realities that are relevant to it. These realities include the facts that exist outside the organism, the external world, the 'environment' as seen from the perspective of the organism, and the internal reality of the organism itself, its hidden 'inner world'. The psyche is a highly complex information processing system based on substance and energy. Because the environment is multi-layered, the psyche must also be multi-layered. It is 'multimodal'; in other words it uses different channels of access to receive the information it needs from the different environmental realities.

These psychological processes fulfil specific functions enabling the self-support of the organism and the survival of the species to which the organism belongs. The information-processing programs have an extraordinary ability to adapt to changes in the organism's environment. They guarantee the organism's ability to cope with different and constantly changing natural and species-specific social contexts. A particular quality of the psyche therefore is its ability to manage these changing realities 'intelligently', with the help of these highly complex information-processing procedures.

The psychological programs are not only adaptive but also extremely creative. They are able to co-ordinate information from within the organism as well as create new information. In some cases they are even able to comprehend their own existence and are aware of their own inner logic.

As we humans are evidently not alone in having a psyche, we can say that the psyche represents the relevant reality for the different sorts of organisms in a way that is unique to each species. In other words, only that part of reality that is relevant to the self-support and reproduction of a particular species is psychologically represented in the psyche of that species. For us humans different aspects of the environment are relevant from those that are relevant for fish, birds and apes for example. Each species has its unique and highly specific forms of information reception and processing.

In species that reproduce by sexuality, the female and male have different functions for ensuring the survival of the species, and therefore the female and male psyches are also different. The age of an organism is also a factor. This is why men and women have different psyches, and a young person has a different psyche from an older person.

The species-specific environment and inner world can never be completely reflected in the psyche, but only in parts of it. The particular personal world of each organism is psychologically reflected to the extent necessary for its particular phase of development.

Different organisms have different degrees of awareness of the multimodal, selective, adaptive and creative psychological representation of their environment and personal worlds. Much of this takes place completely unconsciously in the form of psychological control processes, but to some extent the organism will have some awareness (e.g. a pain signal in a physical crisis), and only some sections of reality are represented internally in images or words, which we can describe as conscious knowledge.

From the traditional perspective of a psychologist, the differentiation between unconscious, semi-conscious and completely conscious psychological processes is part of the concept of the psyche. The unconscious portion is probably very much larger than the conscious portion. Seen from an evolutionary perspective, the unconscious mechanisms are the older ones; consciousness is a later product of evolution. For example, in the history of mankind the knowledge that children are created by sexual intercourse is relatively new. In this sense, no conscious decision has to be made in order to conceive a child. On the contrary, the conscious mind may even be more of a hindrance. With our growing knowledge of how things work we have to make more and more conscious decisions.

Animals too are evidently conscious of their situation in life to a degree. The more highly developed and 'social' they are, the more their consciousness appears to exist. Frans de Waal describes remarkable displays of consciousness in chimpanzees and bonobo monkeys (de Waal, 2010). Without denying the conscious psychological accomplishments of animals or plants, within the different species of living organisms known to us, the human psyche has reached the highest degree of consciousness of its external and internal reality:

- We have achieved a highly differentiated knowledge of our environment, as far as the farthest galaxies.
- We can enter the realms of consciousness of other species of living creatures.
- We have the ability to access our own subconscious by different forms of psychotherapy.

Psychological abilities

If, during one of my lectures, I ask my audience what they think the word 'psyche' means, I am frequently told that it means subjective feelings. However, feelings are just one aspect of the whole system of the psyche. The human psyche consists of a vast number of specific abilities:

- 'Psyche' means different forms of sensory perception. We can see, hear, smell, taste and touch within certain ranges whatever exists in reality; we can perceive the different qualities such as a solid object, energy waves or chemical substances.
- 'Psyche' includes our emotional reaction to our sensory perception. We are aware of our body and we can feel fear, anger, pain, love, pride or shame towards the things we perceive. It is through such sensations and emotions that perceived realities become meaningful for the perceiving organism. Without sensations and emotions the perceived reality remains external and there is no motivation to act. Our feelings form the basis for our

subjectivity and individuality. Out of sight, out of mind – that would be life for us if we had no emotions. Emotional reactions play an important role in the further evolutionary development of a species: an intensely experienced relationship to other living creatures is established via the feelings, and emotions also establish a unique relationship to oneself. Feelings are derived from environmental experiences, and they allow the development of lasting relationships to the environment and other living creatures. For example, even if a person we love or are afraid of is absent, the feeling of love or fear is still present psychologically. Feelings maintain our contact with the present and with the past. A person who does not feel anything will not be able to remember much about events in the past. Intense feelings can call to mind past experiences so completely that it may seem as if they had just happened.

- 'Psyche' is built on several forms of thinking. Thinking can be associative, connecting perceptions and internal situations that exist next to each other in space and time, more or less intuitively or arbitrarily via imagination or fantasy. Thought processes can be focused on the short-term solution of problems. Analytical and logical thinking are also possible, where the basic characteristics of perceptions and feelings are examined, and an attempt is made to identify causes, reasons, conditions and results. Analytical thinking tries to understand everything around us and separate what seems important from the unimportant. It pays attention to precisely defined concepts. Vague concepts and logical contradictions indicate to the analytical mind that the particular reality has not yet been sufficiently clearly recognised.

- A fundamental element of the human psyche is its ability to express itself in language. The use of language means that a deeper awareness of the environment and internal world can be created and communicated. When reality can be put into appropriate words, it is easier to deal with it practically and communicate one's understanding to others.

- The human psyche has at its disposal a number of forms of memory that support perception, feeling and thinking through the storing of information in the short and long term. These systems of memory store patterns of perceptions or feelings, words, findings, experiences or practical routines, thereby accumulating a wealth of experiences for a further enquiry into reality. Memories are either conscious, and can therefore be 'explicitly' named, or they are unconscious and lie 'implicitly' in the psycho-somatic network as an available reaction pattern. We assume today that in early infant development memories are only implicit, and that explicit memories of experiences are only possible from the second year on, when the brain is maturing. How far back the implicit memory reaches is an open question. At least in my psychotherapeutic practice the indications are that pre-birth experiences, as well as the birth process itself, can significantly shape the psyche of a person. It is even possible that processes of procreation and conception leave a trail of information in a living organism. In this regard, we can think of 'body' memory or a 'cellular' memory, which can be accessed via regressive methods of therapy such as hypnosis, or can be seen expressed in children's drawings and games (Eschenbach, 1994), and also in 'the constellation of the intention' (Ruppert, 2014).

- The human faculty of consciousness is included in the term 'psyche'. In other words, the human psyche has, at least in part, an idea of its own existence and the processes by which it functions. It reflects on its own role and is therefore able to change itself consciously and re-program itself. The question 'Who am I?' is a question of identity, and identity can mean different things at different times of life: who am I as a child, an adolescent, a young woman or man, as an adult woman or man, or an old woman or man? A child takes his own parents in the first instance as his point of reference as role models, and orients his identity according to them. A person who does not know who his mother and father are therefore has a major identity problem. Adolescents look for idols to emulate in their peer groups and from the media. The older we get, the clearer it becomes that we cannot live the life of another, but have to find our own unique way of self-realisation.

- The psychological processes can be unique events, or they can become generalised patterns of behaviour and actions. Unconscious and instinctive reactions can be the immediate result of visual or auditory perceptions. Actions can also take place as a quick result of certain feelings, or we act after having deliberately made reasoned decisions. Sometimes psychological coping processes can result in purposely choosing not to take any action.

Perception, emotion, cognition, will, identity, reaction and action – all psychological components are connected through the individual's experiences in life, and are stored as mental states, and remembered. Just like the components of a construction kit, the individual psychological functions can be switched on and off. The processes of perception, feeling, thinking, remembering or self-awareness can vary in capacity between zero percent to a hundred percent. We can see, hear or smell nothing at all, or we can make full use of our sensory organs; we can feel nothing, or be extremely sensitive; we can act without thinking, or we can think about things without ever taking any action, and there are many varying degrees between such minimum and maximum psychological functions.

For the psyche to be able to fulfil its function completely, the specific functions of perception, feeling and thinking have to be connected. Association and integration have to take place in order for individual perceptions to bring together what is separate and, in the course of human development, become a more tightly woven network of psychological structures that allows for a more exact and precise understanding of diverse realities.

The psyche consists of a number of compromised solutions, as does the human body: breathing and food intake, excretion and sexual intercourse make use of the same orifices in the body. There has to be a compromise for the successful function of both processes, and there may also be a danger of accident or infection, and risk of excessive consumption of bodily resources. In certain cases the psychological functions are also compromised in the attempt to reconcile different requirements and needs. Neither the living body nor an active psyche is infallible or perfect. For this reason 'dissociation' – the switching off of the individual psychological functions – is one of the processes of a healthy psyche. Sometimes it makes sense *not* to empathise with everything we experience, *not* to see everything happening in our environment, and *not* to worry about the things other people say.

We also have to take time into consideration when understanding psychological functions, because our mental abilities fade and age with time. Experiences and knowledge have to be continually updated so that a person can remain grounded in his constantly changing reality. Our psychological constructs of reality change during the course of our lives, slowly but steadily; sometimes there are personal or collective crises that force us to relinquish some images of reality that have become obsolete, and keep us looking out for new concepts, thereby giving precedence to more precise forms of reflections of psychological reality.

It is the psyche that forms a specific way of life from what is essential to the particular organism on a daily basis, its need for self-support and the continuance of its species. Determined by these needs, eating, drinking, sleeping and sexual intercourse become the specific behaviour patterns and practical routines of everyday life. If we want to know why people behave in a certain way, we have to understand their psyche. It is the psyche that holds the key to understanding what makes people function in their own particular way. Anyone who does not concern himself with his own psyche will never understand what is happening in his or her own environment.

Consciousness and will

The more complex the psyche of an organism, and the greater the degree of freedom for a variety of different responses to the external and internal worlds, the more there is a need and opportunity for a central construct that directs the perception, regulates feelings, organises thoughts and decides on actions.

From observing babies it is not hard to see that such an overarching inner organisational construct does not exist at the beginning of life. No child is born being able to say 'I'. The child does not even know that his hands, arms and legs are a part of him; he learns gradually to understand that his body belongs to him. Because of this, babies have to be given complete protection so that they do not harm their own bodies. There are plenty of indications that this 'ego construct' develops through contact with other people, in particular the mother, the father and any siblings.

Conscious awareness is also a later product of individual development. As a rule, the psyche processes the influx of information from the outside, and the information that originates from inside the organism in such a way that it does not become conscious. We can assume that about ninety-nine per cent of all psychological processes take place unconsciously. Most happen automatically, and require no conscious awareness. Consciousness is an additional aspect of the psyche for those situations in which a conscious awareness of reality is essential and advantageous for the living organism. Consciousness is particularly important when decisions have to be made, problems solved and realities that appear contradictory have to be understood. Consciousness requires time and effort, which is why scientists currently researching the brain maintain that consciousness is the exception rather than the norm in the field of psychological behaviour (Roth, 2001, Singer, 2002).

The more a person can consciously understand about reality through his environmental and inner experiences, the larger and more complex his consciousness will become. And since human experience mainly is concerned with relationships, we develop a particular awareness of the quality of relationships, and can become very adept at consciously understanding social relationship structures. In normal circumstances, the process of becoming consciously aware is accompanied by the wish to achieve more conscious awareness, particularly when it seems to be advantageous.

As a person develops, a further psychological quality comes into play that we call conscious will. The first impulses of life are directed unconsciously and automatically through reflexes and instincts. Primal reflexes are, for example, grasping, swallowing, blinking, kicking or crying. Some sensory stimulation is sufficient to activate these more or less complex motor reflexes. Instinct plays a major role in, for example, dangerous situations, the search for food, finding a mate or being a parent. Unconscious instincts focus attention quite naturally in the direction essential for survival. As an example, psychologically healthy mothers react instinctively to protect their child when they sense threatening dangers.

The conscious human will, which is presumed to have its source in the prefrontal cortex, is therefore a result of evolutionary, as well as individual development. It provides an 'authority' in the living organism that regulates and directs the psychological processes that run more or less as reflexes, instinctively and automatically. This 'authority' that we normally call our 'will' presupposes consciousness: I can declare my will by saying something, doing something or refraining from action, but only when I know what I want and do not want. We express our will most clearly in decision making. Every conscious decision taken makes a person more of an individual, allowing them to increase their personal identity and autonomy. In favourable circumstances a person can, in the course of his life, develop a clear will that sets goals self-confidently and achieves them of its own accord and by its own means.

We humans mostly attribute the characteristics of consciousness and will to ourselves rather than to other living creatures. We give ourselves credit for being more than just biologically pre-programmed creatures that have to obey physio-chemical causalities. This has advantages but also disadvantages. The advantages are that:

- we are able to perceive ourselves consciously as a part of everything around us and within us;
- we are not helplessly at the mercy of reflexes and instincts;
- we can change things that threaten us;
- we can create things that we think will please us;
- we can be autonomous and also individual

The disadvantages are that:

- we tend to distance ourselves from our body, taking too little notice of its needs, regarding it as an object and thinking we can treat it as we like, subjecting it to our will;
- we misunderstand our conscious 'ego' as being the centre of our universe. This 'ego' may sometimes develop towards an independent existence, inventing its own world and seeing connections that in reality do not exist.

Psyche and reality

The question as to how we as humans see the world, and whether the world really is the way we see it, has a long philo-sophical tradition. Famous thinkers such as David Hume, Immanuel Kant, Karl Popper to name but a few, have contributed important lines of reasoning to this issue, and within the framework of psychology and psychotherapy one should not revert to any previous position (Chalmers, 2001).

By the way in which the psyche, as defined, provides the living organism with access to reality, it also creates its own

25

kind of reality. The psyche functions as a tool by which the organism can make reality accessible, and at the same time it becomes the means by which the organism creates a specific form of reality. In order not to fall into the epistemological dilemma that a reality independent of the psyche does not exist, it is necessary to differentiate between three dimensions of reality:

- the objectively present reality independent of the existence of a psyche ('actual world');
- the reality psychologically processed by the organism, which results from the psychological transformation of the objective present reality into a subjective experience of this reality ('world as experienced by the cognitive organism');
- the fictitious reality created by the psyche, which plays with the perceived reality, and in extreme cases has no connection with the 'actual world' reality. This type of reality can be seen for example in dreams, fantasies, fiction, literary contrivances, films, imagery of gods, witches, angels, goblins or other creatures. A whole universe of mythological visions can result from this, which then may become materialised in the external world through concrete objects, thereby appearing as an objective reality. In this way the personal unconscious world of the psychologically active organism is created. What a person regards as *real* based on the activity of his psyche, does not therefore have to be *true*. It could just as easily be an illusion, emotions extruded from within, thinking influenced by interests, a lie, or even self-delusion.

To illustrate these three different realities, let us take, as an example, a stone lying on the road. This stone exists, regardless of whether a person perceives it or not. It was probably in existence on the earth long before *homo sapiens*. It might be a product of the distant past of the planet we happen to be on, from millions of years ago; it might have resulted from the collision of an asteroid with the earth. Over time, physical and chemical energies have shaped it. Perhaps human forces have altered it, giving it its present size and colour. In any case, its existence is not dependent in any way on whether there is a human psyche. It is a phenomenon of the 'actual world'.

For a person with basic psychological faculties this stone can mean very different things. Even the effort of bending down and picking it up to look at it more closely gives it a special meaning, because it becomes the object of our attention. We perceive its colour and shape to the best of our eyes' ability. If we are short-sighted, we have to move it closer to our eyes; if we are long-sighted, we look at it at arm's length. If we are colour-blind, we might not see the red or green tone that the stone reflects when light falls onto it.

One person with the stone in his hand might think of throwing it; another person might find it so beautiful that he thinks of putting it on his windowsill as a decoration. If we remember what we were taught at school, we might notice characteristics of the stone that enable us to determine whether it is made of marble, granite or flint. If we studied geology or mineralogy, we might be able to identify it as quartz, ferrite or pyrite on the basis of its different chemical elements.

The stone we are holding in our hand might stimulate our imagination. We might imagine that it has magical powers, that it will help us to keep negative energies at bay, even help us overcome illness. The human psyche knows no bounds in its ability to use objective reality to develop its own ideas, thereby creating new psychological realities. To take just one example: the human psyche invented many colourful stories about the sun, the moon and the stars that have nothing whatsoever to do with the reality of these vast rocks in space far from the earth.

If a simple object like a stone can present so many different dimensions of reality, objectively and subjectively, how great is the increase in the potential facets of reality if we look at something like 'the family', 'the state', 'society' or 'the economy'? What then, for example, is the objective reality of a family? What is each family member's subjective reality of their family's coexistence, and what characteristics are read into 'the family'? Objectively, it is those people present: mother, father and children. How these people are subjectively experienced as father, mother or children and how they see themselves, is completely different in each family. Even siblings will usually experience their family in different ways. Ideas about what a family actually is and what it should be can be very far apart. For some 'family' means perfect love, harmony and caring for one another; for others it is a sort of social welfare provider, and for yet others 'family' might be something akin to a prison or even hell on earth (König, 2004).

'Subjective' means that on the one hand we can only recognise objectively present reality through the filter of our psychological reality, our interpretative faculties, and on the other, all of us, whether collectively or individually, construct our psychological reality based on our fears and hopes. However, we cannot assume that there is no objective reality independent of the psyche, and therefore no actual truth. Even though we will never be able to perceive the 'actual world' without it being filtered by our psyche, there are still many ways of unearthing the ultimate truth with the help of technical achievements, empirical verification and logical deliberations.

Within the framework of psychotherapy, facts such as the following are extremely relevant:

- Who is the mother or father of a particular child?
- Has there been any violence, particularly sexual violence (incest, abuse) in the family?
- Did an abortion take place, was it attempted, or was a child killed after birth?

For the psychological well-being and for healing processes in psychotherapy such questions very often need to be resolved as far as possible. To accept such facts as impossible to resolve may play into the hands of those in whose interests it is to keep them unresolved. It is perpetrators who may want their victims' perceptions to remain subjective experiences, rather than having them know the actual reality of the facts. This is why perpetrators attempt to cast doubt on the ability of their victims to remember events correctly, and victims are often loyal to their tormentors by wanting to avoid remembering or knowing about certain events and facts.

The synchronisation of psychological processes

Without parents, no child can survive. Without the support of a social community, parents cannot help their children to become adults. As humans, we are dependent on one another and therefore we are, in a way, 'herd animals'. That is reflected in our brain and in our psyche.

There are many ways for us to access reality ourselves through our psyche, but we rarely make use of this possibility, since if each of us lived only in our own reality it would be very difficult for us to live together. We need something to make us coordinate our psychological processes so that we can live in a common reality. The need to coordinate psychological processes within a group of people is guaranteed in different ways:

- by synchronisation of processes that run unconsciously that we experience as resonance, sympathy and empathy, and which have their physiological basis in 'mirror neurons' in the brain (Bauer, 2005), whereby to a certain extent direct brain-to-brain communication takes place.
- by the subjective wish to belong to a certain group of people, where we attempt to fit our reality construction to the reality constructions of the group, such as the group into which we were born (family), or to which we belong as a result of circumstances. Children adapt to the demands of their parents and teachers, and use the more mature personalities of the adults to enhance their own incomplete psychological functioning. Adolescents and

adults often accept the view of reality that is given by television, radio, the press and the internet.

- for different groups of people living together, public opinion creates its own image of reality, which consists of a particular combination of objectively present, subjectively experienced and subjectively invented realities.

In order that this synchronisation of psychological processes does not hold back the individualisation process, or lead to the negation of individualisation already achieved, segregation mechanisms are necessary to help prevent individuals from merging in the crowd. Only by creating a stable and healthy ego-structure can we counteract the pull to synchronise with everyone else's perceptions, emotions and thoughts. But it is also a question of power and powerlessness, of dependence and independence, as to whether we can use our psyche to create our own picture of the realities we perceive, or whether we have to assume the interpretation of reality given to us by others.

Psyche and reality suppression

Above we have defined the main task of the psyche as making reality accessible to the living organism, but the reverse is also true: the psyche limits our access to reality depending on the species and the level of maturity. For example, we are unable to see infrared and ultra-violet light with our eyes, unlike some insects. We are also unable to hear high frequency sounds that are audible to bats. Babies and school children perceive things differently from each other. The psyche can consciously ignore objective reality if this reality prevents it from reaching its goals, or seems unbearable. It can also add to this objective reality to make it appear brighter and more beautiful than it really is.

Shutting out such realities that might be too demanding or even harm the organism is a function of the psyche. Reality then is suppressed, unconsciously and consciously. What is actually present or actually happens are either not represented in the psyche at all, or only in part. The psyche can even create a substitute reality if the actual reality is so threatening that it cannot be managed or tolerated. In the most extreme case this leads to the psyche denying responsibility for this suppression of reality. Processes of self-awareness and self-examination, such as psychotherapy, then may question the lack of concern with which the perception of reality is at times manipulated according to the organism's own interests and needs.

Even if, from an evolutionary point of view, the psyche was 'invented' to assist a living organism in self-support and survival of the species, it has, however, become independent during this process. It is a vibrant and highly dynamic system that has its own laws. Sometimes the living organism may even have to be of service to particular psychological programs. For example, young women who suffer from anorexia have such a dominant 'food refusal program' controlled by fear, defiance and rebellion, that their self-perception is impaired. Looking at herself in a mirror, the young woman will see her self as fat, even if she is skeletal. Such an insane psychological program cannot be switched off, even if the individual is likely to starve to death. With the help of many examples in this book we will look at why, of all things, the suppression of reality can become a central goal of the psyche.

Psyche and the brain

High amounts of energy are required for intellectual processes such as perception, problem solving and the pursuit of active strategies; these energy currents cause modifications of the material brain. This can be in either animate or inanimate material structures, for example, in a smart phone just as much as in a human brain. If we use the analogy of computer technology, then the brain is the hardware and the psyche the software. Many software programs run in the background, unnoticed by the computer user, and only some of the activities of the different software programs lead to audiovisual displays on the monitor. This corresponds with the difference between conscious and unconscious processes in the psyche.

Nerve cells are highly specialised connections of matter, which can modulate alterations in energy conditions with extreme precision. To a certain extent, the concentration of nerve cells in the brain represents a supercomputer. We can therefore regard 'the psyche' as the various software programs running on the brain computer. Since the human brain computer is also a product of evolutionary development, as is the whole organism, it is not standardised, as if it had been made from one mould, but is put together from different stages of evolutionary development. As we know from computer technology, certain software programs can only run on hardware components designed to accommodate them. Updated software cannot run on first generation hardware. It is too complex and requires too much memory.

Similarly, in the human brain there are several parts of the brain which have different characteristics ('computer perform-ances') and where only special types of software program can run, depending on the different hardware of nerve cells.

The brain stem

The brain structure is designed and adapted to control motor-sensory movement processes such as flight or fight, to regulate body temperature, to set up and maintain digestive and basic sexual functions. The psychological programs running on this hardware are relatively one-dimensional and work to a great extent on the principle of stimulus-reaction. Along the lines of: Eat or be eaten! Kill or be killed! Take what you can get!

Two elementary emotions are generated in this brain: fear and anger, both of which frequently end in actions of aggres-sion. Although the biological classification does not actually correspond to it, this brain is sometimes called the 'reptilian brain' in literature (Vroon, 1993). It is the principal nerve centre for the bands of nerve fibres that run throughout the organism and form the 'autonomic nervous system'. This network of nerve fibres with its sympathetic and parasympathetic divisions ensures that the organism changes its state as necessary, to either active or resting.

The interbrain

It is mainly mammals rearing their young that possess this additional brain structure, therefore it is also known as the 'mammalian brain'. Thanks to its many feedback loops, it is the brain that creates the psychological skills necessary to produce and maintain emotional experiences and thereby relationships to close family members (Damasio, 2006, pp. 178 ff.). Establishing these relationships seems at first to happen unconsciously, by a synchronisation of the brains involved. The limbic system of the mother synchronises with the limbic system of her children and vice versa. Lewis, Amini and Lannon (2001) call this process 'limbic resonance'. Especially at the beginning of his development, the child's internal state is dependent on the presence of his mother. The child's self-regulation ability, which is not yet fully developed, will fail if his mother is not present. His internal state then threatens to degenerate into chaos.

This causes a new dimension of feelings in the interbrain: compassion and sympathy. 'Ich fühle, was du fühlst' (I feel what you feel) is the title of Joachim Bauer's book (Bauer, 2005) about the modes of action of the 'mirror neurons'. We call the exclusive relatedness of one person with another, and the concern about his welfare, 'love'. This is the basis of psychological programs that function along the lines of: Love and you will be loved! Show consideration for the other and he will show consideration for you! Make sure you still belong to the group you came from! You belong to your tribe: make sure it stays alive, it's the way that you'll survive, so fight for it!

The neocortex

The neocortex is connected with the emotional world of the limbic brain system, whilst being different and separate structurally, and different in the type of its nerve fibres. Due to its systematically densely layered nerve cells, this brain structure offers the possibility of recognising the different qualities available in the environment of an organism in order to be able to take appropriate action.

The neocortex is divided into two halves (the right and left hemispheres), which are connected via a band of nerve fibres ('corpus callosum') (Siegel, 2010, pp. 141 ff.). The right hemisphere, probably the evolutionarily older of the two, operates more associatively, i.e. it enables different aspects of perception to be combined to a whole picture. Associative thinking and recognition make use of the following logic: things that happen at the same time and in the same place somehow belong together and form a unit (shapes, colours, sounds, smells etc.). This associative logic also puts phenomena into context that just happen by chance to exist side by side. It quickly leads to types of magical, mythical and irrational thinking that establishes connections that do not exist in reality. A large part of a child's consciousness is still trapped within this associative logic.

The left hemisphere allows linear and focused thought, and enables us to 'separate the wheat from the chaff'. In analytical logic it is a matter of understanding cause and effect interrelations, and of differentiating conditions from cause and effect, differentiating between chance and necessity and of reducing phenomena to a single concept. This also includes detecting contradictions in lines of reasoning and reflecting on the possibilities and limits of analytical thought. However, there is also the danger that these thought processes become too simplistic and one-dimensional, and ignore and suppress more complex connections that actually exist. The human cerebral tissue provides the prerequisites for recognising the world, but whether what is perceived, the feeling or the thought is right or wrong, is another matter. Even though recognising what is true and what is false is something accomplished individually, it also depends to a great extent on the cooperation of several brains and the resulting combined consciousness – ultimately influencing relationships between people, and social coexistence.

The neural structures in the prefrontal cortex are presumed to be those that are necessary for deliberate decision-making, looking to the future and making plans. This seems to be where the neuro-anatomical basis for an ego-consciousness developed in the course of evolution.

The second, left hemisphere has also developed the possibility of making a copy of events that happen in the right hemisphere, so that within the psyche, consciousness of the psyche was able to develop. As humans, we have the potential to identify ourselves as creatures with a psyche and to develop a consciousness of ourselves. In principle every person without major damage to his brain can gradually learn to say 'I' and to become aware of his own 'identity'.

Since all human brain structures have their own psychological programs, the question arises as to how the different brain structures are connected to one another and how the contradictory psychological programs of the brain stem, the interbrain and the neocortex can be integrated and reconciled. If a person just follows the directions of his brain stem, he will become pretty much an animal. If his 'mammalian brain' does not function and he cannot access his compassion functioning, i.e. if only his 'reptilian brain' and neocortex function, then he could become an extremely dangerous and highly intelligent predator. On the other hand, if a person is only controlled by his 'mammalian brain', there is a risk that he will become totally entangled symbiotically, unable to develop a coherent ego or an individuated self. Coordination and integration of the different brains is therefore a task of huge importance for everyone. It can be accomplished; and people can also fail at it.

There are some principles of the way the brain functions, which should also be mentioned here:

- Repeated strong stimulation leads to a longer-term memory of an event; everything that stimulates strong emotions is of paramount importance to the individual.
- The processing speed and the density of synaptic connections increase in those parts of the brain that are active most often. The brain adapts its structure as well as its processes to the use made of it. It can grow in this way, as well as degenerate.
- Parts of the brain that are no longer needed by certain functions are available for use by other programs. Experiences can be forgotten and new priorities set.
- Nerves are enlivened by new information. Familiar things only generate a small amount of stimulation. The brain can easily fall into a state of 'boredom' if it receives no novel external stimuli. It is then even more likely to invent its own images.

The brain is a continually dynamically developing and diminishing organ. The American neurobiologist and professor of psychiatry, Daniel Siegel, has developed a highly sophisticated understanding of the connection between the neurobiological basis of subjective experience and the development of the psyche – he speaks of 'the mind' – from interpersonal relationships (Siegel, 2010). Although our brain is genetically pre-programmed in its anatomical structure, its functions and microstructure develop according to what it experiences, i.e. the genes responsible for the psyche are activated in the brain on the basis of perception, feeling and thinking. The psyche itself initiates the establishment of new brain structures and the increase or reduction of the brain's neurochemistry. (Siegel, 2010, p. 33). The brain is modified by the way it is used. As I see it, this is further proof of the unity of body and psyche.

The attributes of the psyche are determined by the events an individual has experienced and the self-organisation of the psychological programs. They are partly hard-wired as reflexes and instincts in the older parts of the brain, whereas the newer parts of the brain are largely open and inclined to create a connection to the continually changing reality. Mental processes or willpower alone cannot alter the brain structures produced by experience. New all-encompassing experiences need to be made in order to bring about any alterations: experiences that involve perception, feeling and thinking and that initiate new self-organisation processes of the psychosomatic network.

Even though research into the brain can help us understand better and more precisely the anatomical and functional basis of psychological programs, it would be an error to assume that the brain is ultimately the reason for the contents of the psychological data-processing programs. The brain is a prerequisite and an essential condition for human perception, feeling, thinking and the memory of experiences, but it is not the cause of these things. In the same way, for example, a piano is a prerequisite in order to be able to play piano sonatas, but is not the reason for the choice of music played. The brain defines the context for the development of the data-processing programs and mental representations of experienced reality. No investigation, however thorough, of the keys, strings, hammers or pedals of a piano, could explain to a researcher why Beethoven's piano sonata No. 5 is played on one piano and 'chopsticks' on another. Manipulating the individual parts of the piano might mean that the sonata sounds better, but it cannot ensure that the sonata is played on that piano. This depends on the individual the brain belongs to and on the manner in which he lives and what he has already experienced. 'It is not the brain itself, but the living person who feels, thinks and acts' (Fuchs, 2012). His brain is his musical instrument. He can use it or abuse it.

Materialistic monism

Deriving the qualities of the human psyche from brain structures is the most recent attempt to explain materialistic monism. Material monism is the idea that we are nothing more than the physio-chemical processes, where mental processes are defined by their physiology; humans are just complicated physiological processes. For materialistic monism 'psyche' and 'soul' are simply an adjunct of the material, epiphenomena that can be reduced to physical and chemical processes. Other variations of this monism are:

- The theory of humours, from which the alleged character structures such as sanguine (blood) or choleric (bile) follow,
- The concept that behaviour is triggered by the inner organs, e.g. hysteria was supposed to originate in the female uterus,
- The idea that the genes lead directly to human modes of experience, or that metabolic disorders of the brain lead to 'depression' or 'schizophrenia' (Porter 2005).

Materialistic monism is a form of reductionism that historically arose from the attempt to use reasoning to contradict metaphysical constructs and religious persuasion. However, in its own way it created its own ideology and doctrine that presumes to be scientific and objective, but in reality is just based on an anti-belief. This thinking reached its philosophical-historical climax in the philosophy of 'positivism', which was established by Auguste Comte (1798–1857) in the late 19th Century. The practical application of this positivistic approach in medicine, and particularly in psychiatry, which is regrettably still prevalent in many places, leads frequently to a disregard and even a violation of an individual's body and psyche.

'Soul' and 'mind'

'Soul' is a term that is still frequently used in German, in particular in the tradition of Sigmund Freud (1856–1939) in connection with psychological issues. The term has met with very different interpretations in religion, philosophy and psychology (Hinterhuber, 2001).

In the linguistic usage of philosophy, 'soul' is tantamount to the internal life or the essential part of a person. The term 'soul' is rarely used in scientific psychology today because for many psychologists it is linked with a metaphysical 'construct' associated with religious and moral concepts.

In my opinion, the particular disadvantage of the term 'soul' lies in the fact that it assumes integrity and constancy, whereas an investigation of psychological processes shows that they consist of many different procedures and are part of a process of continuous development and change.

The integrity of the 'soul' is an idea that is necessary for a belief in continued existence after the death of the physical body and the concept of reincarnation. In most cases, the term 'soul' contains the assumption that body and soul can be separated from one another and can exist independently of one another. It belongs in principle to the repertoire of a dualistic view.

'Soul' is also a term that is often used in connection with groups: a family soul, a tribal soul or a national soul. Notions such as this lead to the assumption that something is more uniform than it actually is. Families, tribes and nations consist of a large number of individuals, with their particular opinions and decisions that are frequently actually in conflict with one another. Hence it seems to me that the desire for a harmonious society is the origin of the concept of a national ('German', 'British', 'Russian') soul, and the harsh reality of human coexistence, with its differences, contrasts and contradictions, is frequently ignored.

In the Anglo-American language world scientists are particularly reluctant to use the term 'soul' and instead tend to use the word 'mind'. In contrast to my earlier publications, where I frequently used the term 'soul' to point to the interconnectedness of our human condition, I meanwhile prefer to base my 'psychology' on the term 'psyche', and to define this concept of the psyche as clearly as possible as I do in this publication.

3
What is a healthy psyche?

Prerequisites for the development of a healthy psyche

There are many things that we only notice when they are missing. As long as we have enough oxygen, we think breathing is easy, and we do not notice our breathing. Provided we do not have any physical illness or disability, we don't worry about our physical health. The situation is similar with psychological health. It is only when we do not feel comfortable in ourselves, when fears and worries overwhelm us, when we no longer know what to do, that the question arises: What's wrong with me? Why do I have no control over my feelings and thoughts? Why are they dominating me? Why can't I sleep at night? Why do I eat and drink too much, even though I know it's not good for me? Why do I always choose the wrong people to be with, people who make me feel angry and resentful?

The presence of such disturbing symptoms or physical illnesses is what most clearly indicates the absence of psychological health. However, it is not enough to define psychological health just in terms of such symptoms, because then there is a danger of seeing the recovery of psychological health solely in terms of the removal of these symptoms. In my opinion, the symptoms of psychological illness are only the noticeable alarm signals indicating that the underlying psychological programs are not working properly and need attention.

These symptoms have to be understood; however agonising they may be, they give us the opportunity to understand our internal life better. How does our psyche work and what has to take place for us to feel good and healthy?

Integration and coherence

As mentioned previously, psychological processes are similar to software programs that continually update themselves. As with all software programs, they are susceptible to disruptions and problems, and the solutions often are a compromise. The information chosen and processed can be too little, too much or it can simply be the wrong information. There might be no adjustment to environmental conditions, or there may be too much. The individual psychological programs might be unable to keep pace with the physical development or they might be too far ahead. Thus it can happen

- that the processes of perception, feeling, thinking, talking and acting stagnate during growth and maturation;
- that individual psychological programs do not develop fully, because they are not based on experience, or are unable to progress beyond certain experiences;
- that memories are attached to, and remain fixated on, certain experiences.

The programming malfunctions of the psyche can cause damage to the body, and make a person act in ways that actually cause harm to the person and, in extreme cases, lead to a breakdown. There is no guarantee that we humans develop in a psychologically healthy way.

What conditions have to prevail for our psychological development to follow the healthy path? The simple answer is: different psychological functions that are involved with understanding reality and choosing and processing relevant information in a meaningful way have to be compatible. The flow of energy that furthers psychological information-

processing programs must not be interrupted. The information has to be networked and integrated into a meaningful
whole. According to Daniel Siegel a healthy psyche is ener-
gised, stable, integrated, coherent and organised in a complex
way. It is neither too rigid nor too flexible, is extremely
open to new ideas but does not degenerate into chaos (Siegel
2010, pp 352 f.).

The French neurologist and psychiatrist David Servan-
Schreiber regards the smooth and constant interaction of
emotions and rationality as essential for our well-being: "To
live in harmony with other people we have to find and maintain
equilibrium between our immediate – instinctive – emotional
reactions and the rational responses that preserve our social
ties over the long term. ... We pursue our objectives effort-
lessly, with natural concentration, because our actions are in
harmony with our values." (Servan-Schreiber, 2010, pp. 45).

According to Servan-Schreiber, to achieve this objective
there needs to be harmonious interaction between the
emotional brain that delivers energy and chooses the direction,
and the cognitive brain that regulates the implementation.

So psychological health means that the body's energetic life
forces are able to flow and express themselves. The different
psychological functions complement each other whilst retaining
their own distinctive way of regarding the external and internal
world. Every life experience is capable of being integrated.
Nothing that concerns the individual's biography has to be
suppressed, denied or split off. There is no fixation on certain
sections of reality, no ideas set in stone or ever-present
feelings that continually require and use attention and energy.
In summary: a healthy psyche moves with the flow of changes
in reality. It is not trapped in past experiences and it does not
race too far ahead with images of the future.

It is a sign of psychological health when we use our psyche
to recognise and endure reality in all its complexity, its depth,
its tensions and its contradictions. We then have no need to
substitute primitive psychological mechanisms such as general-
isations, black and white thinking, attributing blame, looking

for evil, escaping into false worlds and many others, none of which offer progress and which serve only to increase problems.

The qualities of a healthy psyche

When I ask participants at my lectures what being 'psychologically healthy' means to them, I receive many different replies: "being at peace with oneself", "being able to be happy and enjoy oneself", "being able to empathise with others"... From my years of therapeutic work I believe the following characteristics of psychological health are of particular importance:

- Curiosity: a thirst for knowledge and adventure are natural impulses in order to orientate oneself well in one's environment and be aware of what is happening around one. Making use of all one's senses means turning towards life and enjoying it to the full. It is fun to make new discoveries and it awakens the desire for more. Intuitive knowledge and rational distinctions both lead to a continually improving insight into complex reality and, if the psyche is healthy, they do not contradict each other. Feeling and thinking access reality in different ways. We can make equal and alternate use of the right and left hemispheres of our brain to anchor ourselves in our environment and in our body. It is part of a healthy awareness of reality that we can differentiate between the various levels of reality I described above: what is reality regardless of whether I perceive it or not, whether I like it or not? How does our psyche alter this reality and how does it process it for us selectively? And what is the pure fantasy output of the psyche?
- As we grow older our ability to distinguish between the objective and subjective levels of reality should increase. When children believe in Father Christmas, when they think they cannot be seen if they cover their eyes with their hands, when they think that by wishing for it, they

can make their mother or father healthy, these are forms of magical and mythical thinking appropriate for their age. The older we become, the more we ought to be able to recognise what actually exists, what emanates from our fears and fantasies, what we can and cannot influence. There is a childish awareness of the world and there is an adult one.

- It is a sign of psychological health to be in good contact with one's body and feelings, and thereby with oneself. Someone who experiences his feelings, who can feel, who can distinguish and name his emotional states, who has a sense of his own body, whose emotions flow through his body, who is aware of the source of his feelings, this person is essentially at peace with himself. Such awareness gives him an inner stability that is constant and reliable, even in stressful situations and moments of tension. The sense of his own existence is conveyed via his body and feelings, and for that reason this aspect of himself must be examined more closely, looked after and tended to. Connection with one's own feelings, their form, intensity and direction, is a basic prerequisite for becoming and remaining psychologically healthy.
- If a person has a basic sense of a right to his existence and is sensitive towards his errors and weaknesses, he can accept and love himself. He can then make mistakes and learn from them.
- I believe that a major characteristic of psychological health is the ability to have contact with others while at the same time to stay oneself. A clear feeling of oneself is the basis for our ability to establish good contact with others. This includes the ability to maintain a good distance if another person intrudes too much. Another factor is not being upset by inappropriate demands and accusations from others. A person can feel and decide for himself how much intimacy is good for him, how much space he needs and how much he wants to accommodate the needs of others.

- Mental alertness and clarity also result from the need to recognise what is important for oneself and not to become bogged down in the problems of others, nor to value others' perspective on life more highly than one's own.
- Having good access to the memory of one's personal experiences is a further sign of psychological health. Conscious memory begins from about the eighteenth month, and as far as it allows, important and formative experiences can be retrieved from memory into waking consciousness. We not only know what has happened, we can also feel our reaction to it. We have a feeling for our own life history, which we can talk about and piece together into a comprehensible whole. We have our own biography at our command.
- Everyone has basic sexual functioning that becomes activated at certain ages. Healthy sexuality is a component of psychological health when it is compatible with the relevant age of the person, and no inner psychological split occurs when engaged in sexual activity. Healthy sexuality is based on healthy relationships; it must not be confused with a childish need for bodily contact and affection that is inappropriate and will be overtaxed by sexual stimulation. Mature and appropriate sexuality means to assume responsibility for oneself as well as for the sexual partner.
- In my opinion, a person is psychologically healthy when he assumes full responsibility for his actions and possible mistakes, and does not shift responsibility onto someone else. Thus he does not become rooted in the role of victim or perpetrator, but tries to compensate for any damage and find the best lasting resolution for existing conflicts.
- Healthy psychological structures do not increase stress; on the contrary, they reduce it. Even if some problems prove to be very difficult, a healthy psychological structure possesses the basic optimism to assume that adequate solutions will be found. A person with healthy psychological structures does not attempt to overtax himself, and achieve

the impossible, nor to fight all resistance with violence. The optimism of assuming that his own problems can be solved, is a sign of an individual's inborn trust in himself, in his fellow humans and in life in general.

What has emerged in my psychotherapeutic work with many clients as 'healthy psychological structures', corresponds to a great extent with the essential results of resilience research. Michelin Rampe (Rampe, 2012, pp.16 f.) for example, lists the following resilience factors:

- Optimism and the expectation of self-efficacy,
- Acceptance and realistic assessment of one's own situation,
- Focus on finding a solution and the search for constructive new paths,
- Not being caught in the role of victim,
- Accepting responsibility and recognising one's own perpetrator self,
- Building up stable and well-intentioned relational networks,
- Making careful plans for the future.

The scientific approach, which deals with the resources for creating and maintaining psychological and physical health, also follows the same lines. Aaron Antonovsky (Antonovsky, 1997, pp. 34 ff.) has spent considerable time looking into the question of what allows people to remain healthy despite having been dealt severe blows by fate. He identifies the following main factors:

- the individual's experience can be explained and is understandable,
- it is manageable for the individual; he can influence it,
- the actions the individual takes are significant and experienced by the individual himself as important and meaningful.

In my opinion, an individual's own psychological structures are the most important resource for overcoming traumas he has experienced. Healthy psychological structures grow from within the person; they cannot be replaced by external guidelines or skills. No partner, medication, doctor or healer can take the place of a person's own internal healthy psychological structures.

Everyone who contemplates the human psyche must be aware that he approaches the topic from within his own psyche, with all its particular characteristics: linguistic, cultural and autobiographical. No one can rise above his own psyche, looking down on it from a superior vantage point. Accordingly, for an individual to believe that he or she knows what 'the psyche' is, and what is right and healthy for another, is not proof of a healthy psyche, but rather an expression of naivety, delusions of grandeur and narcissistic superiority.

I therefore regard my list of healthy psychological structures as neither complete nor irrefutable. It is simply my contribution towards what I see as a very important question; essential criteria that I have discovered over the years for my professional therapeutic work with clients as well as for my own life. This list can be regarded as a suggestion, encouraging everyone to find their own criteria for psychological health and to confirm consistency by validating them again and again in everyday life. We experts can provide a definition for psychological health so that psychological laymen can find their bearings accordingly. But it is a central characteristic of psychological health when I, as a human being, wonder about what psychological health means to me.

I was therefore impressed by the following outcome of a constellation. The client had formulated the intention of being able to feel her own vitality and zest for life. A child part within her knew exactly how to achieve that: "I don't do anything that feels wrong to me." Conversely this means: We feel alive and happy when we do what feels right to us.

Fulfilling symbiotic needs

Healthy human development can be understood as the successful interaction between the symbiotic needs and the needs of autonomy. We human beings are social animals; social contact is just as important to us as eating, drinking, sleeping and protection from heat and cold. Being on our own, being excluded from a community, not belonging, not being liked: these are all things that we humans fear. Our need to have contact with other people is therefore as a rule undeniable and it is not a good sign if a person prefers to avoid other people and mistrusts them.

Symbiosis is a Greek term that consists of two words: 'sym' = together, and 'bios' = life. So it simply means "living together". The word 'symbiosis' was used in the late 19th Century by biologists to describe *different* species living together to their mutual benefit. For example 'cleaner birds', who venture into the mouths of crocodiles in order to clean the remains of food from between the crocodile's teeth, without the crocodile regarding them as prey. However, symbiotic relationships are not restricted to different species. Individuals of the *same* species can also live in symbiosis with each other. The opposite of symbiosis, from a biological point of view, is the hunter-prey relationship or parasitism, whereby one species feeds and multiplies at the cost of the other. A parasitic relationship can also occur within the same species.

In psychology the word symbiosis has negative connotations. It is associated with dependent relationships and a lack of independence. But if we look at it from a neutral point of view, in symbiosis one organism is so attuned to the needs of another that its own requirements are also met. This implies mutual dependence, but it does not have to mean a negative relationship. Whether a symbiosis is regarded as positive or negative depends on the type of relationship between the parties involved. I have therefore differentiated between constructive and destructive symbiotic relationships (Ruppert, 2013). Constructive symbiotic relationships constitute

49

'win-win' situations, while destructive symbiotic relationships are normally 'win-lose' or even 'lose-lose' situations.

We have symbiotic needs, in other words the desire to have contact with other people, our whole life. Symbiotic needs are directed towards other people. We want from others

- security, protection, assistance and safety,
- nourishment (food and drink),
- to be seen and recognised,
- to be understood,
- to be allowed to belong.

What we humans fear most is to be left alone, to be forgotten, neglected, overlooked, rejected, excluded, abandoned or even betrayed. All these make us experience the most unbearable feelings.

The original fundamental symbiotic relationship for human beings – as for most mammals – is the mother-child relationship. A growing unborn child and a newborn baby are totally reliant on, and at the mercy of, the mother. If the mother dies, the child will die as well without help from outside. If his mother is ill, he is likely to become ill as well; if his mother is weak, he is also in great danger. The child has no choice other than to adapt to his mother and her physical and psychological constitution as well as he can. For children, 'the world' is what they experience with their mother. The mother is the first environment in which the child grows. He has to stand the test of this environment. For this reason the child's psyche is totally oriented towards this 'mother reality'. A child's psyche sees the mother and feels her; in his early development this is unconscious and instinctive. The mother's body, her scent, her voice, her eyes – for the child these are *his whole world*. This world is his central point of reference, the goal of his longings and needs. And it is towards this reality that he directs his aspirations and desires. He adapts himself to this world. He needs this world and so he tries to preserve it with all the means at his disposal: with his voice, his gaze, the movements of his body, with his emotional energies, his imagination, fantasies and thoughts. His whole being is oriented towards his mother. His primal need is his mother and the satisfaction of all his other needs depends on her.

Whether the mother is full of life or full of fear, then, plays a key role in the development of her children. What can a small child do, other than go along with the way his mother experiences the world emotionally? It also makes a significant difference, whether a mother is able to separate her experience of life from that of her child, or whether she completely involves the child unconsciously and unthinkingly in her own life experience.

In most cases the quality of the mother/child attachment plays a decisive role for the child in the development of those psychological problems that lead people to seek therapeutic help. Each person's experience with their own mother forms the foundation for their psychological development. This is something I have observed that seems to become increasingly obvious the longer I work as a therapist. And because the most important relationship for the mother is her relationship with her own mother, it must come as no surprise that the grand-mother's life has a psychological effect on her grandchildren. Sometimes this applies to the great-grandmother as well.

As a result, it is only when the mother is accessible and available that her child can turn his or her attention to the rest of the world, which is of course also there: the father, if he is present, possibly siblings or grandparents, aunts or uncles; or the many unknown things that he can investigate with his mouth, hands or ears. All of that becomes insignificant to him if there is a danger of the mother leaving. In such a situation an inner alarm is activated that brings forth childish behaviour that attempts to restore closeness to the mother, for example, crying, screaming, protesting, running after her, looking for her. It takes several years for the child to be able to build up that much trust in people who are not his mother, and in himself, for him to be able to cope with a longer period of his mother's absence without suffering from inner turmoil and stress. Becoming detached from dependence on the mother, which is not only physical, but also highly psychological, is a long process of development that requires not only physical growth and an increasing ability to be independent, but also a considerable psychological maturity. Basic emotions such as fear, anger and love have to become defined and any tendency towards generalised overstimulation has to be decreased. The child is confronted with the challenge of having to calm himself down, to understand his feelings and regulate his emotional state. Allen, Fonagy and Bateman have described the ability to regulate one's own feelings as 'mentalisation': "Mentalising emotion includes identifying emotional states and their meaning, modulating the intensity of emotion, and expressing emotion externally and internally; crucial for emotion-regulation, mentalising emotion includes mentalising while remaining in the emotional state." (Allen, Fonagy and Bateman, 2011 pp 432).

A mother also has many psychological traits that assist and support her in satisfying the needs of her child. The mother's psyche begins to be reprogrammed towards motherhood during pregnancy: speech alters so that the pitch of her voice and the melody of her speech match the child's ear, usually becoming higher and more melodious; infant-like features – large head, large eyes, small nose, smiling mouth – trigger spontaneous and automatic nurturing reactions and feelings of joy. Feelings of happiness or pride do the rest, so that a psychologically healthy mother focuses her interests predominantly on her child.

As the child grows and develops the mother also needs to disentangle herself gradually from this close symbiotic relationship that has developed physically and psychologically to benefit the child's development. The mother has to turn back the clock psychologically, so that she is able to reclaim her life independently of the child in her perception and feeling, as he separates from her. My experience has shown that the mother who is unable to be psychologically present to her children is also not able to let go of them.

As humans, we search all our lives for the pleasant symbiotic qualities that define a healthy mother-child relationship. We want to be warmed, stroked, caressed, massaged, kissed, rocked, comforted, listened to, taken care of, understood and taken seriously. In a good adult couple relationship, the partners can generally fulfil these needs for each other. Good physical contact even allows us to enjoy moments when ego boundaries melt away for a while. Saunas, massages, singing and playing together, being outside in nature, these activities also provide many opportunities for creating a psychological state in which we feel at one with our environment, and attempts at isolation recede into the background. In my view, one essential criterion for the fulfilment of symbiotic needs is that they are not connected with any feeling of loss of self, or abandonment of the self. On the contrary, our feeling of selfness is realised in a particular way through interpersonal encounters as well as through experiences in nature. When we are in contact with other people and with nature, we feel and learn who we are. In meeting other living beings, we encounter our own aliveness.

Secure attachment patterns

In my opinion, attachment theory provides a fundamental answer to the question: What constitutes a healthy psyche? Attachment theory was developed by the English paediatric psychiatrist, John Bowlby (1907-1990) (Bowlby, 2006 a, b, c). Much research has since been carried out which has confirmed his findings to a great extent. The theory concludes that the human psyche cannot be understood on its own, but only in its interaction with the psyches of other people. We are not solitary individuals; we live in relationships and in groups. Relationships with other people, social interaction, are the central focus of our lives.

The core statement of the attachment theory asserts: The basis for an individual's healthy psyche is a secure attachment to his mother. How does a secure mother-child attachment develop? 'Attachment' in the psychological sense means that two living beings relate to each other reciprocally and are dependent upon one another. Looked at it purely biologically, the human embryo is basically a parasite, which establishes itself in the woman's body and takes what it needs from her body. Its growth directs impulses to the body of its mother to make the changes necessary for the embryo to continue its development. Programs are also activated on the psychological level that give the woman support in tolerating the parasitic presence of the unborn child and gradually make her into a mother. The growing child and the mother-to-be continuously communicate and interact physically and psychologically with one another. The basis of an individual's psyche is therefore what develops from the relationship with their mother.

Ideally, a mother's psyche is oriented towards nourishing her child, keeping him warm, looking after him, protecting him from danger and helping him to discover the world, and every child is oriented towards his mother, needs contact with her, lets himself be fed by her, seeks her protection and learns from her.

The cord of psychological attachment between mother and child that develops from the moment of conception consists of many separate threads: physical touch, smell, taste, voice and sounds, eye contact, facial expression and reciprocal interlocking feelings. If the mother is a stable attachment figure for the child, helping the child and always being there for him in times of danger or if he is afraid, if he feels alone, if he is in pain and needs comforting, then the child develops an entity within himself that, just like his mother, wants the best for him, has patience with him, tolerates his imperfections and is pleased with every small step in his development. But if a child feels neglected by his mother, criticised and rejected, then the inner 'entity' that has developed within him is a judgmental ego that also becomes dismissive, unkind, and rejecting.

Through his mother's mirroring, a child learns to distinguish between himself and his mother. To do this, the mother has to be able to react appropriately to the child's behaviour, feelings and attempts at communication, and to help him understand his inner world, his feelings and thoughts. For example, if the child starts to cry, an understanding mother will suggest some possible causes: "Why are you crying? Are you tired? Are you afraid? Do you feel lonely? Have you hurt yourself?" In this way the child learns to identify the inner causes of his behaviour and recognise whether he is crying because he is exhausted and needs to have a sleep, or because he is afraid and therefore unable to go to sleep. For the child to be able to understand his feelings and behaviour better, his mother needs to have the ability to empathise with him, while at the same time not putting her own feelings, for example her worry or exhaustion, above those of her child. Allen, Fonagy and Bateman (2011) describe this in the following way: "The mother is attuned to the child's emotional state and expresses his feelings, while at the same time making it clear that the emotional expression belongs to him and not to her" (p. 280).

Fulfilled autonomous needs

Symbiotic needs must have as their counterpart autonomous needs, otherwise development is impossible. Every child has to disengage himself sooner or later from the symbiosis with his mother otherwise he cannot become a separate individual. Autonomy means:

- being able to do things himself,
- having his own perceptions,
- experiencing his own feelings,
- developing his own thoughts,
- expressing his own will and implementing it.

Autonomy means making one's own decisions, living one's own life, freeing oneself of old dependencies and obligations and owning responsibility for creating new interdependencies. Autonomy means having the ability consciously to say 'yes' and consciously to say 'no'.

The development of autonomy also begins very early in life. My therapeutic work with children who had a difficult birth leads me to believe that it is the unborn child that gives the signal that it wants to leave the womb and be born. It is not only labour pains that push the baby mechanically out of the mother's womb. The child itself contributes actively with the way it presents itself and twists its body to make its way through the narrow birth canal. After the birth, a healthy child seeks eye contact with the mother and actively moves towards the mother's nipple (Klaus und Klaus, 2003, pp 37 ff).

The more secure a child feels with his mother, the wider his range of action is, and the more curious he is about his environment (Mahler, 1998). In a healthy person's development, the ability to feel, think and act autonomously increases with age. It is only when a person reaches an advanced age that physical limitations may again lead to a reduction in autonomy.

Healthy autonomy is based on the symbiotic needs being satisfied. Someone who has developed a healthy autonomy has no fear of dependence. He can be in a relationship without worrying about being patronised, controlled and dominated. He can win others over to satisfy his needs in a healthy way. He can let others be the way they are, and has no need to change them.

I would like to use the term 'pseudo-autonomy' to define autonomy that is only experienced if a person avoids contact with others and does not enter into any deeper relationship. The 'lone wolf' is not autonomous, just alone.

Someone who is genuinely autonomous does not hide behind group opinions or delegate responsibility for his actions to others.

Egoism or healthy autonomy?

For a child, his or her mother is naturally the most important person in the world. This should not be the same for an adult. During lectures and seminars I am frequently asked if it is egoistic to focus on oneself rather than on the good of others. A client who set up his new girlfriend in a constellation and focused all his efforts in the constellation on taking care of her needs and looking at her in admiration, afterwards said the same thing. His girlfriend's representative made it extremely clear that she felt very uneasy about this situation. She felt she was under tremendous pressure, which was encroaching on her own space. Even when her boyfriend pointed out that he gave her all the freedom she needed, she observed that he was expecting her to look after him as if he was a child.

An adult who makes someone other than himself the centre of his life, reaps several consequences:

- He makes himself dependent on that person and has to adjust to their needs and expectations.
- He exerts tremendous pressure on that person.
- He has no faith in his own abilities.
- He does not take responsibility for his own life.

This applies not only to partners, but to children as well, who should also not be made the sole focus of a parent's life. This puts too great a burden on the children, who are then responsible for the parents' happiness. But if children feel that their parents' own wellbeing is as important to them (the parents), then the children feel the support they need from the parents.

I experienced an extreme case of children being burdened with inappropriate expectations when working with another client. A psychiatrist had advised the mother of this client, after she had had an abortion, to have another child in order to cure her depression. It soon became clear that a child cannot fulfil the function of an anti-depressant. For this child the situation was hell on earth. His mother was disappointed with him because he was not making her happy She was also angry with him and would have liked to be rid of him. She even put him in a children's home for a while. It is not surprising that the boy ended up in psychiatric care and needed many years of psychotherapy before he was able to free himself from the entanglement with his mother.

When clients come to me maintaining that they are suffering from 'helper syndrome', it usually becomes apparent during the therapy that they are so deeply entangled with their traumatised mother that they have completely lost sight of themselves and their own needs. It is therefore important to understand that no amount of attention is going to help traumatised people. Unless they take their trauma and the resulting splitting seriously, they cannot be helped. To accept this, it is extremely helpful to have a sound understanding of trauma and how it can turn a healthy psyche into an unhealthy one.

4
Trauma as the cause of psychological 'disorders'

In my experience traumas are by no means infrequent phenomena. Assessing how many people have suffered trauma depends on the definition of what we understand by the term 'trauma'.

The word 'trauma' originally comes from Greek, meaning 'wound' or 'injury'. But what is the actual meaning of 'psychological injury' or 'psychological wounding'? It will be the aim of the next chapter to clarify this point.

As I see it, traumas are not just one of many possible causes for the development of psychological disorders, but are the main cause. The longer I practise as a psychotherapist, the more confirmation I receive for this view from my work. Colleagues who work seriously with psychotraumatology have, independently of one another, confirmed the experience that traumas form the basis of psychological 'illnesses' or 'disorders' (e.g. Fischer 2011, van der Hart, Nijenhuis, & Steele 2008). Consequently, I have based my theory and practice on the principle that most psychological 'illnesses' or 'disorders' are symptoms resulting from a trauma. The same is true of many physical illnesses and most relationship issues that cannot be resolved without therapeutic help.

The states of feeling good, feeling stressed and being traumatised

The human psyche can produce three basic states:

- A state in which we feel good, we cope easily with our daily life, we explore our environment with curiosity and learn new things, and we have fun and are able to relax and recover. In such a state we feel secure and well. No existential danger threatens us, we feel entirely at home with and open to our surroundings. In this state we are easily able to develop psychologically.

- The second state is caused by stress, which is a reaction to present threats. Two things happen here: all psychological channels immediately open in order to identify the threat accurately and comprehensively, and perception, feeling and thinking are acutely focused on the danger. Every effort is aimed at removing the danger or escaping from it. So much concentration is focused on the threat of danger that other functions such as digestion, recuperation, regeneration or reproduction, are almost completely shut down.

- The third state is the trauma emergency state, which kicks in when the stress programs are unable to deflect the dangers and the threat becomes unbearable. In the face of such a hopeless situation, any continuation of the stress strategies would lead to a mortal threat. For this reason, the stress programs have to be interrupted at their peak. If, for example, our spontaneous impulse to cry for help in a dangerous situation would draw the pursuer's attention to us, then we have to suppress the cry. In order to survive in a traumatic situation, we have to freeze the stress reactions that are running at full speed, and block other psychological functioning.

Traumas are life experiences that, when happening, can only be endured by interrupting the stress programs, and by masking or avoiding reality rather than by a greater connection with reality. Trauma represents such a fundamental emotional shock that the experience cannot be integrated into the psyche's information processing functions, and so, has to be split off.

The psyche thereby loses its primary function of making reality coherently accessible to the organism. Experiencing a trauma means that aspects of the psyche are used in order to prevent a full understanding of reality. After a trauma the organism lives with a narrowed view of reality; the person only has access to information from the environment that avoids as far as is possible the reality of the trauma.

A healthy psyche can switch quickly and easily between feeling good and managing a stress situation. Stress programs keep the psyche alert, and focuses the psychological functions on coping with any danger. The stress program restricts patterns of perception, feelings and thoughts as long as is necessary while danger threatens. Once the danger has passed, the psyche switches back to the psychological state of feeling good. However, if a person has experienced a trauma earlier in his life, he will not be able to alternate between feeling good and stress states, instead he will find himself back in the trauma state. The trauma states stored in the psychosomatic network constitute a continuous background stress that makes it extremely difficult to revert to a state of feeling good for any length of time.

In relation to reality, these different psychological states mean that our psyche is either

- open to reality, curious, but also well defined, or
- alert and restricted to areas of reality that are associated with danger, or
- engaged in psychologically concealing a reality that is overwhelming as far as is possible. In the case of a trauma, psychological programs are more focused on *not* recognising reality: to experience reality as it is would be overwhelming. (fig. 8).

State of feeling Good — No existential danger / Open to reality

State of feeling stressed — Threat of existential danger / Narrowed view of reality

State of emergency reaction to trauma — Overwhelming existential danger / Denial of reality

Figure 8: Three main states of the psyche

Some situations are unbearable, and this is the reason for these strategies: in order to keep unbearable realities away from psychological experience. The fact that these experiences are stored below the threshold of consciousness, in the nervous system and in the body, and can therefore be recalled, is an attendant problem. The states of over-excitation and over-burdening that are stored as a result of traumatic experiences do not simply disappear with time. They make it necessary to expend psychological capacity and energy on containing them and keeping them out of consciousness.

The fact that states of trauma remain permanently within a person if they are not specifically resolved encourages the tendency to react to a situation with stress strategies that a psychologically healthy person could manage with his normal strategies. A traumatised person gets into psychological states of stress much more easily and frequently than a person who has not experienced a trauma, and finds it much more difficult to return to a normal state of equilibrium.

General definition of trauma

This is the core of my trauma definition: the traumatisation of a person takes place when all stress-processing mechanisms and strategies fail to produce a means of escaping from a dangerous situation, and the mortal danger may even increase if these stress behaviour patterns continue to run. This means:

- A trauma begins with a situation that threatens the life, health or psychological integrity of a person. It could cause his physical, emotional or psychological death.
- The person goes into a stress reaction. The body becomes ready for action, and the psyche is totally focused on the danger in order to avoid it or render it harmless.
- If, while in this stress state, the person realises that nothing he can do will remove the danger and that, on the contrary, the risk of being harmed will actually increase, he falls into an ambivalent state of conflict, and from there into a state of hopelessness. He is unable to react or not react. Whatever he does is wrong and life-threatening. Since he has exhausted his psychological and physical options, he is faced with a situation of absolute hopelessness and powerlessness.
- This also means that different people experience the same kind of situation differently, and therefore the question as to whether a situation is traumatic or not for a person is *relative*. While one person is unable to take any action against a particular threatening situation, another may find a solution at the last moment. So whether a situation is traumatic or not depends on the age, experience, ability and knowledge of the person concerned. Babies and small children are especially in danger of being traumatised, owing to their vulnerability and their extremely restricted ability to defend or protect themselves.
- Whether a person survives the life-threatening situation after he has stopped trying to escape from it depends on external circumstances, and no longer on his resources and actions.
- The only psychological action that a person can take in this situation is to switch off the stress programs instantly. This requires drastically reducing perception, thinking and ego-awareness, freezing all movement,

suspending emotions and feelings, and making use of the 'playing dead' reflex to the point of reducing all energy expenditure in the organism to a minimum.
- By switching off the stress programs no action can be taken that would increase physical risk, while at the same time the risk of dying of overwhelming emotional overload is also reduced.

As a rule, the switch to the trauma emergency mechanism is unconscious; the same is also true for activating the stress programs. It appears to be taken at a sub-cortical level and is thereby outside the control of our will. This is one of the reasons why switching on this emergency mechanism cannot easily be reversed.

Someone witnessing another person in mortal danger, perhaps even dying, and who sees that he can only help this other person at the cost of his own life is an example of a hopeless situation that instantly switches off the stress programs and switches on the trauma emergency program. This is why, for example, children are traumatised if they witness their parents or siblings being seriously harmed.

Switching off and splitting the psyche as the result of trauma

In a trauma situation, the psyche has two possibilities:

- To shut down the psychological system in order to prevent the total collapse that might occur if there is increased activation of the stress reaction.
- To split the psychological system into sub-systems because it is impossible to function as a whole.

My therapeutic experience leads me to believe that the splitting of the psychological system is the essential process that enables a person to survive a trauma situation physically and psychologically. If the psyche is in a state of extreme stress, and anything the person does in the situation only worsen matters, a way has to be found to resolve the dilemma between extreme stress and doing nothing. There has to be an emergency mechanism that kicks in to shut down the psychological alert and the stress programs connected with it.

The integrity of the psyche has to be abandoned in such a moment, leading to a splitting of the psyche: one part remains in a stress state and the other part splits off, thereby no longer perceiving or feeling the threat.

Painful Operations on Babies

One example of the splitting process is this: babies intuitively seek bodily contact, however if they experience the touch of another person as extremely painful an insoluble psychological conflict arises. The child wants to go to someone for comfort, and at the same time the movement towards that person is connected with the expectation of pain. In such situations, the solution for the child is to split his psyche – to split off the experience of pain through freezing and stiffening and internally to withdraw from the adults who hurt him. The child dissociates and abandons contact with his own body.

A child who has been psychologically traumatised by painful operations in the first months of his life, for example by a doctor giving him an injection, or by an operation, or by having tubes attached to his body, can transfer his reactive attitude to all people who approach him. This is particularly true if his mother did not support or comfort him during the original traumatic situation.

Fear and trauma

Such examples show the way in which fear and trauma interact. If we see that something is dangerous and could cause us pain, our perception is focussed on this danger, resulting in a high state of vigilance. As long as there is a possibility of escaping or preventing the danger, the person can stay in contact with his body and his fear. His response to this danger and his fear signals direct his actions. However, if the danger becomes overwhelming and the person has no chance of protecting himself, dissociation takes place and his body becomes numb. The psyche floats free, separate from the body.

As a result, the person's fear system is programmed onto a higher level of sensitivity than before. From then on it scans the environment more exhaustively for possible signs of danger in order to be able to switch off feelings early enough in an emergency, thereby pre-empting the experience of pain. This is the reason why people who have suffered a trauma are likely to become stressed in situations where non-traumatised people see no cause for alarm, and become dissociated far more quickly and easily than people who are psychologically intact.

The model of split parts

The essential mechanism that enables a person to go on living after experiencing a trauma is, in my opinion, general dissociation and permanent psychological splitting. The name other trauma theoreticians give to what I call 'splitting' is 'structural dissociation' (van der Hart, Nijhuis and Steele 2008). In order to illustrate the way in which a person undergoes lasting changes through a trauma experience, I have developed the following model (see Fig. 9). It shows three separate psychological states of a traumatised person's personality:

- the healthy part,
- the traumatised part, and
- the survival part.

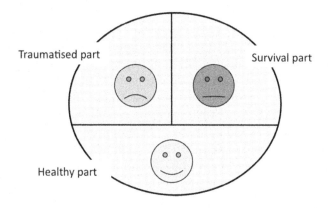

Traumatised part

Survival part

Healthy part

Figure 9: The model of personality splits following a trauma

The healthy part: I have already talked about the healthy part in the previous chapter: these are the parts of the self that represent well-functioning psychological structures even though having experienced a trauma. I am always happy if my clients are able to derive their therapeutic goals from this part of themselves. One client, who had already worked out a lot for herself, put it this way:

"My topics are still the ability to trust myself, to appreciate myself, to stand up for myself, to dare to show myself, to be able to speak up in a group without panicking. I want to have a clear head and I want to be able to see and understand clearly. I want to escape from the role of either perpetrator or victim. I want to feel my emotions and to be able to distinguish them from the emotions of others. I want to experience healthy sexuality with healthy boundaries. I want to be able to master difficult situations without fear or agitation. I want to have a clear memory, to live without stress and fear and without the belief that I am responsible for everyone else. I don't feel as responsible as I used to, but my automatic response is still very strong. It is still much easier to say 'yes' than to say 'no'. 'No' used to be impossible for me. I want to have a healthy body and to emerge from this overload and exhaustion so that my head can function properly again."

The traumatised part: This is what I call the psychological structures in which the perceptions, images, sounds, smells, physical sensations, feelings of fear, anger, shame or disgust, and all associated thoughts are represented that flood through a person's body and head during a traumatic situation. In order to cope with the immediate trauma, these experiences are isolated as much as possible from the remaining psychological states. The connections to these experiences and patterns of agitation are interrupted, curbed, numbed or frozen. The psyche tries to wrap them in a cocoon of forgetfulness. They are encased in thick protective walls.

However, this is only partially successful. The traumatic experiences and energies cannot be removed completely by forcing them out of conscious experience. For this reason, during periods of inactivity such as sleep, the cocoon can break open and the traumatised person may suffer nightmares. Characteristics of an everyday situation that may evoke memories of the original trauma situation can become triggers that re-induce the state of traumatisation. A smell, image or sound may be sufficient to reactivate the split off trauma. The person will then experience flashbacks and intrusions of the trauma experience, which swamp his current consciousness. It is even possible for the protective defence strategies that have been erected around the trauma to break down so that the trauma surges back into consciousness decades after the original trauma occurred. When people with terrible war experiences get older and their ability to defend against them breaks down, they can be overrun by these experiences. The person then is re-traumatised.

The survival part: The task of survival is a fundamental requirement for every living creature. An organism that does not fight for food resources is rapidly at a disadvantage since others will supersede it; others will force out a creature that does not stake a claim to its living space. The biological purpose of life is to survive for as long as possible, and for as long as the survival of that one organism contributes to the overall survival of the species. In other words, survival is the ultimate raison d'être with many other factors being subordinate to it. Health, well-being and a good life are biologically of secondary importance to the individual organism. Someone who is dying of hunger will eat almost anything; a fussy gourmet would not survive in such a situation.

Certain minimum conditions have to be fulfilled in order to secure the mere physical survival of a person: he has to drink every day and he has to eat, he needs protection from heat and cold and he needs contact with other people. Someone who has to ensure his own survival and the survival of others who are either not yet able (children) or no longer able (invalids, disabled persons, the elderly) to look after themselves, has to make use of every possibility available to him. This can cause fear and chronic stress, which, depending on the person's social hierarchical standing, can lead to attitudes such as:

- Always being on guard
- Taking everything he can when he can
- Not setting goals or desires too high in life
- Adapting, and avoiding conflict with those who are more powerful
- If necessary, sacrificing health, and even risking his own life in order to survive.

Even so, we human beings with our highly developed psyche have to ask ourselves whether the chronic stress of the constant struggle simply to survive is sufficient, or whether it might be possible to lead a better life – a life of physical and psychological health with goals that are personally meaningful and achievable.

Surviving material emergencies and times of urgent need is something quite different from surviving a traumatic experience. Surviving a trauma presents an individual with the task of psychologically processing an experience that confronted him with mortal fear and his own inability to protect his own life.

Each form of trauma leads to its own particular types of survival strategies (I use the terms 'survival strategy' or 'survival parts', abbreviated from 'trauma survival strategy' or 'trauma survival parts'). I have listed below the ways traumatised individuals establish and maintain a split in their psyche:

- Suppressing the fact that the trauma happened
- Denying having experienced the trauma
- Behaving as if everything is fine: "Everything's great!" "I'm coping with it all!"
- Believing that the problem lies with other people, not with oneself: "I'm ok. It's the others who are the problem."
- Having memory gaps and lacking visual imagination
- Not talking about the trauma
- Making no attempt to remember
- Avoiding anything that could conjure up the memories
- Looking for distractions when unpleasant feelings surface
- Seeking distraction by looking after others' needs instead of one's own
- Involving oneself more than usual in others' lives in order to protect oneself
- Ignoring symptoms and not seeing them as the result of trauma
- Thinking that symptoms are the problem, rather than a warning signal
- Hoping to get rid of the symptoms quickly and simply
- Reacting aggressively when others tell the truth and remind one of the trauma or talk about it
- Seeking compensation for the inability to experience happiness and joy, for example by addictive need for admiration and recognition and through sex or drugs
- If the trauma cannot be completely denied, downplaying its effects: "It wasn't that terrible." "I've just taken the experience in my stride."
- Escaping into social roles ('masks')
- Inventing new survival strategies

- Using vague and general terms rather than specifics
- Considering illogical connections to be plausible
- Suspending any form of rational logic with regard to oneself and, if possible, others
- If necessary, lying, cheating and deceiving
- Escaping into the alleged higher spheres of 'spirituality'.

Trauma survival strategies put shackles on the psyche, not allowing real perception, feeling or thinking. Instead controlling strategies come into play that switch off psychological functions as quickly as possible if there is any risk of coming into contact with the trauma experience.

Basically, one has to understand that the survival part of the self does not see the problem as a split in the psyche as, for example, a trauma therapist may who can clearly see that the survival strategies are harming the client. The survival part continues to see the split in the psyche and the abandonment of reality as the solution – as it did during the original trauma situation.

Even though the survival strategies were absolutely necessary in the actual trauma situation in order to ensure survival, in the long term they are always dysfunctional and damage not only the individual himself, but also his social environment. They cause unnecessary strain and stress, over-taxing the individual. The survival strategies even increase the likelihood of further traumatic experiences because they prevent the individual from using his psyche's full ability to maintain contact with reality. Traumatised people become numb in fearful situations and are then unable to see reality as it is, which leads them towards harming themselves and others. A vicious circle of stress-trauma-stress-trauma develops and perpetuates.

The survival parts of the self have their own particular linguistic expressions. The words and intonation are a language of stress and aggression, for example the idea that an illness has to be eradicated. Their aims and arguments are usually one-dimensional. When functioning from the survival self a person will often talk endlessly, because as long as they are talking they do not have to feel anything. The survival parts put arbitrary value onto things and moralise. They do not differentiate between reality outside consciousness and reality created *by* consciousness. They believe steadfastly that their own illusory world is the actual reality.

The survival strategies are the biggest obstacle to therapy. Either they prevent a traumatised person from gaining insight into the causes of his problems and seeking adequate psychotherapeutic help, or, during psychotherapy, they sabotage all attempts to allow the patient to integrate his traumatic experiences. The survival strategies are still strongly defensive even when there is a possibility of treating the traumatic experience therapeutically.

Survival strategies ultimately lead to the individual being severely damaged in the long term, and sooner or later he will experience exactly what he has unconsciously feared and been trying to escape: powerlessness and helplessness. The very things the original trauma emergency reaction of splitting was supposed to protect him from, severe harm and even death, are actually brought about by the continual efforts of his survival strategies.

Love

Love and sexuality are so important for human coexistence and the health of the psyche that we need to understand them both. I will try to distinguish between the types of love and sexuality based on healthy structures of the psyche, and those based on trauma survival strategies.

True love is lived love; it is a constituent part of a relationship. It is a matter of loving and being loved. In my opinion there are two forms of loving relationships:

- Relationships of fulfilment
- Relationships of inadequacy

In a relationship of fulfilment, each person has so much love within them that they are willing to give the other of their love and happy to accept the love of the other. Giving love is not considered to be giving away something rare and unusual, which one only gives if one receives something valuable in return, but is an emotional impulse that can also activate love in another person. An individual does not need to avoid another's loving activities, but can accept them because the other person takes any signals seriously if the activities are becoming too much. His own need to love and be loved fits with the need of the other person, who also wants to love and be loved.

In this way, for example, a mother recognises when her child has had his fill of being cuddled, stroked and gazed at. A man shows consideration if his wife has had enough of his declarations of love and, in the same way, a woman recognises if her husband would rather read the paper or watch a sports program instead of spending time with her. Neither worries about losing the other's love if they are not available all the time. Neither has to be afraid of not being loved if they have made mistakes or had the sort of day when they did not even like themselves.

In a relationship of inadequacy, on the other hand, both partners are needy and have too little love within themselves. Their hope is to receive from the other what they lack within themselves. So love is an arduous business. What do I have to do so that the other person loves me? What do I have to look like for him to find me attractive? What job do I have to have, what social status, so that I am worth loving? What will happen if I am no longer successful... if I no longer look attractive... when I get older? What do I have to do to compensate for my deficits, so that I am still liked?

A child's need for love is based upon his dependence on his parents and the associated fear of being abandoned by them. Only when the child realises that his deepest fears are unfounded and that his parents lovingly accept him, is he able to develop a deep sense of trust and his own potential for love without stress.

The love of a child for his parents is one of the strongest emotions. In its raw state it is extremely demanding and possessive. However, if a child receives sufficient love and does not have to exhaust himself trying to be loved, he gradually gains a certain sense of what a nourishing form of love is, and what not.

Love that does not originate from healthy structures of the psyche, but rather from the survival structures, can be recognised by the following characteristics:

- Possessiveness, where the other person wants to possess me. I am supposed to belong to him/her. S/he keeps watch over me as jealously as over a valuable object.
- I am supposed to be grateful for anything I receive from this demanding love.
- In order to hold on to his/her love, I am supposed to subordinate myself to the other person and his/her interests.
- Preserving the relationship becomes the most important thing. It is supposed to be kept alive, even if there are actually many good reasons to end it.
- Love from the survival self is blind to the needs of the other person. It only sees its own needs and fears that these will not be fulfilled.
- With love that constitutes a survival strategy, the person's own concept of love is more important than the lived reality and the reactions of people towards whom this love is directed. An extreme example of this is stalking, when one person becomes the victim of 'love' attacks.
- For the survival self, the love of someone who is absent (someone who has died, or a previous partner) is often more important than the love of a person who is actually present (for example, living children or current partner).

In other words, it is important to be able to differentiate real love from illusions of love. The less that real love is available to the child, the greater are the illusions of love. Some people escape into delusions of love with someone other than their partner because the person they are actually with does not arouse feelings of love in them. It might happen that a woman who has decided against a current lover and takes a different man as her partner for purely rational reasons, outwardly projects the image of a harmonious marriage, but her inner erotic and sexual fantasies involve the other man. The children of this woman are in danger of becoming symbiotically entangled with their mother's illusions of love, and in their own search for a partner may seek the dream partner the mother actually wanted. Being a substitute partner, or a second choice as a child, is extremely painful.

All in all, relationships conducted from the survival self orient primarily on the criteria of functionality. People conducting relationships from their survival strategies have little sympathy with themselves and so, little empathy with others. Ideas about relationships that come from the survival self include the following types of thinking:

- Children should be orderly, diligent and good.
- They should not 'bring disgrace' on their parents, and should satisfy the parents' desire for recognition.
- A partner or wife should be presentable and sophisticated.
- A woman should always be available for sex when her husband wants it.
- A man should be responsible for property and provide money to satisfy his wife's status needs.

Sexuality

Love and sexuality are different phenomena. They are prompted by different psychological and physical processes. Different hormones and psychological needs are at play.

Sexuality is a driving force within humans, so sexual behaviour is steered not so much by conscious decisions, but by sexual signals, innate feelings of lust and sexual fantasies.

Men and women are both sexually driven – but in different ways. For men it is usually sufficient to perceive the physical sexual attributes of a woman as attractive in order to desire sexual contact with her. Men think primarily of the possibility of sexual intercourse and usually no further. Seen from a biological point of view, we can see this as appropriate: through the act of sexual intercourse, men have played their part in reproduction and the next steps are, from a purely biologically perspective, the woman's responsibility.

Women have to apply other criteria in their choice of a man than simple physical attraction. So they will usually check if the man they are considering as a sexual partner is also able to look after children that might result from sexual intercourse.

From a biological viewpoint, the sexuality of men and women has a common goal: procreation. The duties and burdens in bringing up the children, however, are very unevenly divided. The simple fact that babies grow within the woman and so are intensely dependent on the care from their mother means that the main part of the task of looking after the child falls to the woman. This fact can be moderated to some extent by cultural circumstances, but it cannot be completely denied. It leads to an ongoing conflict between the sexes about an even distribution of the burden of bringing up children.

If one goes beyond the evolutionary biological viewpoint and looks more closely at the psychological level of sexuality, one realises that a state of well-being can only be achieved when both men and women feel pleasure when having sex. Both partners must be ready for a sexual encounter and stimulation. The act of sex is also an act of love, an expression of personal affection between those involved. It also encourages this love. If the act of sex is based on willingness and mutual agreement, the sexual drive and the feeling of bonding do not conflict with each other, but can both be present in this intimate encounter.

A pathological and morbid sexuality is the result of a state of stress, and frequently the result of a trauma. When people who are traumatised and stressed have sex, they will ignore their own body, and the body of the other person, whom they are actually using for their own sexual gratification. They will suppress their own feelings and have no concern for the feelings of the other. An orgasm simply serves as short-lived relief of inner tension, likely to leave in its wake feelings of emptiness and staleness. These depressive feelings then can become the compulsion to seek further sexual satisfaction, creating a vicious cycle that leads to sexual addiction. The act of sex can become a traumatic experience for one or both people.

Sexuality practised from the survival self often results in a one-sided sexual satisfaction: only one of those involved has an experience that could be called enjoyable, while the other puts up with the sexual act. This can happen because one of the couple is forced to have sex, or because sex is obtained through prostitution.

The sexuality of the survival self separates the feelings of bonding and love from sexual arousal. The sex act has the quality of a physical abreaction and does not enhance or evoke interconnection. So, eye contact will be avoided during sexual intercourse. One person treats the other as a sexual object, not as a person with emotional needs, and it is then often implied that one person's needs are a fulfilment of the other's supposed needs. For example, based on their own violent fantasies some men imagine that women want and enjoy violent sex.

There are not a few women who endorse prostitution with the argument that men need that kind of sexuality. Sometimes women may argue in favour of prostitution by holding that marriages last longer if men can go to brothels when their marital relationship does not satisfy their sexual needs. This argument ignores the fact that the sex workers are usually women who have been sexually abused as children and for whom selling their body is part of their own trauma survival strategy. Such survival strategies, for example, foster the illusion of the ability to exercise control over the perpetrator, because he appears to be dependent on them. This endorsement of prostitution does not also consider the fact that most men who need to visit brothels are also traumatised as well.

The connection between male trauma and prostitution is most obvious in the case of the military. For men traumatised by war, being with a prostitute represents an attempt to distance themselves from the terrible images and flashbacks of war in their head, at least for a few minutes or hours.

Social roles as survival strategies

To develop a healthy identity, we have to engage continually with ourselves. The survival self hide behind roles: e.g. mother, father, husband, teacher, boss, doctor or therapist. They expect validation for their status as such, and may exert pressure to ensure this: "I've done so much for you as your mother, now you have to... " "Speaking as your father, I ... " "As your doctor, I say to you... ".

When traumatised people hide behind such authority roles it is not possible to connect with the real person. Within the role the person surrounds himself with allies who support his denial of the traumatic reality, and turns his personal problems that have arisen because of his suppression and denial, into generalised problems for others to manage. Thus they will pull others into their trauma survival strategies.

A characteristic of survival strategies is the exclusion of the reality of the trauma experience, keeping it out of consciousness, thereby making it impossible to know one's true identity in terms of real needs and feelings. So traumatised people will search externally for the definition and validation of the Self, rather than internally. They will take on the roles and clichés that they find in their environment, hiding behind different masks, depending on their age. Little boys play heroes, little girls magical fairies and sprites. Our tendency to identify with larger or smaller collectives, a tendency we have because of our symbiotic needs and our desire to belong, is further strengthened by traumatisation. For the survival parts, identification with 'the family', 'the country', 'the state' or perhaps a sports club, is frequently the only possibility available to define individual identity. Because their own emotional basis is missing, all roles played by people in their survival parts are just arbitrary constructs, which they may cling to, but which they could just as easily relinquish or substitute with another.

Normalising trauma

For the survival part, much of life is 'normal' because it is there: war, marital rape, sexual abuse of children, prostitution, exploitation in the workplace and so on. Resigned to it as they are, they cannot imagine that it could be any other way. In some families, generations of children have been sexually abused, and when these children in turn become mothers and fathers, they are again unable to protect their children from abuse. Similarly men have been socialised over the course of many generations to attribute little importance to their own needs and feelings and to allow themselves to be trained as soldiers and work machines.

George Orwell, in his novel *Nineteen Eighty-Four*, coins two phrases: 'doublethink' and 'newspeak', which are typical strategies of the trauma survival self (Orwell, 2004). By using such abstract speech an attempt is made to objectify traumatising relationships that are violent, overlaid with taboos and that create feelings of guilt, giving them the appearance of being normal. For example, prostitution, the sale of a human body as goods to satisfy the sexual drives and fantasies of other sexually disturbed people, becomes a 'service'. The owners of brothels can publicly boast that they are 'creating jobs'. The ostensibly rational end, earning money, justifies all means in a society fixated on making money as a survival strategy.

The fact that all these phenomena are not 'normal', even if most people in their own environment regard them as 'normal', becomes clear as soon as people learn to perceive, to feel, to think and to be aware of themselves from their healthy psychological structures. I find it impressive to see the clear distinction that is usually possible in the constellations process that I work with, between what is possibly regarded as 'normal' in society, and what is actually being experienced as feeling good, harmonious and right. People can only recognise what is good for them if they have gained sufficient access to their healthy psychological structures.

Moral values instead of explanations

Another characteristic of survival strategies is the inability to differentiate between an explanation and a moral evaluation. As the survival strategies render the person blind to the origins of these strategies, the root-cause analysis always ends at the point at which the taboo of recognising their own trauma is reached. The blindness towards their own trauma also means they are indifferent to the traumas of others. It is the reason that their survival self looks for all possible connections, but at the same time subtly avoids the actual causes of the trauma.

Survival parts of the self quickly reach the boundaries of their understanding of the psychological processes associated with trauma. When in their survival self the person can no longer cope with discussions about the results of traumatic experiences, he will break the discussion off with phrases such as: 'All roads lead to Rome!'. Above all, he is likely to refuse to recognise psychological splits as reality – such an idea is seen as far too exaggerated and the model as too extreme. Scientists who are unable to recognise their own trauma, tend to suspect that the causes of their psychological disorder lie everywhere except in the fact of traumatisation. Politicians who have split off their own trauma think they are able to satisfy the needs of their fellow citizens with solely rational strategies. They do not understand that laws and regulations often have the opposite effect to that intended.

On the other hand, an individual who is grounded in the healthy structures of his psyche can resist the temptation to confuse explanations of cause and effect with moral values. A scientific search for the reasons behind a phenomenon is something quite different to the search for culprits or justification.

Narcissism

Another characteristic of the survival self that is very disruptive in relationships, is narcissism. Some people, when they are in their survival self, take everything personally, are easily offended and have a tremendous need for recognition and confirmation. They are unable to believe in their own value, are ashamed of themselves and cannot be open and honest because they have blocked access to their own feelings due to their trauma. They will continually need recognition from others and are permanently under pressure to prove to others how good and lovable they are. They are prepared to do anything for others in order to achieve this.

There is a form of narcissism that is mainly female, that takes the form of unconditionally serving others whom they believe to be superior, in order that these others will have an easier life and become even more successful and more loved. For example a woman may serve a man she supposes to be strong, but who she also perceives to be suffering from great inner distress, and so to be in need of her love and encouragement, becoming dependent on her. This is, for example, what young girls may do for their depressed fathers.

The more common male form of narcissism requires professional success, material possessions, wealth, a beautiful woman at his side and children who are good at school and successful in their careers, in order to cover up his own deepest fear of not being loved and to make himself seem irreplaceable.

Types of trauma

Every form of trauma has its own origins, follows a particular path and results in particular symptoms. We therefore attempt to overcome them in different ways. How the traumatised and survival parts are and develop depends on the type of trauma. It is therefore important to know what type of trauma has affected the psyche of a person in order to select the appropriate form of therapy.

There are many ways of differentiating between traumas

- They can be differentiated by causal groups, e.g. natural disasters (fire, flood, earthquake ...) or man-made disasters.
- They can have violent or non-violent causes (e.g. an injury as a result of war, or a car accident that is not intentional).
- Traumas that originate within relationships are different from traumas which have their origin outside a relationship.
- Traumas that are based on a single occurrence, called by some authors 'mono-traumas', and traumas that are based on an on-going condition, called 'complex traumatisations' (Huether, Korittko, Wolfrum and Besser, 2011).

I differentiate between the following four forms of trauma:

- Existential trauma
- Loss trauma
- Symbiosis/bonding trauma
- Bonding system trauma

Existential trauma

Existential trauma occurs in situations that are life-threatening, caused by another person, an animal, or a natural disaster, where there is no way out. An existential trauma exists, for example:

- When another person who wields a weapon, such as a mugger, a rapist, soldier, threatening neighbour, a classmate threatens us, etc.
- When a vehicle such as a car or motorbike, or other vehicle is racing straight for us,
- When an animal such as a dog or elephant attacks us,
- When natural phenomena such as fire, flood, hurricanes or earthquakes threaten life

Such an experience leads to panic and mortal fear because our life is at risk.

During an existential trauma the fear has to be split off and every impulse to act has to be suspended and frozen: running away, screaming, physically defending oneself, shouting for help, all physical movement and action, even breathing.

This shock-induced paralysis is the first attempt to split off the trauma experience. Further immediate survival strategies are: creating a fog in the mind, having images of leaving the body.

Afterwards it is mainly agitation and mortal fear that have to be suppressed again and again when they penetrate the gaps in the boundary erected to keep them out. Medication is a favourite means of suppression of the hyperarousal; for example, beta-blockers, Valium or Benzodiazepine being offered as supposed anxiety-reducing medication and sedatives.

If the fear and panic become overpowering, 'anxiety therapies' may be tried as an attempt to bring the feelings of panic under control. However, such therapies are only useful if they clearly look at the causes of the particular fears. If the therapy is too focused on the superficial anxiety triggers (e.g. elevators or the underground), thereby obscuring the traumatic origins of the anxiety, they will only deepen the splits, and become an agent of the survival self. The more a feeling is suppressed without dealing with its origins, the situation that caused it, the more tenacious it becomes.

In the case of an existential trauma, fear is an alarm signal connected with the traumatised part, which stays frozen in the emergency state.

For a therapy with fear and anxiety states to be useful and succeed, the original trauma has to be identified. This is not easy, particularly if the trauma happened before birth, during birth or during the child's very early years, and the individual has no real memory of the experience (Ruppert, 2014).

A further obstacle to recognising the original trauma is the fact that traumatic fears can be inherited from the person's parents, or even earlier generations, as part of the symbiotic trauma, and can be confused with the individual's own personal anxieties.

In any event, much courage and confidence are necessary in order to re-visit the original trauma situation, so that existential trauma experiences can be integrated. The experience of helplessness and powerlessness has to be faced by the healthy self, without the many loopholes offered by the ingrained survival strategies.

Loss trauma

Feelings are the connection between a person's internal and external experiences. Our subjective contact with the world takes place through our emotional attachments. If we lose something to which we have built up a deep emotional attachment, we are likely to suffer a loss trauma. Primarily this concerns people who are very close to us, such as our parents, children, partner and very close friends. The psychological pain of separation and loss in a loss trauma is unbearable. Arguably the deepest and most serious loss trauma for a psychologically healthy mother is the loss of her child, for example if the child is killed by a car accident.

If a child's parents die early in his life, this will also represent a major loss trauma. The worst scenario for a child is if his mother dies during or immediately after the birth. My experience with clients has shown me that up to the age of 20 or so, a son or daughter cannot usually cope psychologically with their parents' premature death, and the psychological splits of trauma will occur.

If the parents separate or divorce while the child is young, so that the child ostensibly loses one parent, there is such pain of separation and fear of being abandoned, that the child is unable to cope psychologically, and the situation may lead to psychological splitting. This is particularly true when one parent tries to use the child as an ally against the other parent.

If a child is adopted or given to a foster mother straight after birth, he will suffer a loss trauma, because a psychological attachment to his natural mother has already been established during the nine months of pregnancy and by the birth process. The separation from his natural mother rips through the highly complex psychological connection and fabric that has already been created up to this point. The contact the child has with his mother abruptly ends, completely incomprehensibly for the child. The child has been preparing for the external meeting with his mother for nine months, and suddenly she is not there! No child can be expected to give up this first relationship with his mother. He does not have any psychological alternative concept available and so is unable to endure the absence of his mother. The only way he can survive the loss of his mother is by splitting, even at this early stage of his development, and a part of him will be searching for his absent mother all his life.

Another situation is if there are complications during the birth, and mother and child are separated for some hours or even days. For example, if the mother has to be anaesthetised during a very painful birth, then the child's contact with his mother is abruptly ended. The fear of abandonment, and for his life, that the child then experiences at this early stage of his psychological development can lead to a split, leaving a permanent experience of panic in this person.

With a loss trauma the following emotional experiences have to be isolated from the rest of the psyche:

- the fear of being lonely and alone,
- the psychological pain of the loss of such an important attachment figure,
- the fear of having to cope with life without this person, and
- the anger at having been abandoned by this person.

The immediate trauma reaction to such a loss is to freeze the over-stimulating experience, resulting in numbness, paralysis and a state of confusion. The individual cannot think clearly, and his ability to make any decisions or take action is much reduced.

The loss of a person who is deeply loved leads to an irresolvable psychological conflict. Accepting the loss as reality, and mourning it, would mean accepting that this connection has gone forever and cannot be regained. Psychological survival mechanisms are initiated because the pain and the fear of such finality at the moment of the loss are unbearable.

In trauma of loss the first survival strategies consist of replaying the moment of loss repeatedly. What would have happened if … the person hadn't gone by car, had taken a later flight, there hadn't been an argument beforehand … ? The accident wouldn't have happened, he wouldn't have died, and it wouldn't have resulted in separation … The survivors usually feel guilty, as if they should have done something more, or that they did something wrong. Reality still appears modifiable, at least in their mind.

The bereaved person may behave as if the loved person is still present, as if she has gone out and will be back soon; that she is not really dead but, for example, in heaven and waiting; that she is looking down lovingly from a distant and unknown place, perhaps not of this world. The survival self does everything to avoid accepting the death or separation as something final. They hope that there will be a reunion one day with the person who has gone. Treating the person as really dead may seem to be a betrayal of the deceased person.

For this reason, the survival self may not allow the lost person to be forgotten, keeping their memory vividly alive. One client told me, for example, that her mother reminded her every year of the birthdays of the two siblings who had died before she was born, ensuring that they visited the grave together. In other instances, the rooms in which the deceased lived are not altered in any way. His possessions remain untouched, and his clothes and books are not given away. Every effort is made to avoid a clear line between the deceased and the living. This effort of continual remembrance is presented as being the need of the deceased. In reality though, it is the survival parts of the living that believe they cannot bear the pain of final separation and want to avoid it at all costs.

The deceased and absent are often idealised. Because there is no longer a real relationship, they can easily be elevated to the status of the ideal person, who would fulfil one's every desire if they were present.

Various forms of compensation also function as survival strategies: for example parents conceive another child to replace a child who died; or a child is taken for adoption or fostering in order to replace a dead child; or a new relationship is quickly entered into following a separation or divorce without the attachment with the previous partner having been resolved.

One form of survival strategy that is used in the case of a loss trauma is to diminish the importance of the loss. I frequently find this attitude in those who lost their parents when they were a child. They believe that, because they found surrogate parents, they had learnt to manage their life without their father or mother.

The psychological and physical symptoms of a loss trauma are indefinable fears, subliminal aggression, diffuse headaches or joint pains, feelings of stiffness, and incomplete and blocked mourning. Frequently this results in symptoms of depression, which in turn can lead to increased use of everyday stimulants such as nicotine, coffee and alcohol, or medications such as sleeping tablets or tranquillisers, and in some cases more serious forms of drug addiction.

In order to come to terms with a loss trauma, the individual has to accept the loss as real and final. As long as the survival self fights against accepting the loss, it will try to cope with the symptoms of the trauma through the methods outlined above. Psychotherapeutic treatment of 'depression' that does not make a connection with a loss trauma will collude with the survival self in avoiding the feelings of the trauma. So, as with existential trauma, recognition of the original trauma may be difficult, but if the person is prepared to accept the death and separation as final, and embrace the pain of the loss, appropriate ways will be found to gain psychological clarity and internal stability without any need for further psychological splitting.

Symbiosis and bonding traumas

If the mother is no longer present, or if the father has left, the situation for the child is very clear-cut, at least from an external perspective. It is much more confusing for the child if the parents are physically present but not really there for the child, perhaps because the parents are always at work, or because they occupy themselves with other people, or only concern themselves with their own personal problems. The feelers the child puts out towards his parents do not find any point of contact with them. The signals the child sends out either do not resonate with his parents, or lead to responses that are confusing or cause him hurt. The child is dependent on his attempts to connect with his parents, yet at the same time he may find that it is pointless, and sometimes even dangerous to do so. For the child this is unbearable.

Case study 2

A hotchpotch of basic emotions (Monika)

"I have a strong inner feeling that I cannot describe and that is accompanied by great tension, inner fragmentation, powerlessness, despair, hopelessness and sadness. I don't feel able to recognise what it's all about and what I can do now. I feel a great need to change something, but I don't know how. I feel helpless, without direction or support, overtaxed and exhausted.

"Since yesterday I've been crying frequently and last night I dreamt that some people wanted to kill me. I had to be permanently on guard and active, in order to protect and defend my life. At the same time I was alone all the time. I haven't got anyone I can talk to, who understands my distress. Another thing that makes me despair is the feeling that I cannot get anyone to understand me.

"Even though the crying and the deep despair have eased, the 'hotchpotch' of basic emotions has stayed: the inability

to recognise what's true, what it's all about, what I can do,
the inability to help myself and to 'free' myself, lack of
clarity, powerlessness, hopelessness, despair, etc. It's hard
for me to bear this condition: to know that something has to
happen urgently, while at the same time feeling my own
ignorance and inability. The tension is unbearable between:
I have to do something and I can't do anything and if I *do* do
something, it'll just get worse!"

For such a situation I use the term 'symbiotic trauma', when a
child fails in his efforts to develop a healthy symbiotic relationship with his parents, in particular with his mother. All his
attempts fail. Whether the child is quiet and withdrawn, or he
shows his fears, or he is angry or cries, whether he is good or
tries to gain attention by wrongdoing – nothing helps. He
cannot get the loving attention and understanding that he needs
in order to feel secure and safe with his parents.

The main cause of this is that, due to her own traumatisation, the mother is not able to offer the child a secure and
supportive attachment. She is unable to be open to her child
with her own emotional being because she, herself, is full of
fear. She is afraid that in any intimate contact with her child,
she will be flooded with her suppressed trauma feelings. The
child, with his emotional needs, his crying and his fears, is a
constant source of stress for the mother, because she unconsciously recognises in him her own inner neglected,
traumatised child.

If the child, having failed in his attempts with his mother,
then turns to his father, who is also traumatised, he will experience another symbiotic trauma. This is often the case,
because traumatised people are unconsciously drawn to one
another and tend to marry; each senses something in the other
that feels familiar (e.g. the painful experience of having lost a
parent when young), but they are unable to talk about this
common pain because if they did they would touch on their
own split off trauma feelings. Therefore it is likely that
children who are trapped in a symbiotic trauma with their

mother are also unable to bond securely with their father. This was the case with Susanne:

Case study 3

Withdrawal from the mother and desire to be like the father (Susanne)

When Susanne's mother had to go into hospital, she put the one-year-old Susanne into the care of her father's family. Susanne was not well looked after there, and she no longer had any confidence that her mother would be there for her and protect her from people who did not have her best interests at heart.

In her need, Susanne turned to her father. He had been in the war and had survived the terrible Battle of Stalingrad. Psychologically he was more dead than alive. Susanne turned to him and identified with his survival mechanisms. She wanted to be like him and tried to help her traumatised father. She withdrew from her mother, disappointed, a defining pattern for her life as she grew up. "Endure, keep quiet and put all hope in my father: that's been my survival pattern from that time I spent with my father's family. I suspect that I gave up on myself then, that I withdrew into myself and refused contact with myself, and anyone in my vicinity. My aunts and grandparents also contributed to this. They frightened me; they threatened me, abused me and silenced me. With defiance, denial and silence I withdrew into myself, split off all feeling and put all hope in my father. The last constellation has shown me that part of me is still entangled with him.

"As a representative in a different constellation I was able to access that part within me that had always called out desperately to my mother and didn't understand why she didn't come. This part thinks: 'I am not lovable' or 'I've done something for which I have to be punished.' Until I made the internal decision: 'Now I don't want you (her mother) either!' That is still my 'solution' when something is too difficult for me."

The psychological dynamics of a symbiotic trauma are complex. It contains several processes:

- In his helplessness and impotence at not being seen or loved by his mother, the child splits off his fears, his anger and pain, his despair and distress. The pain of not being wanted by his mother is extremely deep and unbearable for the child.
- He develops a variety of survival strategies: he doesn't like the fact that he is so needy; he despises his dependence and regards his fears and pain as weaknesses, and tries to be big and strong; rather than blame his mother he blames himself for not being accepted and liked – he was bad, did something wrong, did not love his mother enough, etc. He frequently turns to anger to avoid feeling his pain of abandonment.
- Because according to this logic the child is to blame for not being loved, no fault lies with the parents. The child idealises his parents, painting them in rosy colours. He regards them as 'dear mother' and 'dear father' however badly they treat him and whatever neglect or violence he is subjected to. Often the child fantasises about having an ideal mother instead of his real traumatised mother. He passionately defends this fantasy image he has created for himself. He is angry with himself that his relationship with his real mother is so difficult.
- Consequently he identifies with the survival attitudes and survival strategies of his mother and father: 'Life isn't a bed of roses!' 'You can't afford to have feelings!' 'Others are to blame!' 'You have to fit in!' 'What would the neighbours say!' etc.
- He perceives his parents as vulnerable and weak, so he takes on the role of saviour of his traumatised parents. One patient described this as: "This child part in me is

totally stressed out. My blood pressure is extremely high. Fear of failure is huge. If I can't help properly, my mother will die. It takes on really bizarre forms. This child part is very watchful, ready to recognise everything immediately."

- Since the child continues to seek emotional contact with his mother and father, he continues to come into unconscious contact with the split trauma energies and feelings of his parents, digging his way through the walls of their trauma defence strategies. In this way he absorbs his parents' trauma feelings and takes these as a substitute for the absent loving feelings of his parents. If the child is near his parents when they lose control over keeping their trauma feelings split off, as sometimes happens, the child is flooded along with them. For the child needing love, the trauma feelings in his parents' are similar to a black hole that sucks him in.

Inherited trauma feelings

The unconscious connection a child has with the split off trauma feelings of his parents means that he is unable to differentiate between their emotions and his own. So a symbiotic trauma is always connected with an internal confusion of emotions for the child, and since emotions are crucial for the development of the identity, the child becomes confused as to who he really is. Essentially he takes on the identity of his mother along with her trauma emotions, hiding his own identity beneath hers, thereby obstructing the development of his own identity. The bond between mother and child then becomes an entangled relationship.

The child is split into different parts in the same way as his mother is, and his parts bond with the corresponding parts in his mother. So the mother-child attachment is not simple, as it is in the case of a secure attachment, but sub-divided into different patterns of interaction, depending on the type of the maternal trauma.

In such entangled relationships, the boundary between mother and child is not clear psychologically. In parts of himself the child becomes a replica of his traumatised mother. Resolving a symbiotic attachment with his mother in a manner appropriate for the child's age becomes extremely difficult, if not completely impossible.

Traumatised mothers

Mothers can be traumatised for all kinds of reasons, for example:

- because they have had an accident,
- because they lost their parents when they were young,
- because they have lost children,
- because they have experienced violence, neglect and sexual abuse,
- because they had to witness unimaginable cruelty in war,
- because they have become a perpetrator themselves,
- because they are trapped in their own symbiotic trauma.

If traumatised, a mother will have a psychological split with which to meet her child and his attachment needs. Depending on the type of trauma she will . . .

- be over anxious that something will happen to the child,
- turn her child into a substitute mother for herself,
- be emotionally absent and trapped in the past with her feelings and thoughts,
- be blind to real dangers threatening her child, for example she may not see the potential for sexual abuse of the child,
- be over-controlling and not allow her child any space to develop his autonomy,
- play down the child's emotional expressions,
- put up a façade of normality towards her child, thereby preventing him from learning to trust his own feelings.

Case study 4

Three children, each trapped in their mother's trauma

Many of my patients in Germany have mothers who were very young during the Second World War. Mr. M.'s mother as a child had terrible experiences when her family was forcibly moved from East Prussia. Later, in her marriage Mr. M.'s mother unconsciously acted this terrifying experience out in her relationship with her husband and her son, showing them the brutality and cruelty she had experienced; others should feel it too, so as not to think of her as mad. However, she cannot talk about it and does not understand what she is doing.

The mother of Mrs. K. also experienced terrible things during the War, and because of this she is convinced that everyone is evil. It is impossible for her to be happy, and she believes it best for her daughter too if she knows that people are bad and that it is impossible to be happy. In order to be close to her mother, Mrs. K. took on her mother's viewpoint. She literally sacrificed the mother half of her existence – the left side of her body, which as a result was always ill, under tension, and involved in accidents, and she held back her own career ambitions. Only with the right side of her body could she try and live her own life.

Some traumatised mothers expect their children to be a consolation to them. Vincent, for example, was initially a substitute child for his mother for a previously aborted child. On the one hand, he was emotionally too much for her and she wanted to get rid of him, and on the other she expected him to release her from depression. She demanded that he massaged and stroked her back while she lay on the bed naked from the waist up. The more Vincent was able to extricate himself emotionally from the symbiotic entanglement with his mother, the more he accessed his own split off feelings. About having had to massage his mother he wrote:

"I really hated it!" At the same time, he gave her coupons for massages as a present. The massages were the only way of calming her down, and for Vincent, it helped him avoid punishment:

"I find it quite impressive that I can remember it all so well, but up until last Friday's therapy session I thought it was normal and an ordinary thing. It's only now that I realise I actually thought it was wrong and disgusting and never wanted to do it. But if I didn't do it, I was immediately told by my father: 'Just don't expect me to do anything for you. You don't really think that we'll give you something if you behave so selfishly. You know how tense your mother always is. Family is all about give and take. If you don't give, that's the end of our love.' Those were my father's cold, disappointed and aggressive words every time I refused to massage my mother. If I went on refusing he became even more explicit: 'If you don't massage your mother immediately, you'll be under house arrest, not allowed to use the telephone and you can go to bed without any supper. Then you can think about what you're doing to your mother. A child who loves his mother doesn't behave like that.' And that could quite easily escalate to threatening to put me in a home, to beat me, etc. It totally sucked!"

There are also many children of traumatised parents who are unable to find any obvious reason for their psychological disorder: 'If I had at least been beaten,' they may say, 'then I'd know what I'm up against.' They have been well looked after materially during their childhood and youth. It is frequently only in therapy that they come to realise that they were missing love and security. They had become used to the lack of emotion in their family, to the fact that not a lot was said, and that a façade of normality was maintained.

Mentioning the fact that traumatised mothers are the main source of traumatisation for their children is still a taboo topic in most societies and cultures. It has already come to be an accepted fact, at least in the western industrial world, that fathers often avoid their parental responsibility and do not always take care of the children. It is also increasingly recognised as a reality of society, that grandfathers, fathers or brothers in many families are perpetrators of violence and abuse.

For most people, however, still the primary image is that of the mother sacrificing herself for her children, putting her own interests last in order to get her children through life. In other words, every child should be infinitely grateful to his mother for the 'gift' of life and for bringing him up at great personal cost.

The deepest childish fear is not being loved by their mother. From this fear there develops an infinite childish willingness to love and suffer, to forgive the mother any harm she does to the individual, just as long as she accepts him as her child.

It is frequently noticeable in the daily work of social workers for example that the more a child is neglected and rejected by his mother, the stronger he clings to the illusion of a loving ideal mother. 'Mummy is good!' is like a mantra that the traumatised child repeats to himself. He or she would be catapulted into his mortal fear were he to start doubting this, because then the only other option is to blame himself for his mother's shortcomings. During therapy sessions I often see that the more a client has suffered from the actions of the survival part of his traumatised mother, the more strongly he, in his symbiotically entangled survival self, clings to her.

It is not only the terrified child who seeks to excuse his traumatised mother; the mother herself will defend against accusations that she is to blame for any difficulties with the child by accusing the child. She points out the difficult character of the child, his insatiability, disobedience and ungratefulness etc. The mother sees herself as the victim of her own child.

In many societies it is true that children's upbringing is the job of women, and men often take little interest in their offspring. However, in looking at the mother-child relationship

I am more interested in the effect traumatised mothers have on their children than the role of mothers in general. Even if fathers were to contribute more to the upbringing of their children, this could not compensate for the psychologically disturbing effect that a traumatised mother has on a child, especially as many fathers are not free from psychological traumas themselves.

As the topic of 'psychotrauma' is relatively new territory in society's thinking, most people do not understand the concept of a 'traumatised mother'; for many of us, it is difficult to understand that most psychological problems can be traced back to a traumatised connection with the mother. The common view of psychologists, social workers, sociologists and political scientists is that this is too simplistic. Where are the references to the social context, to poverty, exclusion, underprivileged status, unequal educational opportunities, etc.? These objections fail to see that in most cases traumatisation of women who become mothers have their roots in the political, economic and social condition of societies, for example in the tolerance of sexual violence against children or adolescents, in wars where women suffer a great deal, in medical treatments that only take into consideration the physical aspect of a person, and so on.

To assume for example that it was the psychological traumatisation of the child because of the traumatised mother that influenced a person's ability to become a great manager, artist, politician, athlete or scientist, or sent him on a path towards alcoholism, homelessness or crime may not be a very popular idea. One may ask, where does a person's self-will come into this, his own responsibility, his own strength of character and his willingness to challenge adverse circumstances?

I can well understand such resistance to this concept of symbiotic trauma. However, based on my findings from daily therapy work, I believe it to be an important and fundamentally useful insight, helpful for those wishing to understand the roots of psychological disturbance.

The psyche as a four-generational phenomenon

Children of a traumatised mother invest considerable attention and energy in their relationship with her, constantly trying to help, to save her from her perceived suffering and keep her alive. This entangles the child with those other family members with whom the mother is herself emotionally entangled, for example her mother, father, siblings, and even grandparents, and so a large amount of the child's energy and attention will be unconsciously engaged in those relationships his mother is entangled with. The child tries to keep the fragmented trauma-tised bonding system of the family together. Children who are symbiotically entangled in this way will over-sympathise with others who are suffering and in as much need of real love and connection as they are in the hope of getting the good connec-tion and love that they couldn't get directly with their mother.

Conversely, these traumatised bonding systems over several generations unconsciously absorb and feed on the fresh, new energy of the young children. This is only possible until the children break down under the weight of the unre-solved traumas of the family, and then need to absorb energy from others in order to survive themselves. This is how symbi-otically entangled familial bonding systems develop over several or even many generations, and it is almost impossible for an individual to escape without appropriate therapeutic work.

I have learned from my many experiences with clients that the individual human psyche represents at least a four-genera-tional phenomenon, sometimes even a fifth. What I mean is that the human psyche is an entity that is affected by a rela-tional family network spanning four generations. A child may unconsciously resonate with the psychological state of his great-grandparents as if not separate from them. Children usually are more strongly connected with the maternal line. So a great-grandmother's traumatic experience can be reflected in the psyche of her great-grandchild.

Case study 5

Jealousy and Fear of Being Abandoned (Johanna)

Johanna came to her therapy session saying she was utterly grief-stricken and felt totally forsaken because her boyfriend was planning to move to a different town to study. She said she was crying a lot and was extremely jealous because she imagined that he would immediately be unfaithful to her as soon as he had moved. Her boyfriend told her that he loved her and would still be faithful to her, even when he was in the university town, but that didn't help her at all.

In her constellation she wanted to find the reason for her feelings, and the following connection came to light. Johanna had been unable to establish a secure attachment to her mother, because she in turn had had no secure attachment to her mother. Instead, Johanna's mother was entangled with her grandmother (Johanna's great-grandmother), who treated her as her favourite granddaughter. Johanna's mother was pregnant with Johanna when her grandmother died. Johanna's mother told her: "My grandmother was greatly looking forward to the birth of her great-grandchild. But in a way it was a good thing that my grandmother died before you were born. I didn't even go to her funeral because otherwise I would have been drawn into her grave. That was how strong my attachment was to her!"

The background for this was the following: The great-grandmother was separated from her husband during the war; she was pregnant with twins at the time, but they didn't survive. No one knew whether the father of these twins was her husband or whether they were the result of her having been raped during the war, nor whether the great-grandmother herself had assisted in the children's death.

At any rate, the great-grandmother carried this dark secret with her, and small children always seemed to trigger something uncomfortable in her. She had an extremely bad relationship with her own daughter (Johanna's grandmother), and as a result this child suffered from a symbiotic trauma. This caused Johanna, who was seeking an attachment to her mother, to get mixed up in her mother's symbiotic entanglement with her grandmother, and this resulted in Johanna feeling fearful, abandoned, angry and jealous, feelings that belonged to her great-grandmother's unresolved trauma feelings.

Entangled identities

Symbiotic entanglement involves the process of clinging out of fearfulness to someone who is frightening, who actually instils fear. Such a situation creates a confusion between fear and love, making them difficult to distinguish; one is afraid for the person who at the same time frightens one.

A symbiotic entanglement is the result of a child's thwarted attempts to develop a secure attachment bond with his traumatised mother. This leads to the child's developing what we could call 'an entangled identity'. In other words, the child cannot distinguish his real self, and so cannot develop into the person he would have been had his mother not been traumatised. Instead of his own distinct identity, the child develops an entangled identity. He is confused with his traumatised mother, living in her trauma feelings and copying her survival strategies. This can be disastrous for boy children, because it makes it very difficult to access their male identity. It is a slightly different, but even so a considerable burden for girls, because they cannot clearly become a woman since they are confused with the trauma their mother suffered.

Only after a therapy that succeeds in helping them become aware of this entangled identity, can people then begin to discover their own true identity, separate from any confusion with the traumatic fate of their mother or father.

If we assume in principle that the traumatised mother has the split structure discussed above within her psyche, giving a healthy part, survival part and traumatised part – then the child dependent on her will also develop these three parts as a replication of the mother's splits. If we then go on to assume that the relationship between mother and child takes place in parallel and successively on all three psychological levels, then there are basically nine possible relationship forms between these two people, as shown in Figure 10:

Person 1 → Person 2 ↓	 🙂	 😐	 🙁
 🙂	HS-HS	HS-SS	HS-TS
 😐	SS-HS	SS-SS	SS-TS
 🙁	TS-HS	TS-SS	TS-TS

HS – Healthy Self
SS – Survival Self
TS – Trauma Self

Figure 10: Relationship forms based on splits in the personality

- The mother's healthy psychological self can cooperate with the child's healthy self
- The mother can remain in her healthy self while her child is in his survival self or trauma self
- The child can remain in his healthy self even if his mother reacts from her survival self or her trauma self
- Mother and child can communicate from within their survival parts
- The mother's survival self can react to the trauma part in the child

- The child reacts with his survival self to comments from the mother's trauma self
- Mother and child communicate from their respective trauma selves

The relationship between a traumatised mother and her child can have a broad spectrum of differing qualities. It can occasionally be very good, when both are in their healthy psychological structures. Or their relationship can be completely chaotic if both slide into their trauma selves.

When the survival selves in both meet, there are the following likely characteristics:

- there is usually endless and pointless talking and arguing,
- there are accusations, self-justifications and recriminations,
- issues of rejection and anger are played out,
- there are also attempts at reconciliation, and
- as part of this, illusory glimpses of a deep love are imagined.

A symbiotically entangled relationship remains just about manageable so long as at least one of the parties concerned returns occasionally to his healthy psychological self.

Case study 6

I want to help my child (Kerstin)

It is usually a case of symbiotic entanglement if parents come to my practice wanting to do something for their child but do not consider their own contribution. When Kerstin came to me, her intention was to help her daughter, who frequently suffered from stomach-ache, which had no apparent physical cause. If she played with her daughter, the stomach-ache would suddenly disappear.

Kerstin placed one cushion to represent her daughter, and another cushion on top to represent the stomach ache. I represented her intention "I want to help my daughter" (see Chapter 6 for more on the method of the Constellation of the Intention). Kerstin leads me as the representative for her 'intention', to the two cushions. I immediately notice that I feel shortage of breath, dizziness and have a headache. I find that I am fighting for breath and I can barely think. These are all symptoms of a panic attack. I feel hemmed in and don't know where to go or how to extricate myself from this condition.

Kerstin looks speechless at my behaviour and observations. I tell her that I am going to come out of the role so that we can sit down and talk about what has happened. We sit down and I ask her where this fear of hers might be coming from. After some hesitation she says that she was often beaten brutally by her father. He had pushed her to the ground, kicked her and pulled her hair. Her father had been a soldier in the Second World War and he often told her when she was a child about his war experiences, which included once almost being executed. Kerstin went on to say that, as a child, she was always scared when her parents left her at home alone. She was terribly afraid at night that someone would break in and attack her. Whenever her parents got into an argument, she was afraid they would kill each other. Who would have looked after her then?

I then realise how terrible it must have been for her as a child and that she never felt secure – whether her parents were there or whether they were away. "Yes, that's right" Kerstin said. Then it occurred to her that she is still afraid now if her husband is not there, that something could happen to him or that someone could break into the house.

It became increasingly clear that Kerstin had split off her fears, which had been reactivated through her contact with her four-year-old daughter. She didn't feel her fear inside her though, since it was split off, but sees it in her daughter, externalised and somatised as stomach-ache. I explain to her that a bonding through fear exists, firstly between her and her parents, and secondly between herself and her daughter.

In a later constellation, with the intention of disengaging herself from the bonding of fear with her parents, Kerstin succeeds in establishing contact between her anxious child part and her healthy part.

In the integration process both parts, the anxious child and the internal adult, meet on an equal footing and connect emotionally, with each part seeing the feelings of the other and taking them seriously. It is important that the internal child-parent split no longer exists or can be activated, in the sense that the anxious child no longer depends on the adult, or the adult part tries to comfort the sad child, but that they become one.

Women who have had terrible experiences as a child often want things to be very different, and better, for their own children. They often put themselves under enormous pressure to this end, and as a result their stress levels increase. This means that their children in turn come under pressure, which they will often express by means of non-specific physical symptoms of illness and in their behaviour.

Case study 7

Super Mother (Linda)

The following session took place on the telephone. I (F.R.) asked the client (Linda) to make notes of the phone call from what she remembered:

L.: "I have problems with my four-year-old son. He has panic attacks in kindergarten, cries and clings to me when I leave. He doesn't sleep at lunchtime but cries in his bed. He asks for his mummy the whole time and is extremely afraid of being separated from me. He has even defecated three times in his trousers."

F.R.: "Do you recognise panic in yourself and also not wanting to be left alone?"

L.: "Yes. I had a panic attack two years ago for the first time and I've had one a couple of times since. Once I was afraid – because the red blood corpuscles in a blood sample they took from my son were slightly too low – indicating that he might have leukaemia. I was at the book trade fair presenting a program in front of children, and I went berserk because I thought my son wouldn't reach his fifth birthday."

F.R.: "OK then, go and get a cushion for your fear of being alone and one for your son, and stand next to them."

L. (does that): "I immediately want to kick my 'loneliness' away. I don't want anything to do with it. I feel this hard part in me. That's the part that's good when I'm at work, on the stage, which always wants to be superhuman. That part can't bear loneliness. That part can't bear my son being afraid. It wants to be a super-mummy, and you can only be a super-mummy if you have a super-child."

F.R.: "Put down another cushion for this part."

L. (does that, puts the cushion for the part directly behind the cushion for her son)

F.R.: "Now stand in your son's place."

L. (does that): "It's difficult. I can't stand up. This 'super-mummy' behind my back is threatening me. If I sit down it's OK. I'd like her to be further away." She pushes the cushion further away.

L. (as the son): "That's better!"

L. (as herself, amazed): "That's brilliant! I don't have to try so hard to be a wonderful mother if she just gets on his nerves."

F.R.: "Now put the 'super-mummy' and the 'loneliness' next to each other."

L. (does that): "I still don't like the 'loneliness'. I'd like it to be gone."

F.R.: "Now look at your son's cushion."

L.: "I immediately feel like crying and dissolving with pity."

F.R.: "Do you see what you're doing?"

L.: "No."

F.R.: "You don't want your own pain, but you're taking his."

L.: "BRILLIANT!!!"

"After that it was soon over. I looked at my telephone: the constellation had taken from 9.00 till 9.46, after which my son's panic attacks stopped.

"I now feel better in many ways. My relationship with my son is much more relaxed. He now wants to be picked up later from kindergarten, his dry skin is a thing of the past, as are his ear problems (water in the ears), and he's much more active, more open and inquisitive. And my feelings of guilt towards him have actually disappeared – even though we still disagree a lot. But we often have a really nice time together and have much more contact than before. I have the feeling that I can see him now – my view of him isn't altered by the projection of my own issues onto him anymore. It's great, and your sentence: 'You don't want your own pain, but you're taking his' is stamped on my brain and has made me aware of my projections. And I'm so grateful to you for that."

Some months later the client wrote: "A teacher in my son's group spoke to me today and told me how well he was doing, that he'd become really cheeky and self-confident, and that she hadn't thought he would develop so quickly after the drastic crisis in March. I've also altered external things for myself: I'm not doing early shifts any more, my son doesn't stay with the child minder any more but I've found a nice woman who comes and picks him up from home and brings him back again. I'm sure that's made a difference too. But your sentence was at the heart of the change."

Case study 8

Survival parts in symbiotic entanglement (Viola)

Just how entangled the relationships in a family can be is shown in the following account by a client who, although she was already married and the mother of three children, was still psychologically trapped in a murky network of confusing communication within her family. Everybody in her family reacted to each other through their survival self, so no real clear relationship was possible. There are many unspoken expectations that no one can or wants to fulfil. Speculation is rife as to the motives of the others, and there is no clear understanding of what anyone else really means or wants. One person is concerned about the other's condition, but does not see what is really wrong with them. Viola writes: "My brother rang me yesterday and told me my mother was going to have an operation on her shoulder today at 7am. She's got a torn tendon, a torn muscle and osteoarthritis. She seems to have been walking round with it for four weeks now. I was a bit surprised that my brother gave me such short notice of the operation. He rang me yesterday evening to tell me. It was 9 pm and my mother was already in hospital. I noted that I thought I should ring her because there was a chance she might die during the operation. But I also noticed that I didn't want to. And I noticed that, once again, I felt I'd been excluded and ignored by my family, with my brother only telling me at such short notice what was going on.

"On the other hand I'm glad I don't have to bother about them, because I can't stand my father. My father always rings me when something's wrong with my mother, to suck me dry emotionally. That happened on Saturday morning. There's absolutely no reason for my mother not to have rung me herself and no reason for her not to take charge of her body and its condition. But she passes that off onto my father because he understands medical things a bit better, and she opts out of everything, so that I have to deal emotionally with my father. That's the problem! My father pretends to be grown up, but continually drains energy from me during our contact and overwhelms me with his neediness. You can't see it, but that's the way it is!

"And that's the way it's always been and it's the reason for my problems in relationships with men. That's the reason I feel weak. My father's afraid of my mother dying because he doesn't know how to manage on his own. My brother's done quite a good job. At least he keeps my father away from me. I can still remember the way my father got at me and hurt me when my mother was diagnosed with cancer the first time. He accused me of having no feelings for my mother because I annoyed him with the way I reacted. I was 21 at the time and shocked by his outburst. He has never apologised for any of his outbursts. He just says he doesn't mean it like that. I don't want this anymore. I want communication that communicates what's meant, and that's it!"

We can only communicate clearly and resolve any misunderstandings from our healthy self. Our survival self is unable to do that. It only creates more misunderstanding and entanglements because it is trapped within itself and not only has to avoid true feelings but is also forbidden from thinking certain things. Later in therapy with this client it turned out that she was sexually abused by her father as a child.

In my opinion, the model in Figure 10 showing the interaction of different self-parts can be used to understand all personal relationships. Frequently couples come together because they intuitively sense the traumatised part in the other and are unconsciously drawn towards it. They recognise something in the other that they have unconsciously split off and buried deep within themselves, and they feel understood by the other person, and they see in the other a reflection of a core part of themselves. Though of course in such a symbiotic entanglement no one sees the other as they really are.

Also it seems to me that traumatised clients are drawn to therapists with a similar trauma to theirs, and therapists become particularly interested in certain clients because they unconsciously recognise similarities in psychological structure to their own. From my work with many supervision groups I know that it is helpful for therapists to recognise that they are very likely to become entangled with clients with similar traumas to theirs. It is extremely important for therapists to be able to remain in their healthy structures if the client reacts with his survival strategies or from his trauma part.

How does one detach oneself from a symbiotic trauma?

The splits and entanglements resulting from a symbiotic trauma cannot be overcome as long as the person is still dependent on his traumatised parents, or feels dependent on them. In other words there has to be a spatial separation from his parents, or his parents have to be in therapy themselves working with their traumas, and have to allow their child the space to experience his own feelings.

In the case of a symbiotic trauma, the vast range of survival strategies developed over time present the main obstacle to overcome in therapy. To actually recognise that one's own parents are traumatised, and therefore incapable of loving the child in the way he needs means accepting that this love will never be forthcoming. It means giving up on the hope that has determined his interactions with his parents his whole life. The child has spent his entire life attempting to tear down the wall of his parents' survival strategies in order to reach the holy grail of parental love that he imagines is hidden behind it. It is incomprehensible for a child that the only thing hidden behind these massive defences are his parents' traumatised, anxious and disturbed structures.

I have described in my book *Symbiosis and Autonomy* (2013) the way a person can detach himself from a symbiotic trauma step by step. It is helpful to repeat this briefly here:

- to accept his own symbiotic trauma as a reality,
- to bring his own healthy parts increasingly into the foreground,
- to develop a healthy will of his own,
- to relinquish any illusion of a quick solution,
- to give up on wanting to save his parents and wanting to be saved by them,
- to distance himself psychologically and emotionally from his traumatised parents,
- to let go of the symbiotically transferred emotions of symbiotic entanglement,
- to dissolve any later entangled relationships (e.g. partnerships),
- to be able to be content with himself,
- to do work on his other traumas (besides the symbiotic trauma, e.g. a birth trauma or trauma of early separation).

The survival self uses every means possible, even in therapy, to achieve the connection that was, and still is, impossible. For example, other people are put in the position of the person's actual parents and reconciliation rituals acted out. I believe that the great attraction of family constellations as developed by Bert Hellinger is fuelled by the wish of the symbiotically entangled survival self to experience the parents' love, and allow the individual's own love for his parents to reach them through the enactment with representatives in the constellation. To achieve this the traumatised parents are extremely idealised, and the person's own traumatised parts, which know what the traumatised parents have inflicted on him, are banished, silenced and not taken seriously. One of the most striking characteristics of this illusory attempt at reconciliation with the parents in the family constellation is the gesture of submissively bowing to the parents' representatives. This can even be extended into the ritual, in a similar way to a priest at his ordination, of children lying down on the floor with their arms outstretched in order to receive their parents' blessing.

Only when all such illusions of hope of being able to get love from parents, who are severely traumatised, have been relinquished, does it become possible for the healthy psychological structures of the person to come into contact with their split-off traumatised child parts, thus allowing the experience and expression of fear, anger, despair and grief without reservation and without the worry of any attempts by their parents to silence them, reject or punish them. Only in this way can psychological splits gradually be integrated.

Mobbing and discrimination as a bonding trauma

A symbiotic trauma is a particular form of bonding trauma. But it is not only bonding with parents that is important, but also belonging to a peer group, a school class, a team at work and to a larger collective such as an ethnic group or national community. Belonging is a question of survival for human beings. All such bonding relationships can fail if the people who mainly represent these groups are not prepared to accept a certain person into their society. Such bonding trauma situations can be recognised by

- mobbing in school classes or work groups,
- discrimination against people because of skin colour, gender, religion or nationality.

For the people discriminated against there arises a terror of abandonment and even fear for their very life and safety. They become caught in what is for them an enduring contradiction that the more they are rejected the more they try to fit in, and the more they beg to be allowed into society.

This leads to a split in their psyche: the fears, anger and pain caused by their injuries and humiliation are suppressed. For example people from immigrant groups who are not accepted by the society in which they are living are likely to develop the following survival strategies:

- They become submissive in their behaviour towards authorities
- They pass on any humiliation they have experienced themselves to others weaker than they are, for example their children
- They retreat from society and escape into illusory worlds
- They cling rigidly to their old ways of life and beliefs, traditions and legal concepts
- They secretly cultivate a feeling of superiority, a feeling that their own moral standards are better than the society that rejects them
- They fantasise about violence towards those who reject them, even to the extreme of terrorist activities

It is not possible that the splitting can be resolved while the situation of mobbing and discrimination exists, because those of the excluding groups are themselves traumatised, and the mobbed individuals have no chance of becoming independent of the groups they would like to belong to.

However, if the survival strategies of the excluded individuals originate from their early life (for example a symbiotic trauma), and if they can strengthen their healthy self by confronting such earlier traumas there is a chance for them of finding a good way through. It is always helpful for a person to resolve their old scars rather than allow resentment stemming from them to restrict him, involving other innocent people in his personal fight with such earlier wrongs. If the process of healing old psychological wounds is successful, doors that were previously closed to him will be opened; groups that excluded him are more likely to include him. So for victims of mobbing it is always helpful if they look at their part in the symbiotic entanglement and not only see themselves as the victim of the others' persecution. Victim behaviour patterns will always attract perpetrator behaviour patterns.

Bonding system traumas

Symbiotic traumas can result from existential traumas or loss traumas in the person's mother, and these in turn can lead to the traumatisation of an entire bonding system over several generations if symbiotically traumatised people then have children. For example, if a mother has lost a child, she will normally be unable to build up a secure attachment to a child born later on. This child then will suffer from a symbiotic trauma. If, later in life, this child finds a partner who also suffers from a symbiotic trauma, it can happen that the mother neglects her child or even rejects it and this child in her symbiotic need then turns to the father, who in his own symbiotic need might take advantage of the situation and make inappropriate demands on the child, even perhaps abusing her sexually. This leads to situations that are so laden with taboos and cause extreme feelings of guilt in those concerned, that they are not able to integrate them into their identity structure. In this way bonding systems develop over generations in which all relationships are characterised by traumatisation, and continually produce new traumas (Figure 11). I refer to these cases as bonding system trauma situations.

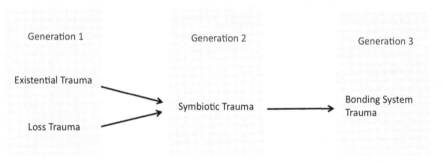

Figure 11: Conditions for the development of a bonding system trauma

In such families there are always some members who mainly function as perpetrators and some who function mainly as victims. Often there is a high degree of indifference, ignorance, thoughtlessness and violence, and frequently both parents partake in acts of violence towards the children. As a couple they will tend to have a destructive relationship, and because they were both usually victims of neglect and violence themselves, they control and abuse their children through their own sense of victimisation. Because of the perpetrator-victim split in their own psyche, they become perpetrators towards their own children.

A bonding system trauma is primarily defined by the simultaneous presence of both perpetrators and victims within the system. Perpetrators and victims live under the same roof and are dependent on each other, materially and/or psychologically.

Perpetrators and victims, perpetrator and victim attitudes

The defining question here is: How does someone become a perpetrator; and how does he become a victim? He becomes a perpetrator by inflicting serious harm on another person, physically or psychologically, or both at the same time.

With this definition, for example a person becomes a perpetrator in a traffic accident where he injures another person, thereby making the other person a victim. Both perpetrator and victim have to deal with this event. The perpetrator has to cope with the fact that he has injured another person, and the victim has to come to terms with his injury; each has to deal with the other if the event is to be handled well:

- The question of guilt has to be clarified,
- There has to be an admission of responsibility, and
- There has to be compensation for the damage sustained.

If perpetrator and victim reach agreement on all these points, they can lay the matter to rest after a certain time. The victim might suffer with his injury for the rest of his life, if he has, for example, lost an eye or a limb in the accident. The perpetrator might have to live the rest of his life with the knowledge that he has inflicted lasting damage on another person. But for the event to be gradually forgotten, the victim cannot harbour any thoughts of revenge, nor can the perpetrator hold any thoughts of atonement. That way, they both avoid becoming trapped in a permanent victim/perpetrator state.

If the three points mentioned above are not clarified, there is a high risk that the perpetrator will be caught in a perpetrator state and the victim in a victim state, and it is then very probable that perpetrator behaviour patterns/attitudes and victim behaviour patterns/attitudes will be developed.

A person who has harmed someone else takes on perpetrator attitudes if:

- He denies responsibility for his act, his own culpability,
- He tries to justifies his act,
- He feels he was compelled into committing the act,
- He does not offer the victim any compensation,
- He puts all the blame for what happened onto the victim,
- He has no empathy with the victim,
- He goes so far as to ridicule the victim.

Conversely, someone develops victim attitudes by:

- Telling no one about what happened,
- Blaming only himself or wrongly taking responsibility for part of the blame,
- Thinking that the fact that he has become a victim is justified, he deserves it,
- Not asking for any compensation for the harm,
- Being ashamed of the harm he has had to suffer,
- Protecting the perpetrator, blocking out the act or minimising it to save the perpetrator.

Thus it is not only the perpetrator who shirks his responsibility; both shield each other. Victims, out of dependence on and fear of the perpetrator do not dare to speak openly about the act, and so allow the perpetrator to continue to perpetrate.

Whether someone becomes a victim and remains in that role depends on how much control the perpetrator can continue to exercise, and on whether the person harmed has someone who helps and supports him, so that he is not permanently forced back into the victim role. This means that it depends on the reaction of his environment as well, whether a person can avoid falling into the role of victim and remaining in it permanently.

In this way, for example, people are wrongly put into the perpetrator role by some psychiatric and psychological diagnoses, and then held in the victim role by the type of treatment imposed. So, for example, if a girl who has stopped eating is diagnosed with 'anorexia', the following takes place:

- She is defined as ill by classifying the fact that she refuses to eat as an illness, namely 'anorexia'.
- By isolating her refusal to eat from its origins, the girl is blamed for not behaving in a 'normal' way.
- This type of diagnosis is regarded as justifying the use of force to make the girl eat 'normally', even force-feeding her.

However, if we understand that the girl's refusal to eat is a reaction to rejection and unkindness from her mother, who is traumatised, or to violence and sexual abuse from her traumatised father, then the absurdity of the diagnosis that the girl is 'addicted' to being 'thin', becomes apparent. What the child is actually doing by refusing to eat, is expressing her internalised perpetrator-victim split by using her own perpetrator part to suppress and control the victim part, as represented by her body.

In a traumatised bonding system perpetrators and victims are dependent on each other. They are trapped in their perpetrator or victim role. As a result of this perpetrators have to live with a guilty conscience that they try to ignore, and victims have to struggle with fantasies of revenge and their suppressed rage. Thus the perpetrator and victim behaviours are actually survival strategies that perpetuate the destructive relationship rather than resolving it. Neither perpetrator nor victim knows any other form of relationship. They accept the destructive relationship because they are more frightened of what happens if they are not in such a relationship, and do not have someone to fight with or beat up. Being alone seems a greater horror than the existing relationship.

The perpetrator-victim relationship, which initially is an external relationship, becomes a permanent internalised split in the psyche of those involved. All those concerned internalise and develop both perpetrator and victim structures. Through the presence of the victim, the perpetrator feels under pressure and perceives himself as the victim, and the victim also develops perpetrator behaviour patterns which they enact on those weaker than themselves, since it is impossible for them to enact in this way against the actual perpetrator.

These perpetrator-victim splits are found in all those involved in such a destructive bonding system. Within a family these dynamics continue from generation to generation and are likely to spread out into the larger relationship systems within which these families exist, because it is not possible in a perpetrator role, or in a victim role, to lead an autonomous life separate from the system. Perpetrators need victims for their survival and victims are fixated on perpetrators in their survival strategies. In extreme cases within a society this results in war.

Incest, violence and delusions of love

The things that have taken place in the past within a traumatised bonding system, and that may still be taking place – such as violence, abuse or even murder – are socially unacceptable. However, to put a stop to them would mean recognising them as such, and talking about them, but that would arouse the fear that things would then get much worse. If, for example, a woman realises that her husband is sexually abusing their daughter, she ought to tackle him about it. However, if she does so her husband would likely deny it. If she then turns to someone outside the family, she knows it would mean the end of her marriage. Whichever course of action she takes, she would create a new situation that she thinks might be even more distressing than her present one. So as a rule she chooses the means of denial and suppression, which she is already familiar with from her own traumatisation. She looks the other way, turning a blind eye to all the signals her child gives to alert her to what 'papa' is doing to her. She diverts attention by any means possible, aiming to present a perfect façade of a normal family to the outside world.

The perpetrator also behaves as if nothing is amiss. For example, he creeps out of the marital bedroom into the child's bedroom at night, uses the child to satisfy his sexual desires and returns to the marital bed as if nothing had happened. He knows that his wife is his silent accomplice. If necessary, he can accuse her of not satisfying him sexually which, bearing in mind that this man is a liar and child abuser, is not particularly surprising.

For such absurd arrangements to work, the children have to go along with it, and as a rule they do. When children grow up with traumatised parents, who not only neglect them emotionally, but also may inflict extreme physical and psychological pain on them, they sometimes survive by taking the blame themselves for everything that happens to them and not blaming their parents at all. In this way they can retain the illusion of having good parents. This childish survival strategy is also encouraged by the adults, who blame the child for the fact that he is not loved but tormented instead, on the basis that: 'We have to punish you because you're bad and evil'. Another frequently practised survival strategy of abused children is to imitate the behaviour of the perpetrators, for example they may also find what is being done to them 'funny'.

The perspective of perpetrators

Incest is usually based on the perpetrator's delusional concept of love, which allows him to draw a child into his psychological splits and delusions. The perpetrator sees in the child something that the child is not. Usually he is looking for the love and attention he did not receive from his mother, and his adult relationship does not provide. He projects fantasies onto the child that have nothing to do with the child. He wants to devour the child symbiotically and to be one with him or her. He wants the child to confirm to him that he is lovable and desirable.

The perpetrator wants to leave his own traumatic past behind him, so he fixates on his own child and the child's fresh, new life, which he wants for himself. He identifies with the child, and he wants to have this child all to himself. I have observed this dynamic many times with fathers who were severely traumatised as soldiers in the Second World War and who started a family after the war with the idea that this would help them forget the insanity of war. They saw a new and unencumbered life in their daughters that they wanted to have as their own.

Some perpetrators lead a completely double life. Part of them appears to the world as perfectly normal and good, as a respectable citizen, as a hard-working tradesman. Some even attach great importance to being morally, ethically or spiritually superior. Such perpetrators in their 'normal part' can be, for example, the mayor of a town, director of a school, singer in a chamber choir, amateur painter, stand-up comedian, etc. Their other part may be obsessed with sex. He may systematically bring up his daughter or son as a 'whore' or 'rent boy', who is more or less submissively at the beck and call of the father's sexual fantasies and actions. He grooms the child, buys him or her nice clothes, jewellery or expensive toys. He finds more and more excuses to be alone with the child by including him or her in his hobbies, taking him on hiking tours or doing exciting activities with him, going on holiday alone with the child. To outsiders this is supposed to look like a particularly loving father-daughter/son relationship.

For the perpetrator, the act of sexual satisfaction is in most cases a mixture of his attempt to satisfy his symbiotic need for love and union, combined with his erotic fantasies, sexual stimulation and the release of his inner tension by means of orgasm. Before arriving at incest and sexual violence, an initial phase of varying length can take place, during which the perpetrator finds out the child's preferences and his psychological susceptibility and uses them to make the child more dependent on him.

One strong motive a perpetrator has for staging such strategies is a fear of being alone. He or she cannot rely on someone else naturally wanting to be with them, wanting to stay with them, putting up with them and giving them the connection and love they have an almost insatiable desire for. They think they can only attain and keep what they want by devious and forceful means. For this reason it is clear that in the background of many perpetrators of violent crimes lies a childhood of symbiotic trauma, during which they felt abandoned and neglected by their parents. Accordingly most perpetrators consider themselves to be innocent; they regard themselves as victims who have not received what they deserved.

For many perpetrators of incest, delusions of love and excessive violence alternate. First of all the child is cajoled and tempted with care, attention and presents. If he or she resists the perpetrator's subsequent sexual advances, the perpetrator will try to convince the child that he or she really likes what is happening. If necessary, violence may be used to force the child to submit. As a result, the dynamics of a bonding trauma and an existential trauma (due to the violence) are often simultaneously present in a person who has been sexually abused.

Male perpetrators of incest transfer their split perception of women onto the female child. They idealise women as possessing all good characteristics, as being the 'good mother', while at the same time denouncing them as a whore and a slut. In many cases the perpetrator's mother has already been the victim of sexual abuse. A *female* perpetrator of incest has usually suffered sexual abuse as a child herself. With her daughter she will play out what happened to her, or she will repeat with her son the sex games to which she was originally subjected.

Sadistic perpetrators in particular are intent on convincing the child that he is not only completely dependent on them, but also evil. According to the perpetrator, only if the child does as he demands, does this child have a chance of not being abandoned by the perpetrator, and of then becoming a good child again. The perpetrator projects onto the child his own guilt and bad feelings. A sadistic perpetrator also repeats his own experiences with the child, of having been treated as a bad and dirty child by his parents.

A child's perspective

To begin with, a child frequently sees the perpetrator as the person who gives him or her the love he or she does not receive elsewhere. She likes the attention she receives before she is sexually abused. The child willingly accepts everything the perpetrator offers her by way of kindness, flattery and the feeling of being important to the perpetrator. Psychologically, perpetrator and child often have common feelings of loneliness. Both recognise the feeling of abandonment in the other and the sense of mirroring attracts them. Many female patients who have experienced sexual abuse report that their father's sadness and neediness underneath the sexual aggression touched them, and that they felt sympathy for him. In the symbiotic entanglement the child connects with the father's or grandfather's trauma feelings, unconsciously absorbing them. A part of the child holds onto these trauma feelings since they provide a very strong emotional tie between child and perpetrator.

Nature in her thrifty way has combined excretion of bodily fluids (urine) with the sexual organs, and as a result, we humans often associate sexuality not just with feelings of pleasure, but also with feelings of disgust, and excretion is often connected with shame. Therefore, if sex is unwanted it is often experienced as painful, disgusting and shameful, as is the case with most sexually abused children. A child will never agree to the perpetrator's sexual assault of his own accord; he or she only allows it to take place because the perpetrator dominates him or her physically and psychologically, often with the use of violence. She lets sexual stimulation happen or, under pressure from the perpetrator such as the threat of not being liked or being abandoned, performs sex acts on the perpetrator.

So we can understand that children who are already split from a previous trauma, such as a symbiotic trauma or a trauma of loss, are particularly liable to become entangled in a perpetrator's delusions of love, because they know they cannot get emotional contact and protection from their mother. In most of the cases that I am aware of the primary precondition for a child being susceptible to contact by a sexual abuser is having a prior symbiotic trauma with the mother .

Some daughters who are abused by their fathers believe they understand their father better and love him more than the mother does. The perpetrator usually creates or strengthens this feeling within the child. The mother's open rejection of the child is the final straw in driving the child into the perpetrator's hands.

The thing a child is totally unable to understand is why her mother does not protect her from such sexual assaults. She assumes – often correctly – that her mother is aware of what the perpetrator (father, grandfather, brother) is doing to her and she feels forsaken by her mother, but sees no way to confront her openly about it.

Thus, another situation is created in which there is no solution for the child. The abused child is unable to say anything; she cannot leave, nor can she defend herself. Whatever she does, she will only make the situation worse. So the child starts creating further splits. She pretends, for example, that the abuse only happened in a dream. As if what was done to her in the darkness of the night was only a nightmare and not brutal reality. She idealises the perpetrator as the good Papa, Grandpa, dear Auntie, etc. and completely obliterates the person's dark side.

While being sexually abused, the child may leave his body or despise it if he feels any pleasurable reactions. Frequently the child becomes a 'day child', who behaves as if nothing has happened, and a 'night child', who is not sure if what he experiences is actually real. Consequently, the child lives in a permanent state of stress and panic.

A patient of mine described this insanity very touchingly and in great detail, the insanity acted out by perpetrators on children when the child is completely at their mercy. One of the many survival strategies of an abused child's psyche is turning reality into a nightmare. A vital step in healing an abuse trauma is recognising reality as reality; that the individual actually did suffer sexual abuse and it was not a dream, a fantasy or their imagination. If the individual does not take this step, they will remain in their splits, preventing their own healing and protecting the perpetrator and their accomplices.[1]

Case study 9

Actual memories – not a nightmare (Anna)

"I dream that I'm lying in bed and that my mother's watching me sleep and dream. And I think: she's watching me dream and she can see what I'm feeling. She must be able to see it!!

"My father gets into my bed and he moves towards me, so tenderly and lovingly, and I think: well, perhaps he is kind; of course he's kind. And he whispers things in my ear:

---

[1]   This case history is printed with the kind permission of its author, who intends to write a book about her childhood experiences. This extract remains the property of that author.

that I'm his best girl, his prettiest girl, his princess and that he loves only me and that I can help him feel better, because his wife (my mother) is so nasty and unloving. And anyway he's only doing all this because he loves me so much and he knows that I like it too. He promises me that. And while he's saying that he gets closer and closer to me in bed. His mouth is very close to my ear – I hate it!

"I move towards the wall and he moves closer to me and I can feel him touching my back. And in a strange way I like that. I so want someone to cuddle me, to hold me and stroke me. To feel bodily contact, physical closeness. To feel a person. Anything warm. Not just the hate, coldness and humiliation I get from my mother.

"And he goes on talking in my ear – oh, how I hate that – that I am the only one for him, the best, the greatest, the prettiest. That no one can understand – only I can – how much he loves me, and that we can't tell anyone. Because the others simply wouldn't understand. It's something only we two understand. Just us. You and me – he says.

"To be honest, I don't understand it – but that's probably because I'm simply too stupid. He says that too as well, quite often in fact. Which doesn't seem to fit together somehow. How can I be his best girl and the greatest if I'm stupid? It's another thing that doesn't make sense, but like I said – I simply don't understand because I'm just stupid.

"I start to have my doubts again. Perhaps my dear Papa's right and the others just don't understand how much he loves me; the others are the bad guys. After all, why should my dear Papa lie to me?

"Again I start to enjoy his closeness and I relax, which is when I suddenly feel the hardness of his penis in my back. Now I definitely know, no, this isn't good. When this happens, something really bad follows. No, I don't want the horrible thing to happen today. All I want today is to be cuddled.

"But his embraces get stronger and more demanding and I feel his arousal. Oh shit, I think, this isn't good. I have to do something to appease him, to de-escalate the situation. Papa, I say, no, I don't want that. Stop it – you're hurting me!

"His smile disappears. 'It doesn't matter what you want, do you understand?', he says. 'You can't tell me what to do. I already have to listen to your mother telling me what I can and can't do – I'm not going to let myself be told by you as well. You're not giving me orders!', he shouts at me in a whisper.

"I lie there stiffly. He grabs my arm and turns me round so that I'm facing him. He grips me roughly. I become more and more rigid, my body is rigid and tries to protect itself. I start feeling cold. I gradually leave my body. The coldness spreads – I'm bitterly cold, as if I'm in the middle of a block of ice. Frozen!

"But today it doesn't seem to work because my body is reacting with other feelings. Warmth. And I can't completely leave it. I hate my body for doing this – I feel betrayed. Why is it doing that?

"I feel his hands between my legs and I see the way he's looking at me – lustfully, as if I'm not a human being but simply an object that is there to satisfy his lust and his needs. Yes, that's exactly how I feel: like an object that's only there to fulfil the needs and desires of other people. Like an IT -there is no ME – I'm not an 'I'.

"He goes on stroking me and he wants me to touch him. He forces me to hold his penis in my hand. I hate my hand for doing it! Another betrayal. I know exactly what he wants – he wants to bring me to orgasm. He wants to do that so that he can justify what he's doing. If I come, then what he says is true, isn't it? That I enjoy it and he's only doing it for that reason? And he always looks at me while he's touching me. It's horrible. Being exposed like that.

"I feel my arousal and I simply can't understand why my body does this. He goes on stroking me and grinning maliciously and says: 'Come on, or does the little miss want me to beg?'

"I feel so humiliated and exposed. And he says: 'Come on, show me that you like it! I know I can make you come.

Your mother is just frigid, but I know I can satisfy a woman.'

"I have no idea what the word 'frigid' means, but my mother must be a very bad woman. And that's why my Papa is like this, because Mama doesn't understand him.

"'Come on! What's taking you so long?' At this moment I want to kill him! But he pushes me down onto the bed with one hand and strokes me with the other. I know he won't stop until I've come and I give in to my physical feelings. I surrender to my own body, which has betrayed me. And I have to make a lot of noise otherwise he squeezes my throat. He wants to hear that he can give a woman pleasure, because he doesn't succeed with my mother.

"I see myself dreaming all this and in my dream I see that my mother is watching my dream, seeing everything, hearing everything, seeing my feelings! And I think: she can't possibly not notice! How could she?

"When it's over he's nice to me first of all, and then he says: 'You see, I knew you liked it – all you have to do is trust me.' I turn away from him. He doesn't like it when I turn away – he sees it as rejection and he gets enough of that from my mother. His expression changes and it feels as if something sharp is sticking into my back. It feels like a knife. It feels as if he's sticking a knife into my back.

"And then he says: 'And don't think for a minute that anybody would believe you if you told them. Your mother certainly wouldn't, and no one else would either. Don't even think of telling anyone. You're a whore and that'll be visible to everyone. You're nothing and no one. You can do nothing. You are nothing. Just a dirty little whore. And if you breathe a word of this to anyone, I'll kill you.'

"He squeezes my throat with both hands. I'm completely frozen, turned to stone; my limbs are sticking out away from my body. He forces my head backwards, choking me, my tongue hanging out. I gasp for air, my eyes swivel. I am completely frozen and stiff and he comes up really close to my face. I think, now he's definitely going to kill me, I'm going to die and then he screams at me in a whispered, threatening tone: 'If you say anything, if you mention even the slightest thing to anyone, I'll kill you. I'll kill you with my bare hands; it'd be easy for me. Remember how I killed the kittens? I'll do the same to you. You're dead if you breathe a word!'

"Suddenly I feel something again. A wave of heat floods through my body; I am covered in a cold sweat. I'm still gasping for breath, his hands are still squeezing my throat. Everything becomes blurred. All I can see are black and white dots. I'm going further and further away. I feel so sick, I think I'm about to throw up. Cold sweat runs down my body and all I can see are blurred outlines and then this unbelievably awful feeling fills my whole body: every cell of my body feels mortal terror. Not having any control any more, in complete hopelessness with the feeling of utter terror; certain of death and feeling the imminence of dying. And with these words he leaves my body and my room.

"And I know that in a few hours I'll get up and go to school as if nothing had happened. Because Anna who will get up tomorrow and go to school, it didn't happen to her."

Victim/perpetrator reversal

The self-esteem of children who have been abused and rejected by their parents, sometimes even handed over or sold to others to be abused, is systematically undermined. The attempt is even made to destroy it on purpose. These children are rendered speechless, and feel worthless and incapable because their parents continually tell them that they are stupid, that they know nothing and are completely depraved. The author of the text quoted above writes:

"Wasn't allowed to scream. Was beaten and sexually abused until I was silent. My way of adapting was to say to him/them what they wanted to hear. That they are wonderful. That they should take me roughly. That I am a good girl. That I am a completely wild/naughty girl. That I deserve the way Papa is hurting me. And because I'm a bad girl Papa has to hurt me a lot. It's my fault and Papa will like me again if I turn round. And then he enters me anally. I wasn't allowed to cry, wasn't allowed to scream; had to smile, otherwise the bad girl would be raped anally again."

The perpetrators therefore succeed as a rule in convincing the children that they are the bad ones, and the perpetrator is the good person. So the child tries hard to be good and do everything the perpetrator demands of her so that she is seen as being good. These children try hard to adapt to the desires and needs of the perpetrator, to second-guess them and serve them as required, regardless of the price to themselves.

Children who have been sadistically tortured in this way have to create several internal splits. The symbiotic needy survival part longs for the mother's care, and experiences this perverse form of attention from their tormentors as proof of their love, grasping at the smallest hint of attention as a drowning man grasps at a straw.

Consequently such children develop inner parts of themselves that have a slave mentality. They admire their 'lords and masters' for their power and strength and the way they assert themselves in life. The children have no confidence in themselves and feel dependent on their tormentors for everything. They want to belong to the perpetrator and to the family. Not belonging, being without the family and on their own, seems to them much more threatening than the physical and psychological torture they have to suffer for staying within the family. The emotionally numbed body of the child is offered in appeasement to the perpetrators for them to abuse sexually, so that they can affirm: Yes, you belong with us.

Sexually abused girls often retain this inner appeasing attitude and, as adults, seek out those whom they think will be strong protectors. In a sexual sense, they will do everything men expect and demand of them. They try their utmost to fit in, denying all their own needs and interests. They endure being raped and accept it as normal. They don't see the fault as lying with the other, who ruthlessly satisfies his needs, but only with themselves. In their victim survival strategies they are unable to differentiate between normal, healthy sexuality, and perverse, sadistic and masochistic forms of sexual acts.

Case study 10

'Madness is raging inside me' (Ursula)

A patient describes her inner struggle between the part of her that does not want to go on (she calls it her 'healthy part', although in reality it is still a very adapted survival part), and the part of her that is loyal to the perpetrator:

"It's total madness inside me. Healthy part versus perpetrator part. Absolute chaos! The perpetrator part commands me to be intimate with my husband several times a day. Once isn't enough! It's just crazy. I don't know what to do. The healthy part in me says: once is enough. It's so crazy that I think the best thing would be for me to kill myself. Nothing makes any sense. My body does what the perpetrator wants. I try to distract myself with exercise and reading. If I give in again it'll never get better. I want to get away from it."

In my therapeutic practice I have come across many cases of sexual abuse of girls and boys. There are studies that show that 25% of all girls have suffered sexual abuse. But the number of sexually abused boys is also considerable, estimated as 10%. The percentages depend on the definition of sexual abuse and the method of data collection. The age of the sample, their level of education and social class all play a role, as do regional differences (Kloiber, 2002; Finkelhor, 2006).

Based on my work as a trauma therapist and my publications, many male and female clients who have experienced sexual abuse come specifically to my practice, which explains the number of cases of sexual abuse I deal with and which I have been able to use as examples in this book. Many of those concerned are unaware of their sexual abuse at the beginning of therapy as a result of splitting off their traumatic experiences. They are only able to recall it during the course of therapy when they try to investigate their many psychological or physical symptoms or relationship issues; their resistance to seeing themselves as victims of sexual abuse is very high. There are always survival parts that vigorously try to deny their own sexual abuse.

Of course it can happen that someone believes he has been sexually abused, despite that not being the case ('false memory syndrome'). However, I see no sign of my patients presuming that it is to their advantage to believe or to claim that they were sexually abused in their childhood and adolescence, and as a result I think the estimates of the prevalence of child sexual abuse quoted above are, if anything, too low.

In some cultures it seems to be acceptable for young boys to be sexually abused by their fathers and older brothers, but mothers who were victims of sexual violence in their childhood, also tend to abuse their sons sexually. These abused boys and the sons of abused mothers then are likely to become the next generation of perpetrators of abuse. They have learnt to make use of sexual fantasies and sexual acts to release their unendurable inner tensions. They can often then become trapped in a pattern of sex addiction and compulsive sexual behaviour. This is a client's description of his survival strategy: "When I fuck someone or someone fucks me, then I can *be*, I am *accepted* and I can stay."

The desperation they experience by enduring the internal tension resulting from their sexual exploitation and humiliation, can even lead to sexually-traumatised men becoming deranged killers and terrorists (deMause, 2002).

Multiple identity splits

There are people who are subjected to such cruel and painful experiences, and so mercilessly made to feel mortal terror by ruthless perpetrators and organised criminals, that it is in a way unbelievable how they manage to survive (Fröhling, 1996;

Huber, 1998, 2003, 2011). I have learnt a lot from the comprehensive and profound publications of Michaela Huber concerning therapeutic work with multiple-split female patients. Therapists are greatly helped if victims of this type of abuse break their silence and write about their experiences.

The development of whole identities with different names is a product of the perpetrators who often earn a lot of money through their exploitation of the children, by selling pictures and movies of the sexual abuse. The perpetrators force the child to switch their identity and give them the different names for the different tasks the child has to fulfil.

It is quite astonishing how some of these extremely abused children can later in life appear externally normal and can, for example, have a job as a teacher or manager. Alongside these seemingly normal parts of the self, there are other parts that retain contact with the perpetrator, are loyal to the perpetrator, or stage suicide attempts because they are unable to endure it all.

The fact that they themselves are somehow aware of their many splits and that their different identity survival parts often have their own names and lead their own lives, is an extremely threatening state for these severely traumatised people. They therefore try to hide it and deny it as much as possible, both from themselves and other people. They are afraid of being seen as crazy, and of actually going insane and ending up in a psychiatric ward, and never being able to be in charge of their own lives again. Certain parts of them know what has happened, so the survival parts have to work hard in order to keep the memories out of consciousness: "Nothing happened to me, because the person it happened to isn't me. And the proof is that that person's name is different from mine."

People with such 'multiple identities', or the diagnosis 'Dissociative Identity Disorder', also have as part of their psychological structure many survival parts that will work hard to prevent exposure in trauma therapy, because of the fear that if everything came to light it would then be completely unbearable for them. The goal of trauma therapy, the integration of the split personality parts, is contrary to their survival program of keeping the chaos under control by continually changing personality and denying reality. The perpetrators often also produce parts within them that sabotage therapy, revealing to the real perpetrators in the background what happens in the therapy.

I was once the representative for the 'intention' of a sexually traumatised female client, and I knew for certain that a part of her was aware of everything that had happened. But all the same, as her 'intention' I was unable to do anything other than show my desire to live to the other part of the client that was grimly determined to remain silent.

The difficulties of disengaging from a bonding system trauma

Bonding system traumas can often end in murder or manslaughter. An incestuous relationship may lead to conception, with an abortion then taking place, or the newborn child being killed after birth. Within such a traumatised bonding system, the situation will escalate until the system is completely dissolved. This can happen, for example, if the perpetrator leaves the family. But unfortunately, some women then introduce the next perpetrator into the family, who continues the abuse of the children.

My therapeutic experience has shown that it is extremely difficult for children to detach themselves completely from a family that has treated them badly. They have internalised this perfidious system because they have learnt and developed many strategies to enable them to survive in such a family. They play their own part in the evil game, by keeping silent and not telling anyone outside the family what they experienced and what they see going on. They are afraid that their family will break up, and that they could end up in a home, and their father could be sent to prison if anything came to light. They are afraid that their mother would abandon them or kill them, or that she would commit suicide.

These are all very real fears, because the parents really are unpredictable due to their own traumatisations. How is a child, living in a hell on earth with such parents, supposed to survive, other than by splitting and relinquishing more and more parts of their healthy psyche? This is why the psychological processes that originate with a bonding system trauma are frequently continued over many generations. One generation traumatises the next and so on.

Case study 11

'It's not my fault!' (Anna)

The patient who wrote the text above (Case study 9 – 'Actual memories – not a nightmare') only realised after many years of therapy that the sense of responsibility for what happened had been transferred from her parents to her as a child, and became aware that she had accepted the blame. Following one therapy session she wrote:

"Since yesterday I have been able to recognise what has determined my whole life. I don't have to tell you about the horrors of my childhood any more. But what I didn't know was that the beatings, the abuse on every level and all the violence, had made me believe that I am so bad that I deserve this treatment. I believed I deserved this treatment because I was so bad that I had corrupted the good adults and made them beat me. My whole life I have suppressed my strength so that I didn't harm anyone with my badness. I reduced myself to an absolute minimum, in every sense, so that the evil that is me didn't rise to the surface. I had it beaten into me that it's me who makes the others treat me the way they do.

"Thank goodness I've reached the end of my tether in suppressing what I am. Yesterday was the first time I came to the surface as ME. I've grasped that I was carrying the entire blame for my mother, my grandmother and my father.

I'd taken on responsibility for their behaviour. Yesterday I realised that *they* were bad (or were themselves entangled with their perpetrators), and I wasn't. The child that was me was totally innocent of the badness and the adults' hate. At the moment I'm completely exhausted and more thankful than I've ever been in my life. I can stop putting myself down and punishing myself."

Disengaging from a bonding system trauma can only be successful if all the obstacles built up by the different survival strategies are overcome. The feelings of shame and blame are usually so powerful that those concerned dare not talk about what they have experienced because they fear further rejection and being socially ostracised. Their mortal terror is also so great that the avoidance strategies mentioned in the chapter on existential trauma are highly developed. And finally, there is such a high potential for anger in those concerned, that they fear they might lose control and kill their parents. This is another form of the strong and lasting survival strategies that idealise and protect the parents and the whole family. Despite everything that has happened, the need to be accepted and loved by their parents, and their loyalty towards the family are such strong psychological forces, that sexually abused children persistently try to understand their parents, to comfort and help them.

Many will then transfer this attitude onto others, whom they also try to help and save. Some will take up social work and even therapeutic professions.

Some children even take it upon themselves to accept the stigma of insanity in order to protect their parents from accusations that they are to blame for the fact that the children are doing so badly. In view of the familial reality, idealising their traumatised parents is often the only protective mechanism available to these children to stop them running amok.

A great deal of clarity is required in the psychotherapy process, which must initially be provided by the therapist, so that the healthy parts of the client that are entangled in the bonding system trauma can disentangle accordingly:

- So that the client can gradually see for herself more clearly what is normal and what is not.
- So that she is able to resist the temptations from her symbiotically entangled survival parts to continue her childish need to protect her parents, and stop taking responsibility herself for the abuse and violence she received.
- So that she can confront the endless longing of the small child within herself for her parents' love with an adult's clear thinking and feeling, and accept the justifiable needs of this child for love, support and security and learn to steer them in a healthy direction.
- So that she no longer sees the problem as resulting from her own split-off trauma self, but as coming from her survival strategies that produce the internalised perpetrator/victim split.

The greatest clarity and determination are necessary for the client to find his or her way out of the prison that is still seen as 'family'. Then it is possible that the picture of the mother gradually becomes realistic, as, for example, with the following patient.

Case study 12

Chasm of Splits (Sabine)

"With my mother I see this chasm of fragmentation, rape, splits between good and evil. My mother had a child for a mother. She was unhappy because she couldn't finish studying medicine because her mother was ill, and her father demanded that she come home and look after her mother. I feel that no one in her family was able to speak about their feelings; that my mother bears a deep hate within her which she has transferred to me; that there were things and situations she kept secret. She splits externally and internally. She is emotionally very confused as far as men are concerned, and she sees in me other people, who are not me. She addresses me by different names. She idolises her father as a hero!"

Those concerned need a clear therapeutic orientation to be able to understand this reversal of perpetrator and victim roles, so that they no longer spend all their time trying to belong to the perpetrator's system. As long as psychological and physical symptoms remain it usually means that there is still some contact with the original perpetrator, or that the original perpetrator has been replaced by new perpetrators, and the symbiotically entangled child parts of the person have not yet found an alternative to ending up at the mercy of further perpetrators. This can even happen in the psychotherapy where the therapist may become the perpetrator.

It does not help those concerned to expect that the traumatised parents will give up the child. They will not do it. They won't do it because they need the child to compensate for their own traumas; the symbiotic entanglement with the child is their lifeblood, distracting them from their traumas. Neither trying to establish boundaries, nor showing understanding for the parents will help such a child. These are simply further variations of the symbiotic entanglement and just keep the destructive symbiosis carousel turning.

Generally clients only realise what they have suffered all their lives when they voluntarily give up any further contact with the perpetrator, in other words, when they no longer invest any feelings or thoughts in the symbiotic entanglement. They can usually only then begin to talk about their split trauma experiences as events which actually took place, and realise the emotional dimension of the whole craziness. They can then develop real personal emotions, and, instead of sympathy for the perpetrator, feel compassion for themselves.

It then becomes obvious that the argument frequently used by clients – that they do not know whether they were sexually abused because they have no images of the abuse – is simply a survival strategy. Images alone, with no corresponding emotions, do not amount to anything. The presence of strong emotions such as disgust, nausea, shame, fear, anger, pain, which are clearly noticeable, and physical symptoms, such as pain in the genital and anal areas, inflammation of the gums, gagging or constriction, abdominal and chest pains, or compulsions, such as washing rituals, hair pulling, nail biting, refusal to eat, binge eating and purging, etc, are much more obvious signs that sexual abuse has taken place than fleeting images are.

Psychosis and schizophrenia

For children who are entangled in a multi-generational traumatised bonding system who don't seek healing, there is a risk that they will become lost in the transferred feelings of the traumas, or manoeuvre themselves into more extreme strategies of reality denial. If one looks at the phenomena known in psychiatric terminology as 'psychosis' and 'schizophrenia' in relation to this theory of multi-generational psychotraumatology, one could say that 'psychotic' means being deeply enmeshed in the symbiotic entanglements of the traumas of earlier generations, particularly within the maternal line. Being 'schizophrenic' means that the individual has adopted extreme strategies of denial, even denying realities that are obvious to everyone else. If a child realises his traumatised mother's pull towards death, either because she wants to give up due to her own traumatisation, or because she is entangled in the death-vortex of her own traumatised mother, the child will try to prevent his mother from dying by latching onto her psychological structures and try from within these to bring about the love she desires.

For example, the child may try to apply his psychological efforts to connecting his mother with her own mother emotionally. Or he may try to find strategies to divert his mother's self-destructive violence away from her towards himself, setting himself up as the target for her hatred and rejection, in order to relieve her. In his psychosis, the child, who really only wants his mother's love, tries to bring love into the family of his mother that in reality is not there.

The child believes himself to be right. He thinks he is doing well, and does not want to be interrupted in his attempts to save his mother. If, on the other hand, he has chosen his father to be a replacement mother because he realised early on that love would not be forthcoming from his mother, then his psychotic attempts might also be directed towards compensating for the psychological damage in his father's family.

If, then, psychiatric intervention prevents the symbiotically entangled child from continuing working on his magical attempts to conjure up love out of thin air, love that doesn't exist, a power struggle will ensue between the psychiatric services and the person. Just as the person uses all his efforts to alter reality so that his mother (or his replacement mother) is loved and loves him, so psychiatrists become entrenched in forcing their patients back into a reality they regard as 'normal' using procedures available to them. The result is a grim power struggle, and the question comes down to who has the greater power and is able to force the other to his knees. No one wins this power struggle in the end. Both end up damaged.

Case study 13

A knife at the throat (Dorothea)

Dorothea had been diagnosed with 'paranoid schizophrenia' and kept having extreme panic attacks. She felt as if something was pressing into her throat. She knew that her grandmother had lost her mother as a child. A constellation suggested that her grandmother's mother, Dorothea's great-grandmother, had been killed by her husband. The client experienced a violent pain when she received this information, but it was followed by a feeling of deep peace within her.

Case study 14

Black magic

A symbiotically entangled woman, in whose family children from incestuous relationships had been killed, wrote to me: "There is such great hatred within me that I am afraid of destroying everything. I've got a small child and I can't love him or be good to him. I feel like an evil witch and it's almost driving me mad."

If someone is trapped in such splits and entanglements, even with appropriate psychotherapeutic help, it is difficult to make her give up her symbiotic survival strategies, since these strategies developed completely unconsciously in the earliest stages of life, and the pull of the emotional chaos of the traumatised bonding system is immensely strong and tempting, and the survival mechanisms that protect perpetrators in the family from being exposed are extremely persistent. The fear of not having a family if the truth were to come out, is often much greater than the desire to lead a normal existence. The pull to belong to a family, whatever the cost to the self, is incredibly strong for the survival parts of the symbiotically entangled person, and they may pursue this even at the cost of their sanity, or occasionally their life.

Flashbacks and intrusions

If a traumatic experience is suddenly re-triggered, one that, for example, was connected with mortal danger, it is called in psychotraumatology terminology a 'flashback' or 'intrusion'. In such situations, experiencing the original traumatic situation may lead to strong emotional feelings and expressions according to the type of trauma, which can come and go in waves. In between there will be periods of recovery phases. The client has to decide for himself when he has had enough of allowing the split trauma emotions to surface.

Case study 15

Quit smoking (Marlene)

Marlene wanted to end her addiction to smoking. But whenever she tried to stop, she felt panicky. In her constellation the part she set up as representative for her addiction to smoking showed a dual nature. The representative she chose was a man, and on the one hand he represented someone who had brutally raped her when she was an adolescent. She had completely blocked this out of her consciousness because she had left her body while she was being raped, but during this constellation she suddenly recalled the event. On the other hand, the representative for the addiction said that he felt like he wanted to die. So Marlene's internalised perpetrator-victim split was reflected in this representative of her addiction to smoking. When she smoked, she re-staged the oral rape by putting a cigarette into her mouth and inhaling poison – sperm and swallowing it – and at the same time inhaling nicotine served to anaesthetise her panic.

Psychiatry of the 19th and 20th centuries

In pre-scientific thinking the phenomena of madness, delusion or melancholy were taken as signs that a person was in contact with dark powers. The belief prevailed that the devil had taken possession of the soul or a woman had bonded with evil and become a witch. In this thinking madness was seen as the result of sin, guilt or a curse. Exorcism, the driving out of the devil or the burning of witches seemed to be a fitting method of punishing a sinner and reverting him to a good person (Porter 2005).

During the last two centuries, psychiatry as an applied science of medicine has developed differently in different countries. It has adapted well to diverse social and political conditions. Today it is a specialised area of medicine and generally interpreted according to somatic medical thinking

(Schneider 1992, Bäuml 1994, Rahn and Mahnkopf 2000). It is therefore frequently called 'biological' psychiatry to differentiate it from forms of social psychiatry, which include the psychological and social context of 'psychological disorders' (Dörner and Plog, 1992, Wollschläger, 2001).

Biological psychiatry takes a decidedly scientific view, according to which the 'psyche' represents the consequences of biochemical processes in the human body and particularly in the nervous system and the brain. In this sense, the psyche has no form of existence of its own and needs no special attention. Instead it is all about genes, neurotransmitters, neural pathways and different areas of the brain. From a psychiatric perspective, psychological disorders are illnesses just like all other physical illnesses, and the aim is to subject them to detailed classification, diagnose them and treat them on a purely physical level. Essentially a psychiatric diagnosis equates the symptom with the illness, giving it a Latin or Greek name. If someone feels he is being pursued, he is suffering from 'paranoia'; someone who lacks energy and feels dejected has 'depression'.

Biological psychiatry, like conventional medicine, is primarily concerned with reducing and suppressing symptoms. It is often solely an emergency medicine that tries to bring acutely disturbed and suicidal people back into reality by administering psychoactive drugs. It is openly admitted that the medication given is not free from unwanted side effects, and patients have to accept a whole range of restrictions if they no longer want to be 'psychotic' or 'manic'. There is also a high probability that continuous treatment with psychoactive drugs will result in neurological damage, with some irreparable physical damage to kidneys, stomach or intestines (Breggin, 1996, Bentall, 2003, 2009, Colbert, 1996, Lehmann, 2001).

Even if some psychiatrists declare optimism, and maintain that they are in control of 'mental illnesses' (Lütz, 2009 et al.), they are deceiving themselves and the public. The constant failures of medication to treat psychiatric disorders tell a different story. Mass consumption of psycho-pharmaceuticals does not improve public health, and many people with psychological disorders who receive purely medicinal treatment become worse in the long run. For the rest of their lives many remain regulars in psychiatric clinics, and end up sooner or later as 'untreatable', as 'permanently psychologically disabled' and as 'chronically psychologically ill' in welfare institutions and in psychiatric care (Bosshard, Ebert and Lazarus, 2007).

My main objections to this form of psychiatry are therefore:

- That it excludes psychological and social realities,
- That it does not have any well-founded knowledge about the patient's psyche,
- That it therefore cannot develop its own proper understanding of psychological health.

Healing madness with medication?

I will give a few notes relating to the treatment of 'psychologically ill' people by means of psycho-pharmaceuticals, as this is currently the most widely practised method.

From the middle of the 20th century an increasing number of chemical substances were developed which had a rapid and far-reaching effect on the human brain, leading many physicians to believe that this was the correct way forward for the systematic treatment of psychological disorders. A wide range of psychoactive drugs was developed – tranquilisers, anxiety-reducing drugs, painkillers, anti-depressants, mood enhancers and mania suppressants. For biologically oriented psychiatry, Hadol (Haloperidol), Tavor (Lorazepam), Abilify (Aripipazole) have become the drugs of choice, and seemed to have proved their usefulness. Straitjackets and electric shock treatment, which had previously given the institution of psychiatry a bad press in society, seemed to be things of the past. In their place came the apparently clean and silent elimination of human anxiety, outbursts of rage and delusions through psycho-pharmaceuticals. A whole industry grew up in a closely-knit network with practising psychiatrists and university departments. If patients are non-compliant and resist medication, then the use of medication can quickly become an issue of coercion.

Practice has shown that the patients who only receive medication, although they may outwardly appear calmer, are actually more tired, more indifferent, less animated and show increased physical signs of decline. Many accept this as their fate because they see no alternative and would rather lack feeling and be more inactive than be delusional. They have often found that not taking their medication leads to the recurrence of their psychotic state. Which results for them in a Catch-22 situation: they cannot manage without medication, but taking their medication means that they make no progress.

In the following case study a client describes the long-lasting psychological consequences after she was admitted to a psychiatric ward, forced to take anti-psychotic drugs and diagnosed with 'anxiety psychoses'.

Case study 16

Compulsory treatment and compulsory medication (Tanja)

"The worst thing about being admitted to the psychiatric ward was that I didn't know when I would be allowed to say no again; when I would have the power to do what I wanted again. This powerlessness was the worst thing. And at the same time being weak and helpless. The absolutely worst thing of all, though, was that, being so helpless, I had to trust these people who offered to help me, and what I then experienced has completely destroyed my faith in receiving help and in other people. The very thing that was supposed to help me actually destroyed me.

"The side effects of the medication were terrible. It was horrible for me to have no choice in taking that stuff and having to maltreat myself. I was aware of the effects and the side effects. During my studies I was particularly interested in this group of psychoactive drugs and had read specialised literature about them. I learnt that neuroleptics have horrific side effects and should preferably not be taken at all because no one really knows where and how they affect people. The drugs were really only licensed because the alternative was electric shock treatment or something similar.

"And what's also terrible for me is the feeling that I've now been stigmatised and I have to live with it. It's the feeling that I've suffered an injury. It was basically medical abuse. I have great difficulty in forgiving myself for letting myself be so afraid and going to the clinic, for not looking after myself better. For needing help and being afraid; for giving in and trusting. For trusting the wrong people. For not being able to prevent this from happening and having to experience it and having to have this stigma. I don't feel I'm on an equal footing with people who haven't been stamped 'psychotic'.

It'll probably take some time until I've worked my way through this problem. I'm glad the medication at least didn't cause any permanent physical damage."

In my therapeutic work with severe psychological disorders, I work on the hypothesis that as a rule bonding system traumas, and particularly perpetrator-victim entanglements, are expressed in the symptoms of the psychological confusion. In this patient's case her experiences in the psychiatric clinic were to an extent a repetition of the abuse of her childhood, her symbiotic trauma and her symbiotic entanglement with her parents, and her resulting victim/perpetrator split. She had trusted her parents and had been emotionally and physically abused by them.

I therefore question whether we professionals are sufficiently able to recognise the unconscious patterns of a perpetrator-victim split in our clients. If we are not able to do so we run the risk of being drawn into and becoming entangled with our clients' perpetrator-victim split, and of unconsciously acting out a perpetrator-victim split that may still be active within us in our relationships with our clients.

So if we can assume that non-integrated traumatic experiences and symbiotic entanglements are reflected in the psychological symptoms, particularly in those symptoms that lead to psychiatric diagnoses such as 'schizophrenia', 'mania', 'depression', 'anorexia', 'obsessive-compulsive disorders' or 'personality disorders', what function does medication actually have? Basically drugs and medication can only accelerate, slow down or stop the processes of the brain. They are unable to actually change the psychological programs, as described in Chapter 2 above, and their specific content.

Medication affects the body's energetic metabolism and can undermine the basis of emotional processes. It is, however, unable to

- alter the content of thoughts and feelings, or
- alter the way relationships are experienced, or
- help the processing of traumas experienced in the past.

In my opinion therefore, medication primarily supports the survival strategies of traumatised people, thereby suppressing the consequences of the trauma that are observable as the symptoms of the illness. Basically, medication proves to be a further resource in the arsenal of survival strategies that helps patients blank out the unbearable reality. The psychological split as a survival strategy following a trauma is perpetuated, even strengthened, with the aid of medication, giving the traumatised parts even less chance of being seen and understood, and to break out of their prison. In most cases, taking psychoactive drugs means that it is almost impossible for the person concerned to heal their splits and integrate their psyche into a stable and dynamically responsive psychophysical system, where experiences can flow freely again, without contradiction.

In my opinion, psychologically disturbed people desperately need a therapist as a counterpart who:

- is familiar with the causes and consequences of psychological entanglements,
- is well versed in the tensions of the unbearable feelings resulting from traumatic experiences, and the many denial strategies of such a reality,
- at times of crisis does not allow him or herself to be subverted by the entanglements and anxieties of the person, or start to panic,
- searches with the person for the real traumatising truths behind their symptoms.

People with extreme psychological disorders need human caring. They need to be able to discuss

- their many experiences of being rendered powerless,
- their constant massive anxieties,
- their indiscriminate anger,
- their strategies for seeking relief by escaping reality.

Psychoactive drugs often dull the emotional senses and block a client's ability to access their emotions, thereby, in my opinion, hampering psychotherapeutic work.

Case study 17

'There's no room for you there!' (Ariane)

Experience has taught me that, in the case of patients with a psychiatric diagnosis who are ready to look at the causes of their symptoms and, for example, take part in a constellations session, the background of their illness can be further resolved. In one patient's case it turned out that she heard a voice inside her head that told her there was no room for her there. It turned out that this message had to do with the fact that before she was born, her mother had had a disabled son, her brother, whose existence she had suspected before the constellation, and for whom there was no place in the family.

Such condemning, insulting and ridiculing voices that a person may hear in their head are often, in my experience, a strong indication of the internalisation of the perpetrator and his or her accomplices, particularly in cases of sexual abuse.

Trauma and the brain

Since the 1990s, the psychiatric mythology of the brain and nervous system put forward in the 19th century has been subjected to scientifically reliable brain research that is better able to integrate the phenomenon of trauma into models of the functions of the human brain and nervous system.

Neurobiology is increasingly able to identify and name the prerequisites for, and substructures of, trauma reactions and the resulting disorders in the brain and nervous system. Guido Flatten talks about the following connections:

- "...the intrusive symptoms... can be depicted as a problem of hypermnesia versus amnesia, in other words over-precise storing of experienced reality in contrast to fragmented or even lost experienced content."
- "...that the traumatic experience is subject to a high degree of resistance to erasure."
- "Emotional numbing is the down-regulation of affective perception; we could also describe it as a dissociation of experience and memory." (Flatten, 2011 b, pp 264f.)

The connections between the phenomena of bonding and trauma are also becoming better understood by neurobiology: "The increased experience of stress and anxiety leads biologically to activation of an increased bonding need, which can be understood as an evolutionary counter-program to the experienced insecurity. According to Fonagy (Fonagy, 2008), the priority of achieving a secure bonding at all costs results in a restriction of frontal and prefrontal brain areas, which leads to a limitation of mental capacity. In this state it is more difficult for the victim to develop a differentiated view of the traumatising perpetrator. At the cost of increased (pseudo) security, the foundations for a pathological perpetrator-victim relationship are laid." (Flatten, 2011 b, pp 270).

Such insights into the complexity of bonding and traumatising processes gives a perspective into what I have termed multi-generational psychotraumatology. Since bonding processes are the start of all human development, and at the same time the foundation of the psyche, traumatisations at this time have such a complete and long-lasting effect that they are still present in ensuing generations, and develop their own momentum.

5
Multi-generational psychotraumatology

Psychotraumatology is a relatively young science, which is developing simultaneously in different locations worldwide. Independently of one another, authors in different fields and countries are arriving at similar conclusions. Three main directions are emerging:

- Research into civil catastrophes such as traffic accidents, workplace accidents and natural disasters.
- Study of the consequences of war both in the armed forces and in the civilian population.
- Analysis of sexual violence in close relationships.

Psychotraumatology has a hard time being accepted socially owing to a great deal of resistance from institutions and individuals to being confronted with the daily reality of the consequences of violence and ruthlessness, and of their feelings of impotence and helplessness. So the research and study of psychotraumatology frequently have to risk breaking social and cultural taboos, and have to work hard not to allow themselves to be diverted from their insights and conclusions by widespread popular beliefs and wishful thinking put forward by those functioning from their trauma survival parts.

Accidents and civil catastrophes

Psychotraumatology has had much resistance to contend with in the field of accidents and civil catastrophes. In the mid 19th century masses of people should have been treated for symptoms resulting from trauma, but the field of medicine was not prepared to recognise the psychological side of people's injuries. Instead of talking about fear, panic and powerlessness, doctors talked about 'railway spine', in other words whiplash affecting the spinal cord, only looking for the physical cause of the injuries. (Flatten, 2011 a).

One positive development of industrial safety and accident insurance in Germany now is that traffic and workplace accidents are recognised as possible sources of the traumas of those concerned, and efforts are made to offer those people rehabilitation in relation to the causes (Drechsel-Schlund, in relation Feddern, Klinkert and Ludwig, 2010).

At least the victims of accidents and natural disasters are credited with not having caused their accidents. However, in many cases when the press coverage of the particular disaster has abated and journalists leave to cover the next disaster, those concerned feel they have been left alone with the consequences of their traumatisation.

Wars

Some attempts to put psychotraumatology into a historical and societal context have placed wars at the centre. Seidler, Wagner and Feldmann begin their presentation "with the controversy concerning the illness status of soldiers in World War I with conspicuous psychological problems and the validity of their illness symptoms" (Seidler, Wagner & Feldmann, 2008, p. 178). According to them, the huge numbers of soldiers suffering from symptoms such as 'shell shock' and 'bomb-shell disease' forced medical practitioners into the partial admission that it was not only a case of the personality of those soldiers, who were thought not man enough to fight a war and endure it, but that war created incidents that could permanently damage the nerves of even the strongest personalities.

Even after the shattering experiences of World War I, the social Darwinist viewpoint supporting the idea that conflict of the strong versus the weak was biologically necessary remained predominant, even if many who supported military confrontation in spirit, when faced with the reality of war despaired of this philosophy:

> "The best are sacrificed, while the physically and mentally inferior, the useless and the vermin, are carefully conserved, instead of using the opportunity for a thorough catharsis to take place, which would also have transfigured the parasites who were draining the nation's strength, through the glory of a hero's death" (Nonne, 1922, quoted in Seidler, Wagner and Feldmann, 2008, pp 179).

The consequences of this refusal to recognise the madness of war, and instead to continue with traditional patterns of thought, are known. They led more or less directly to the next catastrophe, World War II from 1939-45. Anyone wanting to understand the degree of mercilessness, and even pleasure, German soldiers showed in killing during World War II, and how they regarded it as a matter of course, should read the book titled *Soldiers: On Fighting, Killing and Dying – the secret WWII transcripts of German POWs*. After sifting through thousands of pages of wiretap transcripts, these authors have drawn a shocking picture of the psychological state of the soldiers, who seemed to have lost any form of empathy for the people they were pursuing on land and at sea, killing, slaughtering and destroying by the score (Neitzel & Welzer, 2011).

It is scarcely surprising that it was difficult for psychotraumatology to gain a foothold in society, even after the collective madness of World War II. The psychological survival mechanisms of denial of such traumatic war experiences are simply too strong, because they relate to a reality which is too unbearable when viewed directly. Scientists and experts in post-war

Germany actually questioned whether the symptoms of those who had survived the horrors of the concentration camps were a result of their experiences in the camps or whether they might not have their roots in a 'pre-morbid personality' (Eckart, 2012).

As the most severe war catastrophe in human history becomes more distant, society is gradually coming to accept that wars put people into such psychologically tortuous situations that anyone can be broken, regardless of their general psychological condition. The diagnosis of Post-Traumatic Stress Disorder as a symptom of the consequences of war is now at least being considered in the cases of armed forces and civilian victims.

However, those concerned still have to fight hard to avoid the stigma of individual failure. Politicians in almost all countries are still too interested in being able to use the machinery of war as a means of force against other nations. Many politicians will not allow such psychotraumatology findings to deter them from instigating and conducting wars. Even now, in the 21st century, there are few people who object to war, even many journalists and scientists stubbornly attempt to come up with justifications for war. These justifications are no longer as militaristic and socio-Darwinistic as they were at the beginning of the 20th century; when armed forces are sent to war today, the reasons given are 'in order to secure peace', 'fight terrorism' or 'protect the civil population'. Anyone objecting to war is still likely to be branded a delusional pacifist.

In my opinion it is a basic task of multi-generational psychotraumatology to make it clear that the traumatising consequences of war not only affect the people directly involved, but also leave their mark on people even up to four generations later. In many cases the children, grandchildren and great-grandchildren are enormously affected by the war experiences of their ancestors, as I can confirm from the case histories of many clients of mine. And in a way we can also say: the purpose of a war is the traumatisation of so-called enemies.

Sexual violence

Some authors set the historical origins of psychotraumatology in the mid 19th century. Pierre Janet (1859–1947), a doctor teaching and practising in Paris, had recognised that the abnormal behaviour of women, who at that time were diagnosed as suffering from 'female hysteria', could be traced back to their having been sexually abused. As Janet established, these women were trying to cope with their experience of violence through the mechanism of 'dissociation'.

This subject makes it clear that the development of psychotraumatology has to do with the development of society as a whole. It is dependent on the openness with which society regards what is actually happening in families and institutions, homes and schools. To begin with, Sigmund Freud (1856–1939), who spent several years studying with Jean-Martin Charcot in the Hôpital Salpêtrière in Paris, as did Janet, also favoured this concept of explaining 'hysteria' as the result of childhood sexual violence. However, he later overthrew this theory in favour of his 'drive theory'. In the early 20th century, societal resistance was still too strong to break the taboo of intra-familial sexual abuse of children and talk in detail about the massive degree of sexual violence taking place in the home, mostly carried out by men on women and children.

Judith Herman's book, *Die Narben der Gewalt* (The Scars of Violence), opened my eyes to the connection between psychological disorders and sexual violence (Herman 2003). Another book of great importance in my own development as a trauma theoretician and trauma researcher was the *Lehrbuch der Psychotraumatologie* (Textbook of Psychotraumatology) by Gottfried Fischer and Peter Riedesser (Fischer and Riedesser, 1998), in which sexual abuse of children is depicted as a trauma with all its far-reaching consequences.

The many cases of abuse within the church and in pedagogic institutions that have come to light in the last few years in several countries in Europe and in the USA, could only have been exposed in an environment that is no longer willing to look away. In order to reveal the extent of violence and sexual abuse to children and adolescents, even by clergy and teachers, walls of silence have to be broken down, cover-ups revealed, and networks of criminal dealings exposed and individuals brought to account.

In many societies perpetrators are still more protected than victims. The mechanism of trauma survival strategies is still functioning on a societal and political level. Parts of the judiciary, the prosecution services, the sciences, political elite, the press and also many of the victims themselves are continually involved in denying or playing down the amount of psychological disorders caused by trauma. The psychological disorders of victims of sexual violence are frequently presented as individual dysfunctions; diagnoses such as 'anorexia' or 'borderline personality disorder' mask the sexual violence that, as a rule, those concerned have suffered. The relatively few rapists and perpetrators of sexual abuse who are caught are declared to be pathological sex offenders, without going deeper into the social and psychodynamic causes that lead to sexual violence in close relationships.

Transmission of traumas via traumatised parents

Psychotraumatology that concentrates solely on the individuals concerned does not go deep enough. Psychotraumatology that is in contact with reality must put the causal relationships into a broader context. Part of this should be looking at the societal framework of the origins of the trauma and its development, as well as the realisation that traumas can be passed on socially and psychologically from one generation to the next. Psychotraumatology therefore has to look at more than one generation; if not, it might well understand the symptomatology resulting from one individual's identifiable trauma, but it will be puzzled by people with massive psychological disorders but no apparent severe personal traumatisation (Baer & Frick-Baer, 2010).

As a result, a further taboo has to be broken in this context, and that is in connection with the role of the parents, particularly that of the mother. This has to be looked at because the mother is so close to her children, and her children depend on her completely for their existence and safety, she is therefore the central link in the passing on of psychological consequences of traumatic events.

Through the endeavours of the feminist movement and theory, it is understood that women have been rightly seen as victims of societal relationships often shaped by male violence, but they must also be seen and recognised now as being the main source of psychological traumatisation of children; in that sense they are often perpetrators themselves. Even if they do not intend to be, traumatised mothers are one of the main causes of hyperactivity, drug abuse or even psychoses in children and adolescents. Early childhood experiences with a traumatised mother are frequently the underlying cause if adults who have suffered a recent trauma, such as separation from a partner or a professional failure, fall into a deep depression. In all these cases, according to my experience as a therapist, the concept of symbiotic trauma has been shown to prevail. In my opinion, the concept of symbiotic trauma explains why a child unconsciously adopts the trauma experiences of his mother, transferring them into his own psychological system, why he identifies with the psychological splits of his mother and is unable to detach himself from his symbiotic entanglement with his mother.

Cooperation with those concerned

In my view, multi-generational psychotraumatology inevitably requires cooperation between the individuals affected, scientists, and practitioners who have specialised in this field. I would not have achieved my current level of knowledge if I had not repeatedly learnt from my traumatised clients how they perceive, sense and think what helps them therapeutically and what does not. If my clients had not kept giving me clear indicators that one idea I am trying to grasp in theoretical form is comprehensible, but that another is not, my theory would have been in danger of stagnating and becoming trapped in wrong or half-true ideas. A therapist tends to see the issues he expects to see in his clients, depending on his theoretical background and practical experience. The practitioner must therefore always be open to the new and unexpected. It is often something that contradicts his own theory that allows him to make headway.

I would never have been able to identify so many details about the psychological realities connected with trauma without my experience of working with representatives in constellations, these representatives having a unique access to information about the survival strategies and traumatised parts of people. Without my additional linguistic abilities to understand and translate this information however, many of those concerned would have remained trapped in their silence. A central endeavour of mine is to mould the connections appearing in the therapy into a linguistic form that is as precise and scientific as possible, while at the same time intelligible to the clients for whom this knowledge is necessary. Theories that are bandied about between experts and specialists but that are over the heads of the actual traumatised individuals they are working with continue to render the clients and patients dependent, turning them into the objects of analysts and therapists and their controlling use of knowledge. The fundamental goal of multi-generational psychotraumatology in my view is to facilitate and restore healthy independence and autonomy in traumatised individuals, not to perpetuate their dependence and helplessness.

Openness of processing and therapeutic procedures

The adage that one should 'learn from one's mistakes' does not hold true for traumatic experiences. Because the mistakes or damage caused by a trauma are so overwhelming, the memory of it and the circumstances in which it occurred are subject to an extreme process of suppression. Also people who witnessed such events try to forget them as quickly as possible. This individual and social suppression process creates a general 'trauma blindness' (Riedesser 1994), which is the basis for insufficient understanding, which entails inadequate provision being made to avoid renewed and repeated traumatisation. The general suppression and avoidance of reality can even contribute to an unconscious re-enactment of the trauma situation, for example, where adults who were sexually abused as children may work in the context of prostitution.

Traumatised people tend initially to deny their trauma; they frequently blame themselves for the symptoms they experience that are really the consequences of traumatisation. They may think they are not normal. It has become more natural for them to regard their trauma reactions as normal reactions to extreme experiences.

The general view of 'psychological illness' in society tends to increase the tendency for self-recrimination, because the diagnosis of 'psychological illness' is attached just to the individual concerned: it has to be him, his genes, his character, his personality or his behaviour that is at fault. Therefore the causes of 'psychological illnesses' become more rather than less puzzling, so 'psychological disorders' appear incomprehensible to 'normal people'. If these causes are somehow absorbed into the metabolism of those concerned, then 'psychologically ill people' will appear hugely puzzling.

In the last few years, popular research into people who seem able to survive traumas unharmed and seem to be 'resilient' in the face of potential psychological damage, takes the same line. Of course it is important to understand why some people can cope with traumas better than others, however, it still conveys the idea that it is the fault of the individual, and not the circumstances of his life, and therefore also not the wider social context for these circumstances, that influence whether someone is psychologically damaged or not.

It is already questionable as to whether two people in the same situation actually experience the situation in the same way. And just because someone shows no obvious symptoms following a trauma, it does not mean that he has survived the trauma with no psychological damage. Experience has shown that symptoms resulting from a trauma can sometimes appear a considerable time after the event, and occasionally the trauma that a person had apparently split off within himself, will only appear in his children.

Therefore it is essential that the analysis of such traumatic events takes place in an arena that is secure for those concerned, where they are able to work on their suffering individually, but also where they can talk about their trauma in the presence of witnesses. Many people have said that the fact that participants in a group are listening is often more effective as a healing process than the empathetic listening of an individual therapist in private. I therefore believe that groups meeting to overcome the participants' traumas constitute a form of trauma therapy suitable for the social origins of the trauma.

Of course no one should be forced to talk about their trauma in a group, and the protection afforded by a private one-to-one context, with a psychotherapist, plays an important role in psychotraumatology. Trauma therapy groups do, however, have several positive effects:

- Common types of trauma suffering leads to mutual understanding and solidarity.
- The therapist's expertise is complemented by that of the participants in the group, and at times, corrected.
- What one person has achieved and clarified for himself will assist the learning process of others in the group with similar issues.

I have frequently experienced situations where individuals who were only in the constellations group to observe what happens in such a group have told me afterwards that they gained a great deal from the constellations of others for themselves. Based on their common emotional experiences, members of a group quickly establish a basis of trust, and support each other in their therapy process.

Constellations as a central method

In my experience, the constellations method is an extremely helpful therapeutic tool to support clients to identify their multi-generational traumatisation. The constellations process can also help individuals detach themselves from traumatic entanglements with their parents and grandparents, and recognise and overcome their own symbiotic trauma.

For me, this method represents:

- an extremely useful diagnostic means of revealing the causes underlying the obvious symptoms;
- a method of therapeutic intervention that goes hand in hand with the diagnostic process;
- a method which in my opinion also satisfies the requirements of a scientific experiment: by means of the constellation, a therapist's own hypotheses concerning possible connections between symptoms and causes can be checked and falsified if necessary.

6
Psychotherapy based on the constellations method

What do we do, when we as trauma therapists offer psycho-therapeutic assistance? We use our knowledge of psychological dynamics, social interactions, societal structures and historic events. It is beneficial if this knowledge is true and is embedded in a consistent theoretical framework. In addition, a good method is necessary in order to apply this knowledge in practical therapy work. Derived from this method different techniques are used.

In general psychotherapeutic methods should have a good theoretical grounding. The person using these methods has to know what psychological processes they trigger. However, in the development of new methods, there can be times when the effects may not initially be clear, but may gradually become so. Therefore, therapists and counsellors who are working with a new method must be particularly responsible and reflect carefully on their work. Clients who put their trust in therapists must never be made the playthings of indiscriminate psycho-therapeutic experiments.

I have been working with the constellations method since 1994. I learnt this method in the form of 'Family Constellations' in seminars with the German psychotherapist and philosopher Bert Hellinger, and I followed his approach for several years. However, the more time I spent studying bonding and trauma theory the more it became clear to me that behind Hellinger's method of Family Constellations lay spiritual ideas, and an idealistic concept of reconciliation and harmonisation of all conflicts in families and larger social systems.

As I worked with Hellinger's method of Family Constellations, I saw increasingly clearly which short- and long-term effects could be achieved, and which could not, and the clearer it became to me that Hellinger's philosophy and way of working fuelled many illusions concerning parenthood, childhood and family. Many of the critics of Hellinger's Family Constellations, and in Germany there have been many, were right in that Hellinger's way of working offers a kind of 'doctrine of salvation' (Haas, 2005); that he makes use of the hope many people hold that spiritual salvation would be a simple solution to their problems.

I am personally very glad that my contact with Hellinger's Family Constellations gave me the impulse to look more closely at the parent-child relationship, and to explore the constellations method as a psychotherapeutic tool. It is clear to me that one cannot work with the constellations method merely as a technique, but only as a method that continually requires the therapist to question himself, his theoretical thinking and background in the process of his therapeutic work.

However, I disagree with critics of Family Constellations (Goldner, 2003) who maintain that the constellations method per se is manipulative or even esoteric hocus-pocus. It depends on the intention an individual has when using it, and on the theoretical background behind the therapist's therapeutic actions. Through two decades of continuous practice with this method, my experience has shown me that it is capable of reflecting people's psychological state sufficiently well to be an effective psychotherapeutic instrument for highlighting unconscious and split psychological patterns, and making complex relationship dynamics understandable.

Constellations offer a unique means of reflecting the psychological reality of a person through representation by other people. When people act as 'representatives' in a person's constellation, and allow themselves to explore their experiences

161

as a representation of the internal psychological structure of a client, this client can gain unprecedented access to his or her unconscious structure. He can recognise aspects of himself that he already knows well, but he is also confronted with parts that have so far remained unconscious or that he has forced out of his consciousness. Through such representation, anyone who wants to can look into the mirror of his own psyche and understand its structure better. In the end the client always decides what to take from the constellation and what not.

A further advantage of the constellation method is, I think, the fact that it is deeply human. People put themselves at the disposal of others in order to give mutual support in resolving their psychological problems. It is not only the person who sets up the constellation who gains from this; the representatives themselves also gain many insights into complex relationships that may reflect their own situation. It is fairly common for representatives to say that they have learnt something significant about themselves through their role in another's constellation.

One client told me, for example, that through her role as representative in someone else's constellation of a small child whose mother had left immediately after she had given birth, she had gained access to her own feelings as a lonely and abandoned child. Her head had told her that there was this child inside her, but she had not been able to access the feelings. In the representative role she had been able to discern this child's feelings and express them.

From family constellations to trauma constellations

From 1994 to about 2002 I identified in principle with the methodology of Family Constellations because it opened my eyes to the deeper meaning of familial relationships, and to the 'blind' bonding love a child has for his or her parents. Decision conflicts, patterns of behaviour through which people suffer, psychological difficulties and even physical symptoms of illness were possible to track back to the entangled relation-ships with individuals' own parents with the help of the constellation method. The knowledge of a child's bonding loyalty with his parents gave me considerably more understanding than I had before. The 'unconscious' of psycho-analysis became accessible in the constellations process. One could see for example:

- how children were drawn blindly into the fate of their parents and grandparents;
- how strongly a child is drawn to connect psychologically with events from his family's past;
- how such psychological entanglements undermine the individual's own will, and unconsciously influence his life decisions;
- how such psychological entanglements keep the individual's emotions and thoughts trapped.

As a facilitator of the Family Constellation, one tries to achieve these goals with the representatives by, for example, re-arranging the representatives, initiating dialogues between representatives of family members, and suggesting 'resolving sentences' to be said in order to remove the breeding ground of conflicts and entanglements. The facilitator then takes the client into his or her constellation and the client's representa-tive returns to his or her seat in the outer circle. The facilitator then goes through certain rituals with the client encouraging him to say 'resolving sentences' to the representatives of family members with whom he has identified psychologically. The goal in this work is for him to find his 'right place' in the system of this family, the place he deserves according to his position in the generational order. Some of the most frequently used resolving interventions are:

- bowing with respect to one's parents or grandparents,
- recognising the significance of those who died young to the whole family system,

- showing respect for the merits of former partners of the parents, or
- bowing to the fate of those who suffered injustices at the hands of family members.

The main goal is an intact image of the family, and primarily this is effected through reconciliation with the individual's own parents, which is expressed by the client being able to go up to the representatives of his parents and, after overcoming any inner resistance, being able to embrace them. Between 1990 and 2000 Hellinger mainly practised this procedure, which can be termed 'classic Family Constellations'.

My scepticism of such family constellations arose for several reasons:

- The assumption that 'excluded' people have to be re-integrated into the family system can easily be taken to arbitrary extremes. The 'excluded' can equally mean a sibling of the mother, who died young, or the second wife of the grandfather on the father's side. This can lead to an indiscriminate search for 'excluded' people, and the client can be presented with this person to respect, and this being assumed to be the solution to his problems.
- With some clients it seemed possible to support the 'interrupted movement' towards their own mothers, while others strongly resisted this. In my view there must be very good reasons for this resistance which are not taken into consideration. Even for those clients whose 'interrupted movement' towards their mothers appeared to be successful in the constellation, in my experience the psychological problems seen as being caused by the unsuccessful original reaching for the mother did not disappear.
- I became particularly sceptical of the idea that changes could happen in people who were not working therapeutically on themselves, and were not present at the constellations seminar, through the experiences of the

representatives in the constellation, as if a child (the client) were able to alter his parents' psychological state through interaction with representatives of his parents in a constellation.

- I also found it perplexing to be doing therapeutic work with people who were dead, working as it were posthumously. In Family Constellations dialogues are often conducted with representatives of people who have long since died, with the idea of altering their behaviour and emotions. The boundaries between real and psychologically imprinted realities become blurred; they are not clearly labelled and separated, and the impression emerges that there is a parallel world outside the psyche of a client in which the dead could actually still be living, talking to one another and influencing relationships.

- It is true that in many cases feedback following a constellation was that the relationship of the individual with his or her own parents or siblings had become more relaxed, but in just as many cases the basic problems which were the reason the client had originally come, had not been altered in any way by the family constellation.

Since 2003 I had begun to concentrate on the bonding theory of the British psychoanalyst, John Bowlby, and on trauma theory. This knowledge helped me see in the constellations I was facilitating all the attachment patterns of 'secure', 'insecure-ambivalent', 'insecure-avoidant', and 'insecure-disorganised' attachments between parents and children, which were also repeated in couple relationships. I saw textbook trauma reactions in the representatives in the constellations, and the clients. It gradually became clear to me that most problems causing clients to seek therapeutic help were caused by trauma.

So I developed my own constellations methodology, based on the understanding that traumatisation leads to a splitting in the psyche. In this type of constellations the representatives no longer embodied complete people, but instead certain parts of them, for example a mother's traumatised part or a client's survival part. And I did not ask the representative for the client to leave the constellation as soon as the client moved into the constellation himself. So several parts of the client were sometimes represented in a constellation at the same time, and the aim of my therapeutic work was to integrate these parts into a complete personality again. The work was no longer focussed on the client's external family system, but on the internal system of his psychological parts. The end goal was for the client to come to terms with himself, not with his family.

For this reason I gave the book that was published after 'Trauma, Bonding and Family Constellations' (published in English in 2008) the title 'Splits in the Soul: Integrating Traumatic Experiences' (published in 2011). I arrived at the premise that the integration of an individual's psyche is the prerequisite for being able to deal with family members on a solid and realistic psychological basis, and perhaps finding some peace with them.

Since the focus is the client's own traumas, I have been using the term 'trauma constellations' for my way of using the constellations method in therapy. However, this term does incorporate a certain conceptual ambiguity: the term for the theory, 'trauma', is combined with the term for the method, 'constellations'. For this reason I want to emphasise at this point the importance of differentiating clearly between the use of therapeutic/advisory *methods and processes* and the *theoretical background* that shapes the way they are used. Depending on the theoretical background the same method can be used in completely different ways. If the theory is correct, the use of the method will be of benefit; if the theory is not correct, the method used might aggravate the very problem it is attempting to resolve. In order to be scientifically accurate, in my work nowadays I refer to 'constellations based on attachment theory and trauma theory'.

It seems important to me that practical therapeutic work is based on a theory that is explicit, presented in detail, and understandable to everyone who wants to engage with it. Such a theory can be discussed and assessed; it can be deepened, corrected, or in extreme cases if it gets too tangled up in contradictions, rejected.

I have been working with representatives in a 'constellation' over a period of many years with thousands of clients, and I am clear that for me it is no longer a question of *whether* the constellation method should be used in counselling and therapy, but *how* it should be used to best effect. Several factors influence how a method is used: the personality of the facilitator, his experience and training, his ability for self-reflection, gender and age, the way he works with his own traumas; the theory the work is based on and the context in which the therapeutic or counselling work takes place.

The same method in the hands of different facilitators can become something completely different if their theoretical concepts differ. Additionally, although they are using the same method, the personalities of the therapists and counsellors are at different stages of development. Someone who has not dealt with his own traumas and tends to function through his survival strategies is hardly likely to recommend that his clients give up their survival strategies and expose themselves to a confrontation with their trauma. Someone who is still holding onto symbiotic illusions of his own parents may possibly be able to recognise certain forms of traumas as the cause of psychological problems in his clients, but he will not be able to grasp all the implications of a symbiotic trauma.

The constellation of the intention

Several years later, and with my increasing knowledge of the psychological dynamics of attachment trauma, when I began using the term 'symbiotic trauma' with its particular focus on the relationship between mother and child (Ruppert 2010), a further change in my use of the constellations method took place. From the perspective that it was necessary to confront the trauma, I had found it appropriate for the client to choose a representative for himself at the start of the constellation, while he, himself, sat outside of the constellation, next to me, and watched the process. I thought this corresponded with the client being an 'observer' and using a 'distancing technique', which is recommended by many trauma therapists. The traumatised client then would be able to look at what had caused his trauma from outside, as it were, as if watching a film on a screen, thereby remaining experientially at a distance (Reddemann, 2001, pp 107 ff.). If one could find a way via watching the representative for himself cope better with the traumatising relationship, one could expect the client to dare to confront his trauma with the support of this representative.

However, this way of going about things is problematic, in that the facilitator never quite knows where the client is internally: is he in his healthy part? Is he dissociating because of what is happening in the constellation and escaping into a survival strategy? Or is he slipping into a traumatised part? As facilitator I had to try to keep my eye on what was happening in the constellation as well as on my client sitting next to me. So finally, I asked the question: why not put the client into the constellation straightaway, and be able to see directly which of his parts he is in?

Based on my increasing understanding of symbiotically-entangled survival parts, it became clearer to me that some clients are not fully in themselves when they set up their constellation. Many are not firmly anchored in their own identity and, when confronted with emotional conflicts, they often experience themselves as another person, frequently like their mother or grandmother.

It was, therefore, a further milestone in my work with the constellation method, to begin a constellation with a representative for the client's intention for the constellation. It then quickly becomes apparent whether or not a client is even able to set up an 'intention' that reflects his own identity. If the client does not clearly relate to his 'intention', then the obvious question is: why not? Is it a split off part of the client that he does not recognise as a part of himself because he has suppressed it until now, or is it a part taken on from an entanglement with his mother or father, which therefore *is* alien to the client, but with which he is symbiotically entangled? Occasionally it is the other way round: the client identifies with his 'intention', and believes that what appears here is a healthy or traumatised part of him, even though to the observer this is clearly not so. This misperception is most apparent when a client chooses a person of the opposite gender to represent his or her intention; then the symbiotic entanglement and the client's confusion of identity immediately come to light in the representation of the 'intention'.

Since 2009 I have been working with this approach, i.e. starting the constellation with the client himself and a representative for his intention for the constellation. This has several advantages:

- The constellation has a clear goal for all concerned (the client, the facilitator, representatives and observers), namely the client's stated intention.
- The 'intention' defines the context within which a client can progress at that moment, without overtaxing himself.
- The danger of a re-traumatisation of the client in the work of the constellation is thereby considerably reduced.
- As the therapist, I no longer have to focus my attention on two places at once: the constellation and the client. That is a great relief to the therapist when facilitating a constellation.
- Experience has shown that the representation of the 'intention' holds a great deal of 'wisdom of the unconscious', since clients usually have a profound idea of what will help them at that moment and what they can bear, perhaps more unconsciously than consciously, and which may show more in the representative for the intention than in the client herself.
- The 'intention' representative, through his experiences, shows very quickly where the client is; it shows his splits and his entanglements, making his illusory ideas more transparent, and even signals when the end of the constellation process has been reached.

The 'intention' as stated, and as in the representation, show how much clarity a client has gained about his identity, while at the same time marking the boundary which he cannot yet cross. This is where uncertainty begins, lines are blurred, beyond which lies the intangible aspect of his identity, because certain truths from his life and family history have not yet been emotionally acknowledged.

If a person does not formulate an intention for their constellation, I do not begin the constellation. I will not be tempted to formulate a possible intention for the client, even if he or she asks me to, because if I did, I would immediately become entangled and be colluding with the survival parts of the client.

Formulating an intention means that the client accepts personal responsibility for himself and his therapy work, and those who are familiar with this way of working may often spend considerable time prior to a therapeutic session thinking about their intention, looking for a meaningful topic and suitable formulation. This process itself is of high therapeutic value because it encourages the process of self-analysis: Who am I? What do I want? What do I have the courage to do? What do I definitely not want? What am I afraid of?

Basically, the constellation of the intention can produce three different results:

- Survival strategies, entanglements and splits become clearer and more conscious for the client.
- Healthy psychological structures gain strength against the survival strategies.
- Encounters between healthy psychological parts and traumatised parts become more possible.

The client cannot get around this 'intention' as represented in the constellations process. If he has no contact with his 'intention', it is a clear sign that he is trapped within his survival self. This is also the case if the client starts to try and manipulate the 'intention' or any other representatives in the constellation, by talking insistently to them, attempting to pull them away or running away from them.

In terms of trauma theory, the person's intention for each constellation he does is the defined resource for that particular constellation. Without a healthy and stable intention, there can be no eventual meeting with the trauma, and so it is a prerequisite for a meeting with the traumatised part that the intention develops from a survival-oriented intention into a healthy part of the self during the process of the constellation.

My main task as facilitator initially is to suggest further representatives for the constellation, and then to help the client understand what is happening at key points in the process. For the client it is most helpful to perceive, understand, feel and reflect instead of taking action.

I don't think it is useful to use the constellation method to look for a 'solution' for the client. Finding and creating 'solutions' is usually motivated by the survival part of the client, since the survival self prefers quick and easy solutions instead of really dealing with the problem. Finding quick solutions allows the person to avoid the emotions involved, distracting themselves with other things, whereas effective trauma therapy needs people to stand back and endure the truth. This could be by seeing reflected in the constellation how one felt as a small child, how helpless and defenceless one was, and how unable one was to do anything about it, and that no one else really saw and understood this distress; to really see these things is a giant step for the person, and it means a great deal if one no longer flees from these realities.

The 'constellation of the intention' is a therapeutic concept. The 'constellation' shows the actual state of the client's inner being, the goal aimed for, emerging obstacles and at the same time the process for overcoming them. The aim of the constellation is for the client to recognise these things, and have an experience, which can start the psyche on a useful process of change.

One-to-one constellations

Right from the beginning, I have explored the work of constellations in the private one-to-one setting. Initially I offered clients different cushions to use to represent their family, or later to represent their internal parts. This resulted in remarkable responses in some clients, and led to many amazing insights for them. I would sometimes ask them to stand where the cushions were or I stood on them myself to gain information on what was represented and symbolised there.

Since working with the 'constellation of the intention' I let the client set me up as the representative of his or her intention. I stay in the role of the 'intention' until the dialogue between us is no longer useful. I explicitly leave the role of representative if I want to make something clear to the client from my therapeutic perspective. In this way it is often possible for clients to gain deep insights into their symbiotic traumas and their symbiotic entanglements in individual therapy as well.

As I frequently now have guest students present in my individual sessions, constellations with two or three representatives can be done, which comes close to working in a group. However, I still regard larger groups with a wide choice of representatives as the preferred method when working with constellations.

Case study 18

Anxiety or happiness? (Mr. D. – Part 1)

Mr. D. arrived in my practice for his fourth individual session. He is a tall, imposing man with strong hands and the corners of his mouth turn down. He had been seeing psychiatrists for many years about his anxiety and depression before he came to me. He was taking a low dose of anti-depressants.

Before he retired, Mr. D. was a very successful academic. He had been married and is the father of a daughter. Two years previously he had separated from his wife. This led to the worst depression he had experienced, combined with a stay in a psychosomatic clinic. He recovered from this crisis when a woman fell in love with him and he was able to return her love. Both experienced an exhilarating year and enjoyed the physical side of their relationship to its fullest. After the first year, however, his lover increasingly withdrew from him; his desire to be close to her and his sexual needs became too much for her.

The situation as it was when he came to see me was that he had given up his house, which had become too large for him on his own, and moved into a smaller flat closer to his lover. He was very afraid of sorting out his belongings and imagined that he would no longer know where to find anything in the new flat.

On the other hand, he hoped that living closer to his lover would rekindle his joie de vivre and he would once again experience being in love.

Mr. D. was born in 1942 in Germany. He was conceived in the middle of World War II when his father, a soldier, was on home leave. He was eight when he saw his father for the first time when he returned from Russian captivity. His father was like a stranger to him, and remained a stranger for the rest of his life.

Mr. D. was his mother's only child. Shortly after he was born she had to return to work. She left him alone in his cot for hours at a time while she went out cleaning. Mr. D. experienced his mother as very anxious and depressed, but he also admired her for managing to bring him up in the midst of war without the support of her husband. In his youth, Mr. D. didn't have any friends. He felt he was an outsider. Only his success at school and subsequently in his career gave him some inner stability and self-confidence.

His intention for the session was to feel more happiness again. He wanted to see the positive side of his current house move and not just be preoccupied with his fears, thereby sinking deeper into them, which had made him incapable of acting in the last few weeks.

I offered to let myself be set up as the representative of his 'intention' and suggested he positions himself in relation to me as his 'intention'. He positioned me in the middle of the therapy room and stood opposite me, about a metre away. The first thing I experienced was a strong feeling in my stomach; then my hands started to circle in front of my lower body, each palm in turn pushing in front of the other. I experienced this as the two feelings of happiness and anxiety alternating, first happiness, then anxiety, happiness, anxiety. Mr. D. confirmed this. Whenever he was happy, feelings of anxiety followed immediately.

Then the movement of my hands stopped abruptly and it felt as if something in my stomach had become knotted. Something was lying there like a big, heavy lump. My hands moved apart and I looked at them as if they didn't belong to me. They appeared unusually large to me; I could have grabbed hold of something with them, but I didn't know what. Again Mr. D. confirmed my impressions. He knew this feeling of pressure in the stomach. He would be clear in his head, but from his neck down he felt cut off from his body. His hands only reacted to commands from his head. This increased my feeling of being split into three parts: I experienced hands, head and stomach as being separate entities.

I switched into my therapist self, and asked Mr. D. to take two cushions, one for 'happiness' and one for 'anxiety'. He did this and said decisively: "This one is happiness and this is anxiety!" I had meanwhile been looking at the floor, seeing only his feet and hearing his voice. Back in role, I now looked at him directly and was totally baffled. He had chosen a dark, almost black cushion, for 'happiness' and a large red cushion for 'anxiety'. I let him know how baffled I was. The black cushion scared me and the red cushion seemed to me to exude fire, love and passion. Mr. D. was uncertain and said his head had made the decision, but the longer he looked at the cushions, the more he thought I was right. He said that the combination of black and happiness did seem a strange one, and that red could definitely be seen in connection with love.

As his 'intention', when I heard that my intuitive feeling was probably more correct than the decision he made from his head, I suddenly got a fit of shivers over my whole body. It was as if the knot in my stomach had started to loosen. I could look directly at Mr. D. and I asked him to say once more, quite clearly and definitely, in which hand he was holding the cushion representing 'happiness' (the red one) and the cushion representing 'anxiety' (the black one). He did that and I asked him to stretch his arms as wide apart as he could, and to hold the cushions as far away from each other as he could. Still in role, I took a step backwards and leant against the wall. I became more and more relaxed and could listen calmly to Mr. D. as he told me that he felt his girlfriend was putting pressure on him to be happy even when he was full of anxiety and that he would probably have to stand up to her more and let her know when he's feeling anxious and unhappy, and when it's justified. Mr. D. talked for a little while about his current experiences with his partner, and he seemed to find it necessary to get something off his chest in order to find inner clarity. We then ended the constellation.

My interpretation of this constellation: As the child of an anxious and depressed mother, Mr. D. was not able to show his true feelings. His mother probably did not know whether she should be happy or fearful about being pregnant in the middle of the war while her husband as a soldier was away at the front. Faced with his mother's uncertainties, Mr. D. would probably have tried to hide his fears from her to avoid causing her any more distress. All this then led to the emotions of happiness and anxiety being combined and, as a result, to a confusion of emotions within him. He was then experiencing a similar situation with his female partner. She displayed no understanding of his fear of losing her, and expected him to be happy, even if he had no reason to be. Mr. D. has to learn to trust his own feelings, regardless of what feelings others expect from him based on their own experiences.

After we had spent several sessions working on his symbiotic entanglement with his mother, I received this note from him: "I would like to let you know that I am very happy to have made such progress in the last therapy session. Two images in particular have stayed with me: 1. The black cushion of anxiety and pain is not black through and through (i.e. from birth), but only has a black cover, and inside is a light-coloured lining. 2. The cushion of the original child was bright and colourful, was shaped nicely and had a clear frame."

Case study 19

Trapped in the role of Victim (Mr. D. – Part 2)

For the first week after Mr. D. had successfully moved from his house into a new flat closer to his girlfriend, their relationship improved, until he began to feel that she was patronising him over minor matters. He withdrew from her while at the same time expecting her to come after him. He arrived at his next therapy session in a despairing frame of mind, unable to see a way out for himself. For a long time he was unable to formulate an intention for the session. Then he said he wanted to develop more confidence in his ability to be independent.

In the constellation process which then took place, aided by two guest students as representatives, and having gone through several stages, we ended up with the following context: when his mother's mother (his grandmother) was 17, her sister had suddenly died, and this grandmother had been prepared to step into her sister's shoes, marrying her sister's husband and looking after her sister's baby, which she did. However, by doing this she denied herself a life of her own, and her own love.

In the constellation it seemed as if Mr. D.'s grandmother and mother were always unconsciously standing at the grave of their sister/aunt, as if the grandmother's psychological development had become arrested and fixed on this event, and the psychological development of her daughter (Mr. D.'s mother) had remained entangled with her mother and this dilemma. Mr. D. said that his grandmother lived a joyless life, as did his mother. The constellation suggested that the trauma of loss that had taken place two generations previously also affected Mr. D., and had been the foundation for the development of his emotional insecurity and depression.

When Mr. D. was born, he said he had been a lively baby, full of energy and the joy of life, but because his mother was neither emotionally nor physically present for him, and had left him alone for too long when he was little, his basic need for love and security had not been satisfied. Mr. D. had had to split off the internal little abandoned and helpless baby early on, and in its place came a damaged, whining and demanding child that begged for attention. But as this child learnt that he was still asking too much of his mother, he also turned into a good child who adapted to what was required of him, who did not want to worry his mother and who tried to learn that the colour of anxiety is not black, but red (see Case study 18 above). Later on, his success at school became the anchor that enabled him to obtain some care and recognition from others; nevertheless, none of these survival strategies was able to heal the original trauma. In relationships he felt he was dependent on the women and defenceless in the face of their moods. He remained trapped in his victim role and continued to blame himself for pushing his girlfriend away by his "self-centred behaviour".

This understanding of his childhood makes it not surprising that he had again chosen a partner who had lost her parents when she was four, and so was also trapped in a loss trauma. She had probably initially seen a strong man in him, someone who could give her the love and security she had been unable to receive from her deceased parents. But when he started to turn into the insatiable little boy who would really have liked to completely devour his mother, it became too much for her since she already had two children, with whom she lived in a very symbiotic proximity. And so Mr. D. again experienced rejection and abandonment. He was alone again and didn't know how to cope with it.

Case study 20

The rejected inner children seek refuge (Mr. D. – Part 3)

When Mr. D. came to a session a few weeks later with his partner, I suggest that they each set up their own intention. There were also three guest students present that day. Mr. D. set me up as his 'intention' ("How can I play an active part in the partnership?"), while his partner chose one of the guest students for her 'intention' ("Why do I feel guilty so quickly?").

For a while both processes ran in parallel, and then it became clear that Mr. D.'s 'intention' became the abandoned little boy within him, and his partner's 'intention' became the little girl who, following the death of her parents, lived with her grandparents who didn't really want to have the child.

After a while, the representative of this little girl attached herself to me as Mr. D.'s 'intention'.

This moved Mr. D. to tears, while I, as his 'intention', found the child clinging to me to be annoying. Mr. D. had fatherly feelings towards the child, and wanted to help her. At the same time however, he didn't relate to his own little boy part at all. As a result, this part moved more and more towards Mr. D.'s partner and found her "very exciting".

This constellation showed Mr. D. and his partner quite clearly that they each rejected their own split off child parts, and could not relate to them emotionally, and that instead, they then sought refuge with the adult part of the other. When this became so obvious we all burst out laughing.

Validity and reliability of the constellation method

With all scientific methods there is a risk of producing method-ological artefacts; in other words, whatever is discovered by the use of a certain method is created by that method itself, and not by the phenomenon under investigation. A recent example of this was the assumption that there are elementary particles that travel faster than the speed of light. When the experiment was checked, the highly sensitive measurements were found to have been distorted by the voltage of an electric plug, which had given rise to an inaccurate reading.

In the social sciences, methods and processes (e.g. person-ality tests, intelligence tests) are assessed using several criteria:

- Is the method valid as regards content? In other words, are the results achieved by using such a method confirmed in reality? Does, for example, someone who achieves a high IQ in a test actually behave in an intelli-gent manner in his daily life? (the validity criterion)
- Does the method produce reliable measurements? In other words does it produce the same results regardless of the user? If a person takes an intelligence test twice under the direction of two different psychologists, do the results point in the same direction? (the reliability criterion)

How might this relate to the constellation method then? What is being detected here, or even 'measured'?

As I see it, a constellation produces an image of the psychological state of the person setting up the constellation, an image that reflects his internal reality. If so, then the repre-sentatives as his internal parts should reflect these internal parts as they really are. His attachment figures should appear the way he actually experiences them.

In relation to the validity criterion, what the representatives experience, express and say ought to correspond with the inner and outer reality of the person setting up the constellation. If the representatives express feelings and thoughts in a constellation, adopt a certain physical shape or position, or reflect symptoms (e.g. pain in a certain region of their body), then the person setting up the constellation should recognise these straightaway, and say "Yes, I know that feeling", or "yes, my mother, my father does that..."

If 'facts' emerge during a constellation of which the client is unaware until then (for example, that his mother or father had another child, or that someone had a different father to the one he supposed, etc.) then the facts ought to be able to be substantiated when the client checks them after the constellation (for example, by information from family relations or by a gene test etc).

In other words, on the one hand, it is possible to check the validity of the constellation method during the process, and on the other, it is possible to check some things afterwards. During the process one can see how frequently the person confirms what the representatives are conveying, and how frequently he says he does not recognise what is happening, or that it doesn't makes sense to him.

With the constellation method, the reliability criterion requires that valid, sustainable results are achieved, regardless of the person of the facilitator, the representatives and the observers in the group. In other words identical results should be achieved when the client sets up a constellation with the same intention, but with different facilitators and in different groups, with different representatives.

Confirming the reliability criterion by a scientific investigation is almost impossible with the constellation method, because the client cannot set up his intention at the same time in two different groups with two different facilitators. He can only do one after the other, and the first constellation would already have caused some change in him, so he would enter the second constellation in a slightly altered frame of mind, and would then have a different intention.

It therefore appears reasonable to me to concentrate chiefly on the validity criterion in any scientific investigation of the constellation method. In my practice I continually and persistently experience clients confirming what the representatives are saying, feeling or doing during a constellation. It only happens very occasionally that the client is not able to relate to what the representatives are doing or saying, or that they reject it completely. However, to date there has been no scientific study with a quantitative analysis of the proportion of such 'agree' and 'disagree' criteria.

I also experience in my practice remarkable examples in relation to the subsequent validation of a constellation. Below are three case studies that show impressively that representatives during a constellation have felt something that was unconsciously present in a client's psyche, but was not available to him as conscious knowledge.

Case study 21

Disgusting child (Mrs. G.)

During one constellation the representative of the mother of a client continually wiped her arms and said she found herself disgusting. The representative of the mother's smother, Mrs. G.'s grandmother, kept repeating the sentence: "Children are disgusting!"

When the client questioned her mother after the constellation, she was told that she, Mrs. G.'s mother, had been a really disgusting and disfigured baby. She had had pustules all over her body because early on in the pregnancy her mother had taken some medication to cause an abortion. As it hadn't worked, she had then had to take further medication in order to be able to have the child. After she was born, the grandfather had asked why the midwife hadn't kept the afterbirth and thrown away the child.

Case study 22

Attempted Abortion using ergot fungus (Hans-Werner)

I am quoting from a record written from memory by a client following a constellation.

Hans-Werner: "For the first time in years I've got nothing in my order book. My practice and my seminars aren't enough to live on. In the last few years work just seemed to find me. Now I'm apparently going to have to go out and find new sources of income. That thought scares me considerably."

F.R.: "Does this situation of existential anxiety seem familiar to you?"

Hans-Werner: "About 15 years ago I had no money and no fixed abode. But I found friends who supported me. But that can't happen nowadays. I'm too old for that."

F.R.: "And what about your family?"

Hans-Werner: "My mother was still at school when she became pregnant with me. Her parents didn't approve of the pregnancy and advised her to have an abortion. My father was a student at the time. My parents moved out of their parents' homes and went to live together. That must have been a time of existential anxiety for my parents."

F.R.: "And how would you like to formulate your intention?"

Hans-Werner: "My intention would be: To go through the existential anxiety and come out the other side."

F.R.: "Then start by choosing a representative for your 'intention'."

From the group Hans-Werner chose a woman to represent his 'intention' and stood about half a metre away from her.

Intention: "I felt a deep sadness and at the same time a Johnny-Head-in-the-Air carefree feeling. We'll crack it!"

Hans-Werner: "I know that carefree feeling, the Johnny-Head-in-the-Air feeling, but I can't relate to the sadness."

F.R.: "Now choose a representative for your mother, at the time she was pregnant with you."

Hans-Werner chooses a younger group member for his mother and positions her on the left, beside him and his 'intention'.

Intention: "I can feel my heart beating fast and I'm getting palpitations."

Mother: "Me too. I've got palpitations as well."

Hans-Werner: "My mother refused to have an abortion; for her it was a question of ethics. And she wanted to be with my father. She spent the whole pregnancy in hospital because she had cardiac arrhythmia. At the moment I feel love for my 'intention', but I'm also afraid and I can feel strong waves of energy running through my body."

The 'mother' then went to stand in front of the 'intention'.

F.R.: "Choose another representative for yourself when still inside your mother's womb."

Hans-Werner selects a young man and positions him with the 'mother'. This representative immediately sits down on the floor at her feet.

Intention: "I can feel myself slipping into the role of mother. I've got an image of being pregnant and that I want to have the child, and I feel sadness because I'm going to lose my parents by having it. It's an insoluble conflict."

Mother: "I feel pains in my lower body, I have to hold onto it so that I don't lose the child."

F.R.: "Now choose representatives for your grandparents, your mother's parents."

Hans-Werner positions the representatives for his grandmother and grandfather in relation to the other representatives in the constellation.

Grandfather: "As far as I'm concerned, I'm neutral. I'm actually quite looking forward to having a grandchild."

Hans-Werner: "That's exactly right! My mother told me that my grandfather had kept out of the discussion about whether there should be an abortion or not."

The 'mother' looks angrily at the 'grandmother', and says: "I feel the energy of a murderer in the grandmother."

Intention: "Me too! It's like the film *Arsenic and Old Lace*."

Hans-Werner: "That was my mother's favourite film!"

(Author's note: This is a film in which two apparently lovable old ladies poison lonely old men and hide the corpses in the cellar.)

The representative for the 'mother' suddenly falls over as if dead and lies stretched out on her back. The suspicion comes that Hans-Werner's grandmother did something that nearly killed both Hans-Werner and his mother.

After a while the 'mother' stands up again and says: "I survived. Life goes on. I don't want anything more to do with it."

Intention: "I feel sadness, that life can be so brutal. And at the same time happiness at being allowed to live."

Hans-Werner: "I feel there's something horrific which has to do with the grandmother, like a dark cloud, a dark mist."

Intention: "I can relate to the feeling of horror."

The unborn child: "I feel I want to run away."

F.R.: "Choose a representative for the horror."

Hans-Werner chooses a female representative for the 'horror' and positions her close to the 'grandmother'.

Horror: "I have the feeling of falling, being on shaky legs, hardly able to stay upright. I'm caught in a large, dark cloud."

The 'grandmother' closes her eyes: "It's all to do with me and I can't look at it."

Horror: "I'm feeling something like electric shocks." She writhes in pain and her whole body convulses.

The 'mother', who has moved to one side, comments: "It's starting to remind me of the *Rocky Horror Picture Show*."

Hans-Werner: "That's typical of my mother – if anything gets dramatic she makes fun of it!"

Hans-Werner to the 'Horror': "Has it got anything to do with torture?"

Horror: "No, the electric shocks aren't being used for torture. They're being used for resuscitation."

Intention: "I know these electric shocks."

Hans-Werner to his 'intention': "Did we experience them?"

Intention: "Yes, we did, and the mother."

Mother: "I know the electric shocks. They come in waves. It's as if you've died, because your heart has stopped and then you're resuscitated and then you're dead again."

Intention: "I feel sadness and thankfulness."

Hans-Werner: "We, my mother and I, went through this horror together."

F.R.: "Now it's becoming apparent that your 'intention' represents your symbiotic entanglement with your mother. You went through the existential threat of attempted abortion with her; an abortion that your grandmother had secretly caused. Both of you almost died. Because you were still inside your mother, you can't separate your existential fear from your mother's fear. That's why you chose a woman as representative of your intention."

In the meantime, the 'mother' and the 'horror' have sat down on chairs next to each other.

'Intention' to Hans-Werner: "As far as I'm concerned, the discovery that your grandmother tried to cause you to be aborted has fulfilled your intention."

With that we ended the constellation.

The next day Hans-Werner wrote me the following note:

"Ergot fungus was a 'popular' method for abortion for a long time. It causes severe contractions. But taking it is very dangerous because it can also cause problems with the circulation and the heart, coldness of the limbs and delusions.

"It seems plausible to me that my grandmother tried to trigger an abortion by adding ergot to some porridge, for example, that she gave my mother to eat. She took the risk of killing my mother and me with the poison. I don't know if ergot was the poison she used, but the whole thing seems to me to fit, even though it appears so monstrous. Something within me says: 'Yes, that's the way it was' and this realisation gives me a certain sense of peace.

"Several earlier constellations of mine correspond with this too, where it was a case of life or death in the time leading up to my birth, and where there was a terrible secret that was apparently too awful to be confronted for a long time.

"My mother also told me that my grandmother had put pressure on her to have an abortion and that a lot of terrible things had happened. It was only when I had invited both my mother and my grandmother, who was then 84, and who died shortly afterwards, to a constellations seminar in Mallorca, that my mother was able to forgive my grandmother. Now I know why.

"As an adult I felt very close to my grandmother. At the same time I now realise that my granny had split off her perpetrator part because she always seemed to be a dear, kind granny. It was only occasionally in her final years that I felt there was something different.

"All my life I have struggled against the hold of my mother, and for a long time I had felt incomprehensibly hostile towards her, which had caused her great distress. This was despite the fact that my mother had always tried to be good to me. This continual rejection of my mother was possibly an expression of my emotional entanglement with her. On the way home after the constellation [outlined above] I experienced heartfelt love for my mother for the first time in my life."

Following is a case study of a woman called Susanne. She wrote the following account:

Case study 23

The secret of 'success' (Susanne)

This is Susanne's account:

I have described below my own constellation. I can do this in such detail because I have received accounts from other seminar participants from my training group. It was the first weekend of our training with Professor Ruppert in Munich. On my way to the seminar on this Sunday morning I had the feeling: 'It'll be my turn today.' And an hour later this was really the case. My name was drawn.

When it was my turn to make a constellation I quickly formulated my intention, which was a question I had been asking myself for a long time: 'Why do I not allow myself to succeed?'

F.R.: "Tell us a bit more about yourself."

Susanne: "I am an only child. My mother had only just turned 19 when she had me. She died two years ago as a result of a doctor's error. My father died of cancer 18 years ago. For 17 years I was self-employed as a personnel consultant for boards of directors, one of the few women working in a male domain. For seven years now I've been concentrating on psychotherapy. Two years ago I ended my former career and I now work as a counsellor and therapist.

"My mother hadn't wanted to have a child. For a long time she kept bleeding and the pregnancy was only recorded in maternity notes in the sixth month. My grandmother had told me all this. The late entry in the maternity notes was confirmed when I found them in my mother's papers after she died. My birth was difficult and took a long time. I was a breech presentation and I had to be pulled out by my right foot.

"My father worked long hours. My mother wanted me to be a 'typical girl' and I wasn't allowed to go to grammar school, but had to train as a kindergarten teacher. During my training, when I was 19, I was pregnant with twins and had an abortion. I then broke off my training against my mother's will. Then I became a pharmacy technician and later a personnel consultant. I became very successful in my career and my mother, grandma and mother-in-law all made sarcastic comments about it. I am married now and we have healthy twins."

F.R.: "Can you tell us something about your parents?"

Susanne: "My parents met at a party. My mother became pregnant straightaway – the first time, so to speak. They got married in February and I was born in June. My relationship with my mother was very cold and I endured a lot of physical violence until I was about 13. My grandma was very rich. She had married a much older man who already had an 18-year old son. My mother was a product of this relationship. When my mother was two years old, her father died in an accident. My grandma then fled at the end of World War II with my mother, her sister who was two years older, and my great-grandmother to West Germany. In all the years afterwards there was never a man in the family. When my father arrived on the scene he was the centre of attention."

Then I had to choose someone for my intention 'Why do I not allow myself to succeed?' We walked into the circle together.

Intention: "I can't bear this question. My heart's pounding and my throat's becoming constricted."

The 'intention' steps back a little. She is unable and unwilling to say what she can't bear. I know this feeling and I experience anxiety and panic.

Intention: "There are so many people here that I don't dare to speak out in front of them. I find it embarrassing. I'm trying not to let *that* come out and then along you come and want something from me."

The 'intention' sits on the floor, helpless and despairing. I know this feeling well too! I walk towards my 'intention' because I don't want to leave it so alone.

Intention: "Something's pulling at my teeth, something wants to come up. Now I can feel something in my jaw. I feel as if I'm going to black out. I have an impulse to push something away. I'd really like to faint. I feel as if I'm trapped inside an armour-plated shell and I can't get out. I want to be able to free myself with my thoughts. It's a struggle; I want to get out. Who am I?"

Susanne: "You're my intention!"

Intention: "I feel as if I'm breaking up; I'm caught up in a struggle between my head and my heart."

Susanne: "You broke free early."

Intention: "NO! I've always struggled, but I haven't broken free. I can't weep."

F.R.: "Would you like to set up your parents?"

I do that. The 'father' is interested in the 'intention'.

Intention: "It's nice to see a friendly face."

The 'mother' sits down on the floor and says she's completely paralysed. She says something is pressing on her throat, constricting it.

Father: "I know that the intention is a projection of me but I don't want to break it up."

Intention: "Now there's a great coldness in me."

Father: "I've lost my support."

The 'mother' is still incapable of moving.

Susanne to the 'mother': "You've never moved! You always allowed yourself to be waited on."

The 'intention' can't stand the talking any more and screams at me: "Why are you talking about such trivial things with your mother?"

Susanne: "Because otherwise I'm so alone."

Intention: "I'm alone, I'm going mad. I'm what we're feeling."

I move towards my 'intention'.

Intention: "I need you, please stay with me! Promise me you'll stay with me?"

Susanne: "Yes!"

Intention: "Do you know who I am?"

Susanne: "Yes, my intention."

Intention: "We've got to get away from here!" The 'intention' leaves the inner circle.

Susanne: "That hurts so much!" I start to cry.

F.R.: "Now set someone up who represents your success."

I choose a woman as representative for 'success' and stand with her for a little while.

The 'intention' moves into the circle again and says to the 'mother': "You can decide: preferably dead or not, preferably success or not."

Mother: "It surprises me, but I think that's how it is."

Intention: "She has the authority to decide." All three parts of me stand in front of the 'mother': 'intention', 'success' and myself.

Intention: "It's a matter of life or death!"

The 'success' moves over to the 'mother', the 'intention' and I move further away. Now the 'father' is once again interested in the 'intention' and in me.

Intention: "I'd rather live than be successful. Mama is the successful one."

Susanne: "I'd rather live too."

Intention: "Let's live now."

The 'success' now comes up to me and the 'intention'. Life or success? The intention and I leave the circle and embrace. The 'success' stays where it is and complains.

F.R.: "Would you like to set up the parents of your mother?"

I set up the father of the mother (grandfather) and the mother of the mother (grandmother).

The 'success' leaves the circle and stands at the window. The 'intention' moves into the circle once more and lies on the floor. The 'mother' feels contempt for the 'grandmother' and for her husband ('father'). The 'success' leaves the room and comes back in again through the other door. I'm totally wiped out; the 'mother' would love to attack the 'grandmother' physically. 'Grandmother' likes me a lot.

Susanne: "The 'success' is being used in an abusive way and I won't go along with it."

'Intention' to 'grandmother': "What have you done?"

The 'mother' continues to despise everyone.

'Intention' asks me: "What was it the grandmother did that was so successful?"

Susanne: "The grandmother bought a house in M— and brought my mother up on her own."

'Intention' points to her abdomen: "There's something down here; 'success' has something to do with motherhood. The 'success' is a person and he belongs to the family."

Susanne: "Yes, it's about motherhood."

Intention: "It's a person who's missing."

Father: "The grandmother took a child away from the mother, my wife, and me."

The 'mother' feels as if blood is running down between her legs.

Intention: "The grandmother is the key."

Susanne: "The grandmother's lying?"

Intention: "She's keeping something secret."

Susanne: "That can't be true!"

Father: "Say it, say it Susanne, say it!"

The 'mother' starts to cry and says: "My mother!"

The 'success' goes up to her. The 'father' goes to the 'mother' and holds her tight.

Susanne: "My grandmother took me away from my mother."

Intention: "The 'mother' is in despair."

While the 'mother' and I cry together, the 'intention' goes away and becomes angry. It goes to the 'grandmother', where the 'father' is already standing.

F.R.: "Do you want to take someone for the part of you that is so closely attached to the grandmother and has seen a substitute mother in her?"

Intention: "I know the truth and want to say it."

Father: "The grandmother made my wife abort a child."

191

I scream at the representative for my grandmother: "You wanted to get rid of me?"

Intention: "It was twins; one of them is still here, that's you. That's why the grandmother was so kind to you, because of her guilty conscience."

I say again that my husband and I have twins and that we fought so hard for these children. They were premature.

The 'father' says to the 'grandmother': "You got rid of my child."

Susanne: "When I was 19 I terminated the pregnancy, that was twins too."

'Father' and 'mother' now stand together. The parts of myself, the 'intention' and 'success', look over at the 'grandmother' and watch her walk away.

Father: "Now you've had your question answered. Now the truth has come out."

Intention: "It's such a good feeling, when it's right."

The constellation was ended at that point by Franz Ruppert. After my constellation I felt as if I was in a thick fog. I didn't really follow what was said. I didn't feel any anger or fury. I was amazingly calm. As if I had suspected all these things. In the break I rang my husband and told him about my constellation. I felt a huge amount of astonishment and lack of understanding coming from him. Right up until the evening I had a really strong feeling that something wasn't right!! My grandmother would never have done anything that could have harmed me. This feeling was strong and unshakable.

After the seminar, on the way to the airport, I had a sudden thought: "What will happen if I have nightmares now, or can't cope with what I've experienced?" From the airport I rang a cousin of my mother's and told her briefly what I had just experienced. She suddenly raised her voice and told me she couldn't talk just then, she had visitors. She asked me to ring the next day. I had the feeling that this wasn't true. Next day my mother's cousin confirmed it. The night passed completely differently from how I'd expected. I fell into a deep sleep. I can't remember dreaming. And then something very strange happened. I suddenly knew that my grandmother wasn't the instigator in causing the abortion. My mother had forced her to do it.

The next day I rang my mother's cousin, as agreed. She confirmed everything that had happened in the constellation, including my suspicion that my grandmother had acted against her will and out of love for her daughter. She also told me that my mother wanted to live freely. From when she was 16 she had regularly gone to nightspots and other places of amusement. My grandmother didn't have any influence over her. My mother continually put pressure on my grandmother. At some point my mother became pregnant, so she went to my grandmother and asked her to induce an abortion. My grandmother helped her, just like she always did. But neither of them dreamed that it was twins.

I asked my mother's cousin how she knew about all this. Through tears she said that her mother, my grandmother's sister, and my great-grandmother had also played a part in the abortion. She also told me that I was the apple of my grandmother's eye. I knew that. After our conversation I felt the old familiar strong attachment to my grandmother, although she died a long time ago.

The next day my mother's cousin rang me again and said a huge load had been taken off her mind. She was so relieved that the truth was now out in the open. When she was with me she had always felt good, but the secret she was keeping from me had made her feel mean. She thanked me.

Several weeks have now passed since this constellation. I'm looking after a dear neighbour of my mother's, whom I call my 'aunt'. She's 86 years old and we've got a very close relationship. She met my mother when my mother was 14 and she's known me since I was born. When we were having coffee together, I don't know why, but I told her about my constellation. This 'aunt' confirmed everything as well. She also stressed that the women in my family had always stuck closely together, my great-grandmother, my grandmother and her sister. She also said that my great-grandmother, whom I remember very fondly, had been a successful abortionist.

It has become clear to me through my constellation that, to the female line in my family, i.e. my great-grandmother, my grandmother, my mother, 'success' or 'being successful' meant having carried out abortions successfully. My great-grandmother was 'successful' with many abortions, amongst them her own daughters', at their wish. I now know this from my mother's cousin too. My great-grandmother had held a special position in the family until she reached a ripe old age. Her daughters (my grandmother and her sister) felt beholden to her and looked after her. My grandmother had tried to terminate my mother's pregnancy 'almost successfully', at my mother's wish. My mother also felt beholden to my grandmother and had looked after her devotedly and cared for her. When I became pregnant unintentionally my mother 'successfully' found a clinic for me where my termination took place. But I had acted differently intuitively. I had absolutely no feeling of obligation towards my mother. And I now understand why we so often had disagreements. My mother said things to me like: "You're so ungrateful, I've done everything for you!" I was unable to experience my own 'success' as such because I felt that this had negative connotations for me in my family. I had broken the pattern of being thankful to my mother for help with an abortion.

Since knowing all this I've had a wonderful feeling of peace. For the first time in my life I don't feel driven.

I frequently experience such astonishing processes in constellations so frequently now, that I sometimes have to pause in order to appreciate how extraordinary they really are. There is still no explanation for the astonishing phenomenon of representatives in the constellation, who do not know the client in the least, being able to make such detailed statements which the client confirms are true and which turn out to be a real history.

Prerequisites for a constellation to be valid

The question then arises: what are the prerequisites for a constellation to lead to a valid result? The following four points seem significant to me:

1. The facilitator has to have a solid theoretical basis on which to build his hypotheses. If the facilitator does not understand the meaning behind the representatives' expressed experiences and is not able to understand the implications involved, which are frequently unconscious at this stage, he may well interrupt the constellation too early, and guide it in the wrong direction through his interventions, for example by setting up more representatives that confuse the issue, by suggesting sentences for the client to say that misinterpret the representatives' expressions, or by interpreting what the representatives are saying.

2. Anyone working with the constellation method has to trust it; that is, he has to trust that the representatives do not express their own psychological disposition, but show what is fundamentally to do with the client's psychological structure. Of course every representative can only express the psyche of a client through the filter of his own psyche. But when, for example in music, one particular tune has to be played, then the instrument on which it is produced is not so important; the same tune can be played on different instruments. In my opinion, the same is true of constellations. Of course some tunes sound more or less melodic depending on who is singing them, and some representatives can express the psychological structures concerned in a more multi-faceted way than others, because they know the problem (for

195

example sexual abuse) first hand from their own experience. If we give the representatives all the space they need to feel the resonances within them, then they will point to real psychological dynamics.

3. Constellations should not be understood as a means of eliciting answers to factual questions, such as whether a person had been sexually abused, or had a different father, or whether he had been loved by his parents or not. The person who approaches a constellation wanting to receive answers to his questions from outside of himself, without his own real participation, is delegating his responsibility to the facilitator and the representatives. In the end he will find more uncertainty than certainty. Constellations are not an oracle, to be asked questions as those in ancient cultures did when they went to a priest, a seer or healer. The process is not like reading tealeaves or consulting a crystal ball. Valid constellations only occur when the client does not become dependent on the facilitator or the group, but relates to the things only he can feel and tap into. The representatives are only a tool that provides access to the unconscious complexity of the person's own psychological structures.

4. Right from the start, the client himself has to have the will to allow things from his unconscious to become conscious. He has to be prepared to accept responsibility if something appears in his consciousness that might cause him extreme fear or shame. By means of his intention he specifies the limits of what he is prepared to do. The facilitator is therefore not permitted to go beyond this intention or do more than is contained within the intention.

I am now able to recognise clearly if clients formulate and set up an intention whilst still to a large extent trapped in their survival strategies and continuing to make every attempt to retain control over their feelings. In such cases, it is important to recognise and accept that at that time the client is not able or does not want to go further emotionally.

Basically, constellations are no more and no less than a particularly good method of using the sensitivity of other people to access the unconscious, split, suppressed and pre-linguistic contents anchored in the person's own psyche. There are other methods that can help to achieve that, for example hypnosis, EMDR or body therapy. With all methods, it depends on the purpose behind the person's choice of method. Is he someone who

- is trying out these methods with scepticism and reserva-tions?
- or does he surrender himself more or less passively to the therapist's actual or presumed skills?
- or does he make use of the advantages of each method as best he can to achieve more clarity and a deeper under-standing of his psyche?

This means that only when a person is in his healthy self when choosing a method is he prepared to take responsibility for the results that come to light in the process. The survival parts will reject responsibility for results achieved if they run counter to their aim of maintaining the psychological split, ascribing the results to the method or the therapist's intention.

If a therapist doubts the reliability of the constellations method, he or she should not be using it. If the facilitator feels that one representative should be exchanged for another because the representative is allegedly not reacting in the way the facilitator expects, she is then doubting the efficacy of the constellations method. She will then use the constellation to follow her own expectations of 'the solution', and impose them on the client. She is in danger of manipulating her clients.

The ability to be a representative in a constellation does not have to be learnt or practised. Picking up on information from other people relevant to relationships is a natural ability, which even a baby can do in order to maintain contact with his mother. For me, one of the significant results of a study we made of representatives' experiences of being in constellations was their awareness of the extreme importance of differentiating between their own feelings and those of the other person (Ruppert, 2007). To do this there has to be a clear separation between the roles of the representatives and the facilitator, a distinct division of labour:

- It only makes sense for a person to take on a representative role if they feel prepared to feel and sense. Everyone is free to decline being set up as a representative. The representatives must be autonomous in their endeavours to represent the psychological state of another. In doing this, they must not be disturbed or doubted by anyone.
- The facilitator, too, is autonomous in his decision to facilitate the constellation process to a good conclusion. He must not let himself be influenced from his perceptions and conclusions by a representative's affirmative or negative feedback. He has to retain an overview of the whole process, and be able to attribute the contradictions contained in every constellation process to their cause. To do this, he has to be able to differentiate healthy survival parts from survival and traumatised parts in a constellation.

Basically we can say that the constellation method consists of four basic elements:

- the client,
- the representatives,
- the facilitator, and
- the observers.

I believe that in order for the constellation process to succeed, all four elements have to be autonomous. In other words:

- the client has to find and formulate his own intention. He has to follow any thoughts, feelings and images that come to him at that time;
- the representatives have to express everything that emerges from within them through words, body language or movement;
- the facilitator has to follow the perceptions and thoughts that occur to him while observing the constellation process;
- the observers have to watch closely. They cannot interfere in the constellation for example by spontaneously joining the constellation. If it feels appropriate to them, they can let the facilitator know if they have strong emotions that are not represented within the constellation at that time.

The autonomy of the individuals concerned is endangered, for example

- if the client expects the facilitator to choose his intention for him, or if he tries to fulfil what he perceives as the facilitator's expectations;
- if a representative has certain ideas about what the results should be or what the client should be protected from;
- if the facilitator starts trying to please his client or lets himself be misled by the expressions of individual representatives;
- if observers feel forced to take part as a representative in the process although they would rather not.

Provided everyone remains anchored within themselves, and sticks to their particular perceptions, emotions and thoughts something new and, in a certain sense, an objectivity, can be created through the process of a constellation. If this is achieved, the different perspectives will complement and challenge each other, and in the end find a common conclusion that is accepted by all. Then the client is most likely to be able to trust whatever has come to light as being based on reality in his own life and his family history.

It is important to stress that the person setting up the constellation must have the final say in whether he considers what he has experienced in the constellation as real or not. It is his inner self and his relationships with others that are being portrayed in the constellation, and only he can decide whether what he has experienced in the constellation is true and correct, because in the end it is all about enabling his own psyche to perceive, feel, think and decide what is real and what is not. A healthy psyche will not allow itself to be deluded and does not try to fool itself or others.

Pragmatism without metaphysics

The reason the constellation method can be so astonishingly accurate, and constellated representatives can suddenly access information about which they have no conscious knowledge, remains scientifically unexplained. There have been several attempts at interpretation that put forward arguments using terms such as 'morphic field', citing 'mirror neurons' or 'quantum physical' matter-energy-information (Lahore, 2009). It is possible that all these concepts cover certain aspects of the constellation phenomenon, but there are still no systematic experiments proving or refuting any theories of how it works.

I do not advise using metaphysical constructs to try and find a causal explanation for the phenomenon of representatives in constellations. It seems very tempting to fill this gap in our knowledge with an explanation from an alternative or spiritual world view ('everything is connected with everything else'), or claiming it as the latest thing in science ('field theory', 'quantum physics'). In my opinion, such attempts are extremely speculative, and are likely to damage rather than assist public credibility of this method. I believe it is more honest to admit that our knowledge is lacking at the moment and to regard the constellation phenomenon as one of the unsolved puzzles of science, of which there are still many.

For my practical work with the constellation method, the following assumptions seem to me at the moment to be sufficient:

- In addition to a verbal transmission of information (spoken or written communication), there is a non-verbal exchange of information (facial expressions, gestures, body language, physical movements), and an unconscious direct exchange of psychological software, when the 'brains' concerned send and receive messages instantly. Like a smart phone that exchanges data even in stand-by mode, our brains probably send and receive data continuously via waves of as yet unidentified nature. The extent of unconscious data exchange is possibly much greater than we imagine at the moment, and is much more than the half-conscious non-verbal and conscious verbal communications process (figure 13).
- Every person sends and receives information, consciously and unconsciously.
- The client seems to be able, at least to an extent, to control the amount of data he releases consciously and unconsciously into the constellation process, and makes available to the representatives.
- Representatives in a constellation who are open to receive, become aware of the information emanating from a client consciously and unconsciously. They can express this received information via their facial expression, by gesticulation, movement and also verbally.

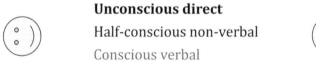

Unconscious direct
Half-conscious non-verbal
Conscious verbal

Figure 13: Three forms of data exchange

Our human ability to empathise and resonate with the psyche of other creatures seems to be considerably more pronounced than we had previously assumed. (Animals also appear to be able to latch onto a human psyche to a surprising extent.) In my view, the constellation phenomenon has opened a new door in the field of psychology in general, and psychotherapy in particular, leading to the recognition of psychological processes in their socially interdependent context. It seems to me that the human psyche is not only a phenomenon of the individual, but to a great extent a collective one. In the course of our lives, it seems we have to learn to sustain our own psychological processes against the influences of the psyches of others, and develop our own personal identity by establishing appropriate boundaries. Symbiotic psychological phenomena seem to precede the personal development of autonomy, and under certain circumstances to inhibit it, particularly when trauma is involved. Constellations can play a part in enabling people who are symbiotically entangled and trapped in destructive relationships to become more autonomous individuals with the capacity to form constructive relationships with others.

7
Case studies taken from one-to-one and group therapy sessions

In order to illustrate my use of the constellations method that I have developed, I have compiled further case studies from one-to-one and group therapy sessions. As far as was possible, I sent a draft of the case study to the client concerned, asking for their permission to use it in this book. They were not only happy to grant their permission to use their case study, but actively added to it with any necessary alterations. At this point I should like to thank these clients for their kind cooperation.

Sexualized violence in male and female relationships

It is mostly women, about 80-90%, who register for my workshops. I am always pleased when there are more men than 10–20% men contributing with their male energy to the whole group and taking the chance to improve their inner state.

It seems to be particularly challenging for men to come to therapy workshops. In most countries where I have worked, the idea that men might have psychological and emotional problems that they can't resolve on their own still contravenes conventional concepts of masculinity. In many societies it is seen as unmanly to expose one's inner self in front of others, showing that one is vulnerable. Although at least a similar number of men as women are traumatised, men often redefine their trauma-survival strategies as an expression of true masculinity, rather than grasping the opportunity to develop a real, stable and healthy type of masculinity. On the other hand, I now know many men who have demonstrated a great deal of courage and perseverance in taking the path of admitting their trauma and finding a way to free themselves of their symbiotic entanglements.

In many cases, when women set up a constellation in a workshop, it becomes clear that it is often masculine trauma survival strategies that represent the underlying cause of women's traumatisation. For example, in women's biographies men often appear as:

- tyrants who terrorise the whole family at home,
- husbands who sexually degrade and rape their wives,
- perpetrators of incest who may even father children with their own children,
- soldiers who may brutishly attack women,
- teachers or priests, or others in authority, who use their superior position to get sexual gratification and act out their own symbiotic trauma on children and adolescents.

When I started doing trauma constellations these facts appalled me. I could hardly imagine how, as a man, one could endure being set up as a representative for a bully or a rapist without experiencing a tremendous feeling of shame. Today I know that the representative roles for men as perpetrators are not nearly as laden with shame and guilt as one would expect. On the contrary, from observing such roles, and from my own experiences as a representative, I have understood a great deal about how masculine trauma survival structures function:

- As perpetrators, men show almost complete emotional indifference when confronted with their deeds;
- they usually maintain that they cannot remember anything;

- they simply look away or diminish the importance of the event;
- they allege that the women and children had wanted sex and that they were the real initiators and seducers;
- they feel so uncomfortable in their own body, having been frequently traumatised by, for example, war, that possessing a new, fresh body (the wife or child's) seems to be the only way out of their inner prison;
- they are looking for physical closeness to their own traumatised mother, but when they are rejected by this mother, they see sexuality as a means of reducing their enormous inner tension and achieving relief for a while;
- they often see it as their natural right to use money to buy 'fun', in other words treat women and children as sex objects;
- they actively seek and provoke violent arguments in order to distract themselves from their own internal hopelessness and pain;
- as violent perpetrators they feel strong and invincible, rather than weak and helpless.

The violence that women experience from men sets off a vicious cycle. Women may then experience all men as threatening, and having sex with them as disgusting and abhorrent. They are likely to react to everything that comes from men as if it is an attack, and internally they are permanently defensive. They may then, unconsciously, see their sons as potential violent rapists, and even feel relieved if their husband leaves them alone and seeks sexual satisfaction with a daughter instead. There are men who can drive women insane and there are women who allow themselves to be driven insane, and who then in turn drive other, psychologically fragile, individuals insane, most commonly, their own children.

At the beginning of my therapeutic career, I found the frequency and range of sexualised violence in male-female relationships, disguised behind the façade of a 'normal' family, almost unbearable. Many violent men and child abusers are highly regarded in their community. Many hold important public positions, and even deliver moral and legal judgements on other men who are accused of such deeds. They are deeply split psychologically, and lead double lives like Dr Jekyll and Mr Hyde: the decent citizen by day and the evil lunatic by night.

Women traumatised by relationships may become cold, dominant and manipulative. Despite the violence many women receive at the hands of their husbands, they frequently remain in the relationship, and then become the source of their children's symbiotic traumas. Outwardly they seem a good mothers, dear grandmothers and decent citizens who work for the good of society, but within the family they spread coldness, stress and confusion.

Dispelling the illusion that male-female relationships can succeed naturally without psychological effort seems to be an essential pre-requisite so that more women and men begin their search for a constructive and truly loving relationship. It is by no means a given for people to be able to do that. The sexual and other needs of men and women are very different, and often do not fit easily together. Bearing in mind the extent of traumatisation suffered by many people, we have to work hard in order to learn how to conduct a good partner relationship. We cannot have fruitful relationships functioning from our survival self, which might simply endure the chaos, and spread it further afield. We can only have a good relationship based on our healthy psychological structures, and these have to be developed, so that the male-female relationship can be turned into a win-win situation. In the power games played out between the sexes, through dominance and submission, or even unconscious revenge against the opposite sex, there are no winners. Men and women destroy each other's potential for developing into healthy human beings.

Case study 24

Allowing intimacy again (Carmen)

Carmen had been working for many years on healing her childhood scars. She grew up in the post-war environment of a bombed German city, in a cramped flat with extremely traumatised parents, and other relatives who were also traumatised. Twelve people were living in 100 m^2 with no bathroom, sharing a kitchen and a toilet. During her childhood, Carmen had no safe area to retreat to. She had to live in her parents' sitting room, which was also their bedroom, and she was unable to escape from her father's sexual assaults, which happened particularly when he had been drinking.

Even now, she has no concrete memory of these sexual assaults. She assumes from her many psychological problems and her body symptoms that they took place, so that she now has no doubts about the reality of the abuse. What she can remember clearly is the unpredictable rages and violent behaviour of her father, and the way he behaved towards her, which she now describes as 'grooming'. It's possible that she was also sexually assaulted by her uncle, who lived in the flat with them, and by her grandfather on her father's side, who had a criminal conviction for child abuse. However, here too, Carmen has only vague memories, and none of any specific events.

Carmen's problems with her father were so immense that she often skipped school and frequently ran away from home. On the occasions when she was on the run, she was repeatedly raped, which she endured with rigidity and without resistance. When she returned home, her father would beat her violently, shout at her and utterly humiliate her. He threatened her mother: 'Either Carmen goes or I'm leaving!' Carmen finally left her family when she was 16 and led her own life, which was very lonely for the first years. She got married when she was 19 and later managed to get a school-leaving qualification and finish an apprentice-ship.

When she was 30, she separated from her first husband and moved out of the marital flat with her two-year-old daughter. It was her way to separate from her partners when the problems became too great. When her second child, her son, was eight years old, she left her second husband. She did not think it worthwhile tolerating and persevering with a marriage as her mother had done with her father, or her grandmother, who had had 13 children with her violent husband.

However now she no longer sees her survival strategy of leaving her husband as soon as possible when problems arose as the only path available to her. In her relationship with her current partner, she recognises that problems are part of the relationship and have to be dealt with together.

Carmen's intention for the one-to-one session I am describing here was being able to let herself be close to someone. She said she experiences again and again how she withdraws from contact as quickly as possible. It is enough for a man to sit too close to her in the underground, or for men to look at her and seek eye contact with her. She imme-diately becomes suspicious and starts withdrawing internally. In groups too, she is unable to present herself as she is. If she has to say something about herself, she is afraid, even panicked, and feels very young.

She works as a lecturer and seminar leader, and she is always confronted with her fears at the beginning of a lecture or seminar. She often notices that she has to split to be able to cope with this situation more easily. She wants to be able to remain present, if only for a few minutes, even though she is afraid.

The constellations process. I let Carmen set me up as the representative for this intention. Just the way she takes my arm and leads me to a place in the therapy room makes me feel very uneasy. For a moment being close to her soothes me, but then again I cannot look at her. Carmen is very unsettled as well, as she stands opposite me, a couple of feet away. We are both confused and disturbed. I feel split. On the one hand I want her to be close and on the other hand I want to get away.

Therefore I suggest using a cushion on the floor to represent the part within her that cannot bear closeness. She puts a cushion down to our right. We both have the same thought at the same time, that this is a child that wants to run away but doesn't know where to go. Carmen has the feeling that there is a suppressed scream within her. As her 'intention', I'm afraid that she might start to scream. I suggest that she puts another cushion on the floor to represent the part in her that wants to scream. She puts this one down to our right too. Now I have the feeling that the constellation is about inner children, and because of her history, Carmen's father should be represented as well. When Carmen tries to choose a cushion to represent the father, she feels rooted to the spot and cannot move. After a while, I suggest she puts another cushion on the floor to represent this frozen state. There are now three cushions in a row to our right.

She is then able to select a cushion for the father. She chooses a sunny, yellow cushion for him and is then unable to decide where to put it. I feel afraid that this cushion belongs on the left, in other words on our side. When she puts it down on the left, next to us, I feel myself drawn to it and am completely intent on this lovely cushion, and I become calmer. Carmen is confused by my behaviour, but can remember that her father also had a fun-loving side and that she sometimes felt secure when she was close to him and that she liked it when he admired her. "I was always his favourite child. Look what a lovely daughter I have created! He showed me off proudly to our relatives."

It now becomes clear that there must have also been another father, the father who was violent, who tried to dominate her self-awareness and her identity, and who abused her sexually. I asked Carmen to choose a cushion for this part of her father too. She takes a brown-black cushion and puts it on the right, behind the three traumatised parts of her (figure 14).

I now start to question which closeness Carmen is looking for. On the left-hand side is the 'closeness to her father', which I find emotionally quite appropriate in my role as Carmen's 'intention', because it can be tolerated, and on the right-hand side it seems completely impossible to establish any sort of closeness to the father and the three other inner parts.

There cannot be any closeness to 'dear Daddy' on the left any more, Carmen is quite certain of that. This has always been an illusion. She puts a small yellow cushion close to the father. She says that this is little Carmen who looked to her father for protection and blanked out his dominance, violence and sexual assaults.

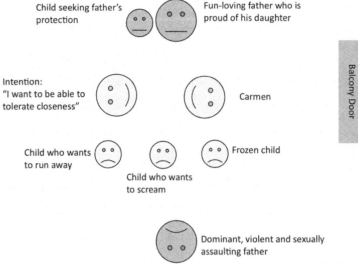

Figure 14: Carmen would like to be able to tolerate closeness

I can see things more clearly now, and I ask Carmen what kind of closeness it is that she wants. She says: "To myself!" She has the feeling that there is a part of her that is truly her, separate from the whole madness she experienced with her parents. I suggest she choose a cushion for this part of her. She chooses an orange cushion, a colour, she notes, that is reflected in the tints in her hair and in the scarf she is wearing. Unprompted, she holds the cushion in front of her belly and is very pleased: "The child's place is here in my belly. Now I know why I never really wanted to lose weight!" As her 'intention' I immediately have the feeling of closeness to this child that is completely unproblematic and uncomplicated. Neither of us feels the need to run away or look away or that something bad could happen. Carmen now remembers that she really used to be an inquisitive and cheeky child who was often up to mischievous tricks. However, to her father, cheekiness was like a red rag to a bull. In his eyes, cheeky children had to be punished.

I now walk to the balcony door in my therapy room and open it. I suggest to Carmen that she goes out onto the balcony together with the child that corresponds with her healthy character. She follows my suggestion and for the first time as her 'intention' I feel as if I'm a healthy and lucid part of her, one that knows which form of closeness is possible and which is not. I now understand that there is a form of closeness that is traumatising (with the father, who dominates, beats and abuses), and a closeness that seems apparently normal based on this childish need and naivety, but includes the cost of surrender to the father and his unpredictable behaviour. Now Carmen realises that her route to recovery has to involve her offering her traumatised parts contact and guidance from the position of security she has now achieved, inviting them to come with her into freedom (figure 15).

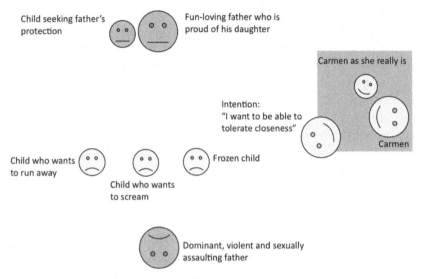

Figure 15: A closeness that can easily be tolerated

Comments on this constellation. The child of a traumatised father who, from his survival self, enacts total control over the child, lives in permanent fear of the father. She grows up in an extremely confusing situation. On the one hand, the father is nice to her, admires her and calls her "his little princess", does funny things with her and gives her presents. Some girls then feel like little princesses who can have everything, and perhaps feel that they are better at making daddy happy than their mother (who often makes him angry). They cannot understand it when this kind and fun-loving daddy turns into a shouting tyrant who lashes out at everything and everyone, and who becomes a lecherous monster, wanting to use their body sexually. At this moment they want to run away from this unpredictable father, without anywhere they can run to. They want to scream and defend themselves, but they haven't a chance against such a perpetrator, who is physically and psychologically superior to them. They can only freeze and retreat internally, trying to make themselves invisible.

However, the physical body remains visible, and is vulnerable, and powerless against the violence and sexual assaults. This is when the child's identity splits; she is present and at the same time not present. Survival mechanisms kick in.

Of course the child still has a great need to be close to other people, but at the same time, this closeness causes her to feel panic. From this time on the child remains confused, as an adolescent and as an adult woman, whenever intimacy is involved. Even when her own sexual desires are strong, the physical proximity of a man will rekindle her childhood memories of humiliation and sexual violence. To this person, having sex can never be a pleasurable encounter with a man, but remains something that has to be endured, something that she wants to get over and done with as quickly as possible. If a woman has had to cope with this problem for a long time, perhaps has had children, she may suppress her own sexual desires and stop having sex entirely. Refusing sexual contact with her partner or husband then can create a breeding ground for the perpetuation of sexual abuse within her present family. The woman's children might even be compelled towards her sexually unsatisfied partner in order to satisfy his desire. Such women often unconsciously choose partners with a high perpetrator potential because they, too, come from an abusive family.

It is therefore extremely important that people who have experienced sexual violence in their childhood clearly understand what has happened to them, that they have been dealing with a parent who is split, and a perpetrator, and that they have split themselves in order to endure the situation. They need to understand that their physical symptoms and behaviour patterns are the result of sexual violence, and recognise that the idea that their childhood was normal is an illusion, that the things they were told were fun, were not fun at all.

Today Carmen sees much more clearly why her father became this monster. His father was convicted of child abuse and his mother grew up in an orphanage, and she had given her children, including Carmen's grandfather, away so that her husband would stay with her. Carmen's father hated and despised his parents, particularly his mother.

Carmen's constellation serves also to illustrate that abused children still have a psychological structure within them that, even though insecure, has adapted to circumstances as far as humanly possible, but was not traumatised. Accessing this healthy child is extremely important to continue the healing of their psychological wounds.

After I had sent Carmen the transcript of this constellation, and she had added her modifications and amendments, she gave as her personal summary: "Healing is possible if we realise that there are parts in us that cannot be destroyed. These parts are connected with values such as the meaning of life, strength, vision, self-care, self-love, being. And with autonomy. I have this image that there are healthy, even somehow autonomous parts within us, that are created at the moment of conception and that are never destroyed and split. My image is that of a person after a heavy storm, standing upright again, brushing himself off and noting what has remained undamaged and whole. He takes a deep breath, looks around and goes on his way."

Everybody has to work therapeutically on his or her own childhood history, but it can make sense to go to a therapist with one's partner. I have developed my own approach to working with constellations in couples' therapy. Each partner can constellate their own intention.

Case study 25

Suppressed anger (Wolfgang and Meike)

Wolfgang and Meike come to a therapy session together. They are concerned about the future of their relationship. Wolfgang says he can't reach his wife any longer, and Meike thinks the same of Wolfgang. Their conversations often end in mutual accusations.

The intention. I let each of them formulate their intention for today's session. Meike wants to try to get more in contact with her self. Wolfgang's intention is to understand how he can get in contact with Meike again.

Two guest students from a training course are taking part in this session, a man and a woman. Meike chooses the woman as her 'intention' for her constellation and Wolfgang chooses the man for his, and sets him up.

The constellation process. Meike and her 'intention' quickly develop a strong degree of closeness and intimacy. Wolfgang's 'intention', on the other hand, immediately says that this is not about Meike, but about him. He feels a great pain in Wolfgang that still cannot rise to the surface.

I can see that the predominant energy in the constellation lies with Wolfgang and his 'intention', so I primarily work with him. It seems that the suppressed emotions are gradually making Wolfgang's 'intention' more helpless and exhausted, so that the representative of his 'intention' ends up lying on his back on the floor. Wolfgang begins to talk about the situation in his family of origin. There was no love and a great deal of violence. When he was ten, his mother beat him brutally, which caused a break in the relationship with his mother.

I suggest to Wolfgang that he sets me up as this ten-year-old. As soon as I am in the role I begin to feel like lashing out in all directions. I would really like to punch everyone in the face. I put my foot on the hand of the 'intention' who is still lying on the ground, and would really like to hear his bones breaking. Wolfgang's expression lights up. He grins at me. He wants to come closer to me but all I want to do is wrestle with him. Wolfgang now explains that he did a lot of fighting as an adolescent and never passed over the opportunity for a fight. It was only after he had caused a serious car accident that this wild phase of his life came to an end.

Meike sits with her intention in a far corner of the therapy room and watches this scene. I step out of the role as representative of the ten-year-old boy. Wolfgang recognises now that this angry boy is still inside him, and he thinks that he withdraws because he is afraid that this anger will cause him to hurt his wife and children. He sometimes slams the door loudly behind him, but otherwise manages not to hurt anyone.

I suggest to Wolfgang that he say to his wife that he is afraid of not being able to control his anger in conflicts, and that this is why he withdraws internally, and gets to where his 'intention' is now, hopeless and depressed. When Wolfgang says this to Meike, an emotional contact between the two of them is established. Wolfgang's 'intention' also gets up off the floor and stands next to Wolfgang. We end the constellation. Meike and Wolfgang embrace at the end of the session.

Comments on this constellation. When couples come to a therapy session together, it is important to ask which of them has come along with an intention. Sometimes it is only one partner who has an intention, while the other has just come along to please the partner. If both have an intention, I ask who would like to begin with a constellation. Often the constellation of one partner creates a new situation for the other, and their original intention alters slightly after the constellation of their partner.

As I knew Meike and Wolfgang from earlier individual and joint sessions, and I knew of their honest endeavours to preserve their relationship, I thought it appropriate to work with both their intentions at the same time. I could then immediately see who or what was the cause of the current crisis in the relationship. Wolfgang's experiences of violence in his childhood threatened the fabric of his marriage. So far he had tried to control and hide the anger that had arisen in his childhood and adolescence. But that led him into depression, and meant that he was unable to take any action. He then felt defenceless and at the mercy of his wife and children. By showing his aggressive feelings and their cause, he became more understandable to his wife.

In the ensuing work with Meike and Wolfgang, a familiar couples dynamic began to emerge: if one of the partners takes a step forward in their psychological development, the other is prompted to follow suit. In Meike and Wolfgang's case Meike was no longer able to hide behind Wolfgang's apparent short-comings. The more he came into his healthy structures, the more Meike was forced to waken from her slumber and confront the question as to whether she had been sexually abused by her father.

Wars as the cause and consequence of traumatisations

The history of mankind is in many ways a history of wars. Tribal wars, civil wars, religious wars, wars between neigh-bouring and distant peoples, colonial wars and world wars – there is nothing that mankind has not used as an excuse for war. Wars are waged to gain power over other people and take their possessions, to exploit and enslave them, to gain control over their land, their natural resources and their trade routes. Eliminating another political and military power using military force is usually the aim, and once this is achieved, the state of war ceases, at least for a while. The purpose of war is to trau-matise others who are merely seen as 'enemies'. Since states are proclaiming their enemies as 'terrorists' the 'war on terror' has become an undefined permanent condition of our whole living (Baecker, Krieg and Simon, 2002).

The Second World War (1939-45) still plays an important role in almost all my constellation seminars that take place in Germany. Either participants were born before or during the war and experienced first-hand bombing attacks, the loss of grandparents, fathers or brothers, or being forced to flee or being expelled. Or the workshop participants are the children or grandchildren of war-traumatised parents and grandparents, who then suffer from the transgenerational consequences of their parents' and grandparents' terrible wartime experiences. For some people their wartime experiences are so terrible that they try to obliterate everything they did and suffered from their consciousness, and never want to speak or tell their spouses and children about it.

Even so, the experiences they suppress have an effect on their relationships because they are anxious, hyperactive, depressed or emotionally absent. In two books Sabine Bode has described numerous case studies of the way German 'wartime children' born between 1939 and 1945 have buried the horror of their childhood deep within themselves and created a façade of normality (Bode, 2004). She also describes with great sensitivity the hardships of these 'wartime grandchildren', the children of wartime children, who struggle hopelessly their entire lives against their parents' walls of silence and denial (Bode, 2009).

In the grandparents and parents of some seminar participants the psychological pain from wartime experiences is so severe that they would shatter internally if they re-connected with it, to the point of going insane. In many cases the burden of angst, suffering and pain is so huge that fleeing from reality is the only escape.

When I visit other countries to hold constellation workshops there, it is also important for me to know more about the wars that are significant for that country. Amongst the other countries I have visited I have seen the following:

- In the Czech Republic, Poland, Ukraine or Romania, Greece, the Netherlands, Belgium, Norway, Russia and Italy, being caught up in the Second World War by invasion of German soldiers has left deep traces of trauma in the families of seminar participants.
- Another factor in Russia is the terror Stalin unleashed over many decades before, during and after the Second World War on the Russian population.
- The 'Troubles' in Northern Ireland (late 1960s–1998), involving republican (mainly Catholic) and loyalist and unionist (mainly Protestant) paramilitaries, and security forces from the United Kingdom and Ireland play an

important role in causing psychological disorders in seminar participants, as does the later violence between these groups

- In The Netherlands the war fought by the Dutch in Indonesia has an effect even now, three generations later. In the war with the Japanese occupiers of the island archipelago (1942–1945), many Dutch were killed, tortured and severely traumatised in Japanese concentration camps. The terrors of war continued for several years for many men, women and children in the Indonesian War of Independence (1945–1949).
- In Spain it is the civil wars between fascists and anarchists/communists (1936–1939) and between Franco-Spain and the Basque Country (1968-1979) that leave an aftermath of trauma today.
- In Portugal there are traumatic repercussions from the colonial wars in Angola, Mozambique and Guinea-Bissau (1961–1974).
- It is also important to know what genocides and massacres have taken place in different countries (e.g. in Turkey, Indonesia, America and China).

Wars do not solve problems. They create new ones. The promise of safety, protection, prosperity and peace that is always trotted out as the ideology of war is an illusion. The consequences of wars are even more wars because those on the losing side seek revenge, and those who start wars are never content with what they have achieved, and continue to feel insecure and threatened by those they have suppressed.

The preparation for war costs immense social resources and money, involving masses of workers and subjecting many to military training. The act of war causes inconceivable death and destruction, and the consequences are poverty and misery for millions.

In my view the desire for war, including planning actions of war, surely does not originate in the healthy parts of our human psyche. They are the expression of the trauma survival selves. Only the trauma survival parts possess the ability:

- to be emotionally numbed enough not to feel human misery as real;
- to refuse to recognise their responsibility as perpetrator, and blaming the victim for the violence they suffer;
- to close their eyes completely to the short-term and long-term traumatising consequences of military force.

War means that human life and health are directly threatened. It means enduring violence, hunger, cold and disease, and it snatches away parents, siblings, children and friends. Wars lead to the brutalisation of men through their actions as soldiers, who then no longer shrink from murder and rape. War uproots people and leaves them with no prospects. War destroys trust in other people and in the future. Wars dehumanise human beings.

From the perspective of psychotraumatology, war is a symptom of the many perpetrator/victim splits in those who instigate war, and those who actively take part in perpetrating it, since those with perpetrator/victim splits in their psyche will tend to shift the trauma inside them onto the external world.

In wartime, those in power attempt to define clearly friend and foe, which is rarely successful. For example, in World War I German manufacturers supplied cannons to England, the 'enemy'; and in the case of Hitler, even his closest Nazi party comrades could never be sure that one thoughtless comment would not relegate them swiftly to the ranks of the enemy. If necessary, those in power will send everyone and everything to the slaughter, in order to avoid coming into contact with their own feelings of trauma. Everything happens according to the ideology that it is for the 'greater good'. No tyrant is honest enough to confront himself with his own trauma before planning a war.

War means dividing people into groups of 'friends' and 'enemies', legitimising the use of force against all those defined as the enemy. Destroying houses that are the centre of these people's lives then appears to be a logical act. How could anyone in their healthy mind drop bombs on towns of innocent civilians?

Wars are started by traumatised people who then draw others into the maelstrom of their trauma. Hitler's symbiotic trauma formed the basis for his delusion of seeing the Jews as the cause of all evil, allowing him to declare himself the master over the life and death of millions of people (Ruppert 2002). The recent mass murder in Norway carried out by one single person, Anders B. Breivik, who declared war on the whole Norwegian society is a further event that prompts me to summarise this insight: people who suffer from a symbiotic trauma can become a great danger to their fellow men and whole societies. This applies particularly to traumatised young men and their inherent tendency to act out their inner conflicts, tensions and splits with violence.

Case study 26

Anders B. Breivik

There are many more categories of psychiatric diagnosis describing the victim than there are describing the perpetrator. For adult perpetrators there are basically two ICD or DSM diagnoses; the first is the 'anti-social personality disorder', which is defined as follows:

> 'Personality disorder characterized by disregard for social obligations, and callous unconcern for the feelings of others. There is gross disparity between behaviour and the prevailing social norms. Behaviour is not readily modifiable by adverse experience, including punishment. There is a low tolerance to frustration and a low threshold for discharge of aggression, including violence; there is a tendency to blame others, or to offer plausible rationalizations for the behaviour bringing the patient into conflict with society.' (ICD-10 F60.2)

221

The other diagnosis is the category of 'narcissistic personality disorder':

> 'The individual has a grandiose sense of self-importance (e.g. exaggerates achievements and talents, expects to be recognized as superior without commensurate achievements); is preoccupied with fantasies of unlimited success, power, brilliance, beauty, or ideal love; believes that he or she is 'special' and unique and can only be understood by, or should associate with, other special or high-status people (or institutions); requires excessive admiration; has a sense of entitlement, i.e. unreasonable expectations of especially favourable treatment or automatic compliance with his or her expectations; is interpersonally exploitative, i.e. takes advantage of others to achieve his or her own ends; lacks empathy: is unwilling to recognize or identify with the feelings and needs of others; is often envious of others or believes others are envious of him or her; shows arrogant, haughty behaviours or attitudes' (DSM-IV, 301.81).

These characteristics are applicable to Adolf Hitler's behaviour and attitudes as well as to the Norwegian mass murderer Anders B. Breivik. However such characterising diagnoses do not answer the question as to where these behaviour patterns come from. Psychology, when it is trying to explain people's thinking, feeling and behavioural patterns, must take into account that people can behave a certain way one day and completely differently the next. According to the situation and circumstances, people can show very different faces and 'ego states' and play different roles. Breivik, for example, had friends and acquaintances who knew him as a nice person, and even Hitler was not always regarded as a monster by everyone and was described by his secretary Traudl Junge as having a pleasant personality. (Junge and Müller, 2004).

So how can we find out what makes these perpetrators treat other people so outrageously? We can start with their own explanation for their behaviour.

Breivik uploaded a 1,500-page 'manifesto' onto the internet, and Hitler wrote his book entitled 'Mein Kampf' ('My Struggle'). In their writings both presented their view of societal relationships, finding scapegoats for everything that doesn't concur with their views. For Hitler it was the Jews and the Communists. For Breivik it was people politically to the left ('cultural Marxists') as well as those of Islamic belief. However, even though perpetrators like to justify their crimes, an intensive study of their texts does not get us much further. Where perpetrators tend to project their dissatisfaction is fairly arbitrary, only a matter of historical circumstances. And perpetrators do not only come from the political right, as Breivik and Hitler undoubtedly do. Such perpetrators may also act out their destructive potential from the left political spectrum, as is obvious in the cases of Stalin or Mao or Andreas Baader of the Red Army Faction in Germany in the years between 1970 and 1980.

So where does such self-righteousness come from that these perpetrators assume to judge over the life and death of other people? Where does their hatred of other people come from and how should we understand the coldness with which they regard their victims?

On the one hand we can understand that the male in general, has a tendency to switch off the brain under the influence of hormones and then to behave more like their ape ancestors. The well-known primatologist Frans de Waal writes, for example: 'Males are built to fight and tend to seek out their rivals' weak spots and to a certain extent are blind to any dangers. Risk-taking is typical male behaviour, as is hiding their vulnerability' (de Waal, 2010, p 70). Anders B Breivik is supposed to have dosed himself up with adrenaline to make himself fit for action. We can therefore presume:

- that the male competitive nature may cause them to create opponents and enemies that they can then conquer and subjugate;

- that the male is often unable to imagine any solution to a conflict that does not involve fighting and violence;
- that they may quickly convert their fears and uncertainties into aggression;
- that they think they are called to lead the group they feel they belong to in fights against other groups;
- that they lack sufficient empathy due to an excess of stress hormones;
- that they are quick to seek revenge.

But fortunately not all males are like that and certainly not all human males. So the next question is: does a violent perpetrator have a biography that indicates the source of his destructive and hostile attitude to life? The little information we have of Anders B. Breivik's family indicates that, although he grew up in an apparently middle-class environment, he had anything but a secure emotional attachment to his parents. Both parents had previous partners and children when Breivik was conceived. He lost his father when he was one year old, following his parents' divorce. According to his own statement, he was unable to develop the loving relationship he longed for with his father, which might have given him some sense of security and direction. His stepfather, who apparently had countless sexual affairs, was not a good male role model for Breivik, who describes him as a 'primitive sexual animal'. His desire for a 'patriarchy', which he mentions at one point in his manifesto, is probably the expression of his deep uncertainty at not having a father to show him how to live as a man.

According to The Telegraph newspaper, Anders B. Breivik wrote in his 'Manifesto' about his mother: 'I do not approve of the super-liberal, matriarchal upbringing, as it completely lacked discipline and has contributed to feminise me to a certain degree'. According to the experts who diagnosed Breivik's psychological state, his mother's mother was paranoid and his mother also had severe psychological problems. Because the mother did not look after her child well enough, the family was admitted to a program for non-residential family counselling for a month. Psychologists even suspected sexual abuse of Anders and recommended separating him from his mother. But no one in the Norwegian social services followed up on this advice (Borchgrevinck 2012, Christensen 2014, Seierstadt 2014).

A mother whom he perceived as weak, an absent father who could not be reached emotionally, a step-father who degraded the mother with his rampant sexuality, and may have sexually abused him too – is it any wonder that Breivik sought escape into the myth of the 'white knight' who has to save the world (in other words his mother) from evil and take revenge for his own humiliation?

I recognise this attitude from some of my male clients who, in similar traumatising circumstances, have experienced massive problems in developing their male identity, and have become entangled in an unsolvable internal struggle between 'good' and 'evil', which are the general categories used so as not to name the real perpetrators and victims. Because such children are unable to show their fear for their mother and their anger towards their father directly, they look for an external outlet for the internal pressure. They feel drawn towards extreme ideologies that confirm their elusive fears and anger, by alluding to existing or alleged social injustices. In the case of Hitler it seems obvious that he had suffered a symbiotic trauma because three of his siblings died within 14 days by suffocation. How could his mother not be traumatised by this nightmare? (see Ruppert, 2002). Looking at the biographies of Hitler and Breivik it is obvious that both of them had suffered a symbiotic trauma.

Something that is carefully avoided by these symbiotically-entangled men, with their profound anger at societal and political relationships and their autocratic attempts to force justice, is a confrontation with their own feelings, their uncertainty and loneliness, their fears and their inability to enter into close emotional attachments. They hide the traumatised child within them behind their many masks of surviving strategies. It is typical for those perpetrators to have the need to talk constantly, because this is an important survival strategy that distracts them from their trauma feelings. They regard themselves as normal and others as abnormal; they experience themselves as victims and the others as perpetrators. Therefore they think they are innocent. They do not want to be seen as 'evil people' (Welzer, 2009). They take refuge in their male fantasy roles (Theweleit, 2000) as 'the greatest leaders of all time', or 'the saviours of Europe from Islam' for example. Instead of living in reality, they live in their illusions to avoid the intolerable pain of their childhood traumas.

As children they did not receive any emotional support or orientation from their parents. They cannot take their mothers (who are caught up in their own victim status) seriously, and their traumatised fathers are unavailable as role models and are often violent. They are small boys who do not know how to become adult men. They play at war and cannot tell the difference between what is playful and what is serious.

Such perpetrators have never learnt to have empathy with themselves, having buried their child anxieties, anger and sorrow deep within themselves, and as a result they cannot feel empathy towards the people they hurt. By mercilessly shooting other children, Breivik is trying indirectly to kill his own desperate inner child. If perpetrators could come to terms with their own entanglements and traumas others would not be drawn into the abyss of their trauma.

The opportunity presented by times of peace

Prosperity for a whole population can only occur in peacetime. It is only peacetime that offers the chance for the healthy parts of the human psyche to develop further, and heal the wounds left behind by the wars of the past. I consider myself lucky to live in Germany at a time during which there has been no war on German soil since my birth (1957). I consider myself privileged to be welcomed, as a German, by other nationalities when holding my seminars and lectures in countries that, 50 or 60 years ago, were being ravaged by the military machine of fascist Germany. I interpret this as a sign that our trauma survival selves cannot obliterate totally our healthy parts, and that the desire for psychological health persists in its own way.

Case study 27

Given to the soldiers (Sylvia)

As a little girl, Sylvia's mother had been handed over to Russian soldiers by her own mother to be abused sexually in exchange for food. The fear this child must have experienced in this situation is unimaginable; she could only survive by splitting off this terror. Later, Sylvia's mother re-enacted this situation by selling Sylvia to a wealthy friend of the family for prostitution. This meant that Sylvia internalised her mother's terror while at the same time having her own terror of being at the mercy of someone else.

Sylvia had realised in a previous constellation that she couldn't see the perpetrator in her mother. So for her next constellation she chose as her intention 'sensing my connection to my mother's perpetrator part'.

As her 'intention' my whole body trembled as I stood in front of big black cushions Sylvia had chosen to represent her mother and the Russian soldiers. I tried to suppress the trembling but my body continued to shake quite beyond my control. My left hand particularly shook very strongly.

The day after this constellation, Sylvia wrote to me:

'When I arrived for my therapy session yesterday after work, I was physically exhausted. But I noticed that it wasn't just from my professional work, but from being stuck with my mother in this huge 'cushion' of mortal terror. I notice now how difficult it is, physically, to sustain such emotional suppression. My body had been doing it automatically up until now, without my being able to relate to it consciously. It is only now that I'm able to recognise how paradoxical it was for me to imagine that I had to establish contact with my mother's perpetrator part. On the contrary, I realise that I was born into this perpetrator part from the very beginning of my life. I had never really known anything else! It's part of my original trauma! As a tiny person, as a child in the womb, I was confronted with over-whelming emotions. I had no frame of reference for these, didn't have any explanation for them later and wasn't able to learn to differentiate them. This state then became 'normal' because I never knew anything else. And because it's all so 'normal', I have never questioned it. Everything in my life is connected to this immense confusion and everything is utter chaos. And my mother's motto, and hence my motto, was: The main thing is, I survived! Over and over again.

On the one hand I was relieved when everything became so clear yesterday. I had finally found an explanation for the chaos, the feelings of terror and the suppression of these feelings. I can now attribute it all to something. On the other hand it made me very sad to realise that there had never been anything except this terror. In order to feel the slightest spark of love from my mother, I took upon myself every-thing my mother had done to me without complaint. My mother only had these overwhelming feelings of terror, and even today that hasn't changed! Struggling for my mother's love, so that I didn't have to feel the pain of realising that there was no love, almost killed me. I now know that there is something else: finding this spark of love within myself, kindling it back to life, and letting it grow.

Women who have experienced violence are commonly drawn to men with perpetrator structures, on the assumption that the man will protect them from becoming a victim. Such women usually despise men who do not behave in a macho-like manner, seeing them as 'weak', instead glorifying 'heroes' and military type attitudes. In this way such female victims will pour fresh oil onto the fires of war, thereby further fuelling conflict. Therefore it is important for such women to learn to relinquish their preconceived idea that they need a strong man to protect them and prevent them from becoming the victim of violence again.

Case study 28

Leaving the family's battleground (Werner)

Male children of parents who were traumatised by war can also suffer in a specific way from their parents' survival strategies. Werner, now 56 years old, was conceived and born to severely traumatised parents after the end of World War II. His mother had been raped during the war and so rejected men. She was using Werner as her protective shield against his father's violence and sexual desires. She made use of her defenceless, male child as a 'safe' way of taking revenge on men.

Werner's father had experienced the typical fate of German veterans of World War II: propelled into war as a young man, burned out and brutalised during the war, he could not come to terms with peace because he could not get rid of the images in his head of the violence he had experienced. For German war veterans, alcohol was their favourite method of numbing their anxieties, laying a mist over these terrible images. Werner's father lived his life in a permanent state of stress. He was afraid of being alone.

Looking at her history it was not surprising that at the end of her life Werner's mother became mentally deranged (diagnosed with Alzheimer's disease); her brain couldn't take the stress any more and she then was unable to remember anything at all. As a young woman, Werner's mother was a nurse in a German concentration camp. She then was taken prisoner by the Russians, but she would never speak about this time. Werner assumes she was probably raped while in captivity.

Werner's life with his parents was permanently stressful from the first moment. Not only did he fear for his own life, but also for his mother's life when his father became violent. Given the circumstances it is not surprising that life made him anxious. In order to endure life with his parents Werner had to split off his fear, and develop survival strategies. But just as with many other people, he couldn't break loose from his entanglement with his traumatised parents on his own without therapeutic support; even when his parents were long dead he remained symbiotically entangled with them.

Werner appeared resigned during our preliminary conversation at a constellations seminar. He said that he was afraid of getting on with life and had the feeling he would rather be dead than accept life. He thought he should have been able to make more out of his life. His intention for the constellation was: to show him a path into life.

Werner thought he had adopted a lot of his father's ways. During the war his father, aged 17, was in Russia, where he experienced a lot of violence. Werner experienced his father as aggressive, short-tempered and sadistic; he was also an alcoholic.

Werner is an only child. He thought he was already afraid in the womb. He said he was very symbiotically entangled with his mother. His parents were always arguing. His mother had often thought of leaving his father, but his father threatened to kill her and Werner if she left him. At the time of this therapy session, Werner's father was still alive, but his mother had already died.

The representative Werner set up for his intention immediately smiled at him.

Intention: "Showing you the path into life – that makes me very happy! What are you waiting for?"

Werner: "I'm waiting for something to happen, for permission."

Intention: "I don't need permission, I want to get on with it."

Werner: "And I don't dare... "

I suggest to Werner that he set up representatives for his mother, his father and himself as a young child.

Intention: "I don't really want to look over there."

Young Werner: "My stomach aches and I've got a headache."

Father: "I'm exhausted. I can't stand these images in my head – blood, body parts ... "

Mother: "I don't like men. I want to crawl inside this little child to protect myself."

Intention to Werner: "Perhaps you have to go there again, then you can come to me. You're not there now any longer."

I suggest Werner say to his intention: "This is how our life started. We came into this world with this burden from our mother and father and we've dragged ourselves through life with this burden."

After he said this, the 'mother' remarks: "I'm two-faced – I'm sadistic and at the same time I pretend to be pleasant."

Father: "I'm thirsty and I want to drink away the pain and the images. And I've got murderous feelings."

At my suggestion Werner says to his intention: "That has been our life up until now." After he said this he asks his intention: "Shall we go out there?"

Intention: "Yes please! How old are you?"

Werner: "I feel that I'm there now. It's not about taking a step into life, it's about taking a step into a different life!"

Intention: "You've been thinking about this for 56 years."

Werner: "I can't believe that it's okay for this to come to an end!"

Werner and his intention leave the circle, walk over to a window and look outside.

Finally, I suggest to Werner that he say to his intention: "There are two spaces to live in – the one we've come from and the life we're going to make for ourselves now!"

This was Werner's second constellation with me. In the first one he had worked on his entanglement with his father. The current constellation shows that he is coming to understand the drama of his childhood and that he has nothing to gain from his traumatised parents. This is why walking away from his old life and into a new one, even at 56, is worthwhile. Only someone who has no symbiotic illusions any more is able to recognise his reality and can reap the harvest: taking the first step into his own life, into a freedom he hadn't experienced before.

A few weeks later Werner wrote to me with comments on his constellation:

> "Up until I was 50 I was in denial about my age – I felt and behaved as if I was 20 or 30. Two years ago (through unemployment, divorce and financial ruin) my age caught up with me, accompanied by severe depression and a fear of dying. Today I see myself as a 56–year-old and accept my age. All in all, I now clearly recognise and feel that I'm in a 'healing process', which will gradually allow me to develop future prospects, new courage to face life and a new zest for life."

The consequences of war up to four generations later

Society as it is has a strong effect on families, and children from traumatised families sometimes have a big effect on society too, as the examples of Adolf Hitler and Anders B. Breivik above show. A vicious cycle of societal and familial events can thus be perpetuated, creating further, enhanced perpetrator-victim dynamics.

In the relationship battles that rage in some families, the parents often act as if they are doing everything for the good of their children while at the same time physically ravaging and emotionally exhausting their children. One basic mechanism for parents is to project their anger and hate, which might have its roots, for example, in the suffering they experienced in war, blindly onto their children. Their survival parts, unable to confront their own suffering, see their children as if they were the original tormentors. This is especially true of mothers who were raped by soldiers in war, in regard to their sons. Their hatred of everything masculine is so deep, because of having been raped, that the masculinity of their own son provokes their hatred, and they torment their son and debase him sexually as a way of relieving their inner pressure. They then experience some inner peace for a while and may even regret what they have done to their child.

This situation is confusing for the children, who cannot be aware of what their mothers or fathers experienced in war. They do not understand that the anger and hatred does not actually apply to them, but to the perpetrators of their parents' suffering, who turned their parents into helpless victims. The children therefore believe that the hate really does apply to them, and think that there must be something wrong with them; that they are not well behaved, or have not worked hard enough, or have done something wrong. Whatever they do, whether they completely withdraw, or try to do everything right, nothing changes the situation, because when the pressure of their parents' trauma builds up again, reaching boiling point, the parents will use any excuse to vent it on the child.

Children cannot bear to feel that they are just helpless victims of their parents, so they split psychologically. The part that carries the physical pain of the beatings and the emotional pain of contempt is split off, and another part of the child tries to do something for the parents so that they will feel better. These parts, which I have identified as 'symbiotically entangled', may even be sympathetic towards the parents, seeing the distress behind their angry despair and taking their parents' side. The child's inner conflict between what they suffer at the hands of their parents and the concern they have for their suffering parents, offering them all the support they can give, becomes bigger and bigger, and they are increasingly unable to bridge the gap. The children commit a 'betrayal of the Self' as Arno Gruen formulates it (Gruen, 2002).

There is also a particular dynamic between mothers who have experienced severe sexual violence and their daughters. Looking at the child's body, and especially the female genitals, may sexually excite the mother. This sexual excitement is transferred to the child who is herself fixated on the mother's intense sexual feelings. The daughter in turn becomes interested in the mother's genitals, thereby she becomes liable to re-traumatise her mother. A vicious circle develops between mother and child, with the child looking for physical contact with the mother through confused sexual feelings, and the mother reacting in panic to the child's sexual advances, and rejecting any form of further contact.

It is a painful process for clients, both women and men, to realise through trauma therapy that they cannot use victim feelings nor perpetrator energies to gain contact with their traumatised mothers. In their confusion about sexual feelings they will often, as children, adolescents or young women, get themselves into situations where they suffer sexual violence themselves, or act it out in prostitution, promiscuity and pornography.

Case study 29

Behind the mask of a clown (Marina)

Marina is 15 years old. She came to the therapy session with her father. She had admitted to him a few weeks previously that she had been raped by a man she got to know through Facebook. She met this man, a complete stranger to her, and went to his flat with him. There he forced her to have sex with him. She didn't put up much of a fight because she thought he would have become more violent. But afterwards she felt guilty because she hadn't tried harder to fight back. When Marina's father told his wife about their daughter's rape, she admitted that she too had been raped by a man as an adolescent.

Marina's intention for the constellation was: "Why did this happen to me? What is it inside me that makes me do something like that?" She chooses her father for this 'intention' and positions him with his back to a wall in the therapy room. He immediately feels extreme loneliness and cold, and thinks that no one is interested in him. Marina stands next to him, to his right, outwardly unmoving: an observer. Tears keep running down her cheeks during this constellation.

I am then set up as Marina's mother. She positions me a long distance away from herself and her 'intention', with my face to the wall. My gaze is directed at a picture that shows people outside in nature going about their everyday tasks. As the 'mother' I feel physically frozen. There's a lot of heat and agitation within me, but because of my body armour this doesn't escape to the outside. I have no sense of contact with Marina.

Marina's father becomes more and more restless in the role of Marina's intention. He complains, feels helpless and doesn't know what to do. I ask Marina to put down cushions for her grandmother (her mother's mother) and her great-grandmother. Her grandmother is still alive and lives in the house with Marina's parents. Towards the end of the war she woke up in bed to find her mother (the great-grand-mother) lying dead next to her. Marina said that this great-grandmother had been raped several times whilst fleeing at the end of World War II.

I asked Marina to release me from the role of her mother and to re-position me as a representative for her grand-mother instead of the cushion. In this role I immediately turn away from all the others and walk to the window. I look out into the countryside and search for something to distract me. I notice a postcard on the windowsill; it shows the picture of a clown with sad eyes holding a patched heart in his hands. Behind me, Marina's 'intention' begins to make faces and behave crazily.

Marina watches her 'intention's' actions. It becomes clear that by behaving like this, a part of her tries to draw the attention of others away from the unbearable tension generated in the family by the split off trauma feelings of the grandmother and mother.

Back in my therapist position I explain to Marina what I understand from the constellation. On the one hand there is the little abandoned child within her seeking warmth and care, and because she didn't receive that from her mother, she played the clown in order to get care and attention. And because that didn't work either, she tried to get attention from men outside the family who found her attractive and told her she was someone special. But then she's unable to set proper limits with these men and protect herself from sexual violence. In this way she is repeating the experiences of the other women in her family. Experiencing sexual violence connects her with these other women.

Marina listened carefully to this and then her 'intention' lay down on the floor and felt at peace with himself. In the role of the 'intention', the father says: "When I have a sense of myself, I don't need any confirmation from outside, I feel good in myself. I don't have to live someone else's life story any more; I can write my own now."

When working with Marina it became clear to me how the rape of an adolescent in 2011 could have its roots in the horrors of the Second World War. The grandmother, who experienced the war, and her own mother who was raped, both emotionally failed as mothers. Externally they both appeared to be caring mothers, however the daughters sensed that something was not quite right, and persistently worried about their mothers, and were unable to separate from them. When Marina's mother became a mother herself, she did not know what it meant to feel as a mother. Her lack of empathy led her to bring up her child according to rules and principles. Such an upbringing is intended to compensate for the lack of relationship. She tells the child to do this and that, but the child never has the feeling of being seen by the mother. Marina, the child of the fourth generation, never grew up, remaining childlike, and playing the clown, putting on a brave front, just as her mother and grandmother did. Marina unconsciously senses the suppressed sexual energies and so seeks attention and affirmation through these feelings. This makes her an easy target for men with a perpetrator psyche. She does not have the inner strength and clarity to create boundaries and defend herself.

It made complete sense when the father said at the end of the session that he saw no point in going on trying to be both father and mother to his children. To do so only encouraged the attempts by the mother and grandmother to conceal the sexual violence they experienced.

The following case study shows that men sometimes cut themselves off from their feelings completely. They try to manage their relational life only through their cognitive faculties, and have great difficulty in recognising that, as long as they do not open up their emotions, events such as marriage, starting a family and professional success do not bring more quality into their life. They cannot understand why their children turn away from them, even though their success in business provides their children with a high standard of living.

Case study 30

Late insight (Mr. T.)

Mr. T. arrived with his wife and a friend who is a doctor. His wife had been pressing him for some time to do something for himself. He has devoted himself to his work, and shows no feelings. Their eldest son (30) had already been in psychiatric care twice. The second child, a daughter, is successful in her job, but does so much sport that it is fairly obvious that she is compensating for something. Their youngest daughter is very intelligent and gifted but she cannot move away from her parents' home. She tried living on her own in the town where she was studying, but moved home again.

Mr. T. came up with the following intention: He would like his relationship with his children to improve.

I offered myself to be set up as the representative for his intention. I immediately felt a massive physical pressure on my right side, which made me move my head to the left, where it seemed to feel lighter, and I had the impression that it is only like this that I could get enough air to breathe.

Mr. T. then had the idea of setting his wife up in the constellation as well. He positioned her on my left, saying: "She could help to make it easier." His wife objected saying that she was not prepared "to take his burden from him".

I then asked Mr. T. to set his children up. He chose the doctor to represent his son, who immediately moved backwards saying: "Something is pulling me back". For his daughters Mr. T. selected a small yellow cushion (middle daughter) and a large, bright red cushion (younger daughter). He put them down to his left and right. The younger daughter was to my right, and as the 'intention' my gaze became fixed on this daughter. She seemed to me to be a beacon of hope, someone who could bring something good back into my life. But I felt incapable of doing anything myself. The weight that I had originally felt on my right side seemed now to be pressing down on my shoulders. I associated this with the business company that Mr. T. had talked about in the preliminary conversation, when he said that it was under considerable competitive pressure at that time.

My experience as the 'intention' was that I was just waiting and had no idea what I could do to improve my relationship with my children. I had the feeling that I was doing the right thing for myself by spreading my burden, so that I could bear it, but I couldn't do any more.

Mrs. T., as herself in the constellation, then said that she couldn't stand it any longer, and she wanted to take the children away from Mr. T.'s negative influence, and she was thinking of leaving the room and taking them with her. Mr. T. and I as his 'intention' had a brief discussion and then agreed she should go and we would then see what happened to us. After Mrs. T. had left the room with the two cushions as the daughters and the doctor as the son, I was surprised to find that my experience had not changed in any way. Even though I now saw the emptiness around me, my feelings hadn't changed. Mr. T. had the same reaction. However, he did say that seeing everything as a whole had helped him a great deal, and he recognised that his relationship with his children was up to him and that he would have to be pro-active if he wanted the relationship to change.

We then asked Mrs. T. and the representative for the son to come back into the room and ended the constellation. Mr. T. said that he saw more clearly that he is also responsible for how his children are and he wanted to do more trauma work on himself.

Mr. T. was born in 1940 and his mother was perilously ill for many months following his birth, and his aunt looked after him during this time. In 1944 his father was killed as a soldier in Russia. His mother was totally distraught after this, and Mr. T. lived with his mother and endured all the difficult years until he was 20, and even then he always remained in close contact with her.

This double trauma of having to do without his mother immediately after he was born, and the death of his father, caused Mr. T. to cut off his feelings and to live mainly in his head. He and his mother bore a common burden of pain, sorrow and grief, which he buried in his body in order to be able to bear it. Up until this session he had been unable to feel this emotional burden. In order to survive he had almost completely abandoned an emotional life.

Case study 31

Blackouts at school (Veronika)

Veronika was 11 years old and in year 7 at grammar school. She came with her mother and father to a therapy session. Her problem was that she would suddenly go blank when she was faced with school tests. Even though she had done her homework well, at school she was unable to remember anything and could hardly write at all, particularly in the subjects of maths, German and geography. Her intention was to get good grades at school again. She had no explanation for the cause of her memory loss.

I asked her mother whether she could explain Veronika's problems, and she said that Veronika had already had problems in year 4, at a very young age. She also said that it was very hard for her to accept Veronika's difficulty since she experienced her daughter's failure at school as her own loss of control. Then she remembered that Veronika had been a very anxious child when two years old, and since the birth of her younger sister had always been very frightened that something would happen to her sister.

I asked Veronika's mother about the family history and she told me the following: her mother's father had died when she was four years old, and this was immediately followed by the death of her younger brother. The grandmother (Veronika's great-grandmother) had given the mother as a child to distant relatives to look after. Later, at the end of the Second World War, the mother had fled with this adoptive family from East Prussia before the Russian army came, leaving the grandmother there. The grandmother apparently survived, but no one knew what had happened to her.

I asked Veronika, whose mother had already explained to her about the constellation method, whether she was ready to set up her intention. She said that she was and chose one of the two female students present at the therapy session to represent her intention. She positioned the 'intention' looking out of the balcony door and stood next to her. The 'intention' wanted to go further outside, down to the meadow in front of the house. I waited until Veronika and her 'intention' had established some good contact, and then I asked Veronika to choose a representative for her mental blackouts when she was faced with school tests. She chose the other guest student, and positioned her a long way from herself, in a corner of the therapy room. This representative said she felt afraid and very alone. Veronika stayed with this part, and the 'intention' then came over to her, saying that she no longer wanted to leave the room and was interested in what was happening.

Then I asked Veronika to set up her mother, who was present, as her mother and to constellate me as her mother's mother. She positioned her mother with her face to the wall in another corner of the room and set me up some distance away with my back to another wall. The 'mother' felt very weak and helpless and I, in the role of the grandmother, felt like a hunted animal. My whole body shook. When Veronika came towards me with her 'intention', I felt even more afraid and hoped that no one would touch me.

In my role as therapist I asked Veronika to place cushions for the parents of the grandmother and the grandmother's deceased brother. She lay all three cushions right at my feet and, as the grandmother, I felt my situation even more hopeless. I turned my face to the wall. Then I noticed a picture of a flower arrangement with a sunny, laughing face. I picked it up and held it to the side of my face, which is turned away from the others, so that it faced them. This was now my survival mask.

In the meantime, the representative for the 'blackouts' had approached the cushion representing the grandmother's deceased brother – which is one of the most beautiful cushions in my collection – and embraced it lovingly. The 'mother' came out of her corner too and gazed at the 'blackout' part of Veronika, and the beautiful blue cushion in her arms. The 'intention' said that the mother should look after the brother. But the 'mother' said that this was not her task, she couldn't, it was completely impossible. The representative for the 'blackouts' gradually paid more attention to Veronika and the 'intention'. She became impatient and angry that no one looked after the brother. She couldn't let go of the cushion because she had the feeling that no one else would look after her either.

I now asked Veronika to set up her father, who was also present. She positioned him with his face to a different wall in the room. The father didn't like that, so he turned around and said that if no one else was going to look after the brother then he would do it. He went to the cushion and picked it up, but after a while he said it was pointless and put the cushion down again. The representative for the 'blackouts' now felt hope that the father might look after her, since her mother wouldn't do anything. The father went up to the group of three: Veronika, the 'intention' and the representative for the 'blackouts' and embraced them all. After a while, Veronika began to sob and rested her head against her father's chest. Both representatives stepped back, and Veronika and her father stood together for more than half an hour. Veronika snuggled more and more into her father's arms, and her father touched her lovingly. Her mother looked on with relief. We ended the constellation there.

In the ensuing conversation, the mother was convinced that school was what had saved her. She had been unable to establish any closeness with her mother, or her father who was an alcoholic. It had been good grades at school that had been her escape and allowed her to feel normal in the face of the wretched relationships within her family. Good school grades had been her support, and that was why it had appeared to her as her own loss of control when Veronika had suddenly begun to have problems at school. She now understood the connection much better, and could see that the situation was different for Veronika, who was looking for security and support, and that if she didn't have that, she couldn't focus on school. She could now see that she still had to focus on her entanglement with her own mother and being more present as a mother for Veronika.

I found this work with Veronika impressive, because I could see immediately how a child would become entangled in the trauma of her grandmother because she had no love from her mother. It happens unconsciously, which is why Veronika would never have been able to explain with words what was taking place in her psyche. But she was able to make her inner turmoil and the relationship to her parents and grandparents clearly visible using the constellations method.

Some weeks later Veronika's mother came to see me for an individual session. She could clearly feel her entanglement with her mother, who in turn was symbiotically entangled with her own mother, and she was now able to make a credible inner decision to disentangle herself from her child role with her traumatised mother. When I asked her how Veronika was now doing at school, she said: "That isn't that important to me any more. I always used to just look at her school grades, to see whether they were good or not. Now I think it's more important that she's happy."

Traumatising deaths and their consequences in a family system

In some families there seems to be a common thread of particular illnesses or events running through them. The example of Caroline, a participant on one of my courses, shows particularly the way that a trauma can be continually repeated if the chain of transferring the trauma energy from a mother to her children is not interrupted.

Case study 32

Fracture of the skull with brain haemorrhage (Caroline)

Caroline's youngest son was lying in a coma with a fractured skull and a brain haemorrhage following a motorbike accident. Three years before, her third son had also had a motorbike accident and was also in a coma with a fractured skull. Caroline's mother had recently died following a fall that had caused a fracture of the skull with a brain haemorrhage. Her older brother had been in a plane crash in which he had fractured his skull and suffered a brain haemorrhage. Her younger brother had had a parachuting accident where he fractured his skull and suffered a brain haemorrhage. Both brothers had survived. Caroline's father had died 25 years previously from a brain tumour following a brain haemorrhage. Caroline's first and second sons died immediately after they were born, both of a brain haemorrhage.

Caroline took part in equestrian events when she was 19 and had fallen off a horse and fractured her skull, and had a brain trauma that confined her to a wheelchair for three years. When she was 25 she fractured her skull in a car accident. When she was 52 she fell from a ladder and for the third time in her life had a fractured skull with a brain haemorrhage.

Caroline's intention for her constellation was: "I would like the brain haemorrhages in our family to stop!" When I asked her about her family she told me the following: Her father's brother, who was his mother's favourite son, died during the war from a shot in the head: he was 19. Her father was in a submarine attack three times when he was 17. He was also shot in the head and from then on he was blind and deaf on one side. The father never talked about his feelings.

Her mother's side of the family had had a shop. Caroline's grandfather had been killed by the shop's roller blind falling onto him following a bomb attack. There were five children in this family. An older brother, the only son, had been killed by a fall from a table when he was a baby. Caroline said she thought her mother had been a substitute child for this dead brother, so that the grandmother wasn't so sad any more. The grandmother had later died of colon cancer.

Caroline's 'intention' in the constellation felt unsure on her legs. Her heart was racing, and she said "Something's pulling me backwards; it's too much, too much! I'm sad and perplexed."

Caroline then said: "I feel better when the 'intention' says it's too much."

The 'intention' noticed an emotion surfacing and said to Caroline: "I would like to lean on someone. We have to run away, escape, hide ourselves away."

The 'intention' and Caroline held hands. Caroline said: "That feels good, nice and warm." The 'intention' said that she couldn't quite identify the emotion that she felt.

As the facilitator I understood that the drama in the family would only cease when the blocked feelings were allowed to flow freely again. I suggested to Caroline that she choose representatives for her mother's side of the family: her grandmother, her mother's brother who fell from the table, her mother and her grandfather. I also suggested that she set up from her father's side her father, and his brother who was killed in the war.

The first person to speak was the representative of Caroline's 'mother', who said that she would have liked to have had contact with her husband, but he obviously hadn't wanted that. The 'father' said he felt lifeless, as if he were cast in lead. The 'father's brother' said he felt powerless and the 'mother's mother' thought the whole scenario "unbearable!"

The 'intention' said she had to be there for the 'mother' and 'father', but she couldn't do that properly and it couldn't stay like that. She had no feeling and she said something had to happen.

The 'father's brother', who was killed in the war, now spoke, saying that he, himself was not important, but where were Caroline's sons?

I asked Caroline to set up representatives for her four children. She set up the son who died shortly after birth, the son who died ten weeks after he was born, the youngest son who is in a coma at the moment and the third son who has also suffered a severe brain injury.

The 'father's brother' then said: "I think it's terrible. With these children it's as if I have to die continually."

The 'mother' said she would really like to scream, it was all so terrible and it made her angry. She didn't know where she should go; it was the same everywhere.

The 'intention' now stood behind Caroline and held onto her while Caroline held her 'third son'. Then she took hold of the other 'son' who is still alive, and he whimpered loudly, and all of them sank to the floor in an embrace.

It now became apparent that no one in this family knew what to do with their grief and pain, and with the pain of all the others. All were flooded with feelings of grief and the whole chaos of feelings was transferred from one to another, from the parents' generation to the children. All felt connected with death.

I suggested to Caroline that she say to her 'intention': "I don't know where to go with this pain and grief. My grandmother didn't know and my mother didn't know either. Pain and grief will be transferred to the next generation because no one knows where to go with it." The following dialogue then took place between the 'intention' and Caroline:

Intention: "It has become too much."

Caroline: "Then it'll get worse and worse!"

Intention: "Now I can feel something."

Caroline: "Then it'll be repeated again and again. The old story will happen all over again."

I then said to Caroline: "You have to start with your own pain otherwise it'll be too much for your children too."

The representative for the son who was in a coma confirmed this: "For me the coma is like a protection from this pain and grief. It gets me away from it for a while."

The 'intention' wanted some contact: "I sense that I'm starting to feel something."

I said to Caroline: "You have to detach yourself from everything that comes to you from another. And then you have to sense your own pain and try to bear it."

Again the 'son in the coma' confirmed this: "For me it's best if my mother doesn't want anything from me and doesn't want to do anything for me, but is simply there."

I said to Caroline: "It is possible for the skull fractures and brain haemorrhages in the family to cease if everyone looks at their own pain and does not try and connect with the pain of the others. Then it'll stop." Caroline repeats this sentence to her 'intention'. Again, the 'son' confirmed that this was

going in the right direction. "That feels good. I can bear my own. Everything else is too much for me."
Caroline agreed to end the constellation at this point.

In such families, faced with so many deaths and tragic accidents, it is not easy to see the overall picture. In my opinion, a central loss trauma in Caroline's family is the death of the mother's older brother who fell off the table and died, and for whom she was a substitute child. It is one of the most painful losses for a woman to lose a baby, and she will probably blame herself for it. She cannot escape from this loss trauma, and it is likely to affect her for the rest of her life. To think that her sadness, her pain and her feelings of guilt would be relieved if she had another child is a typical illusion with a loss trauma that originates from the survival self.

So Caroline's mother couldn't develop a secure attachment to her mother, being entangled in her mother's loss trauma. It would have been an unconscious choice to look for a husband who had also lost a brother. It is likely to be the pain and unresolved grief that are attractive within the other, the mix of love, pain and grief becoming the couple's symbiotic home, their entangled identity, which draws them to each other. They are unable to see the other as a whole separate person.

Caroline was born into her parents' entanglement, unconsciously knowing their grief. For her part, she developed an identity in which both parents are interchangeable for her; the trauma of the one is confused with the trauma of the other. From this comes the tendency for events to be repeated, because everyone is confused as to whom they really are and all are unconsciously drawn to and confused with those already dead. The strongest symbiotic attachment for a new child in this family is to the emotions of pain and grief, and ultimately, death. Caroline herself is a child who is always close to death through her own accidents. She is drawn to risky hobbies, which means that serious accidents are almost inevitable.

As a mother she also loses children. As long as she is caught in her entanglement she will be unable to really feel herself, only living in her head, and the weight of the unre-solved trauma feelings absorbed by her is then transferred to her children, who are likely to repeat the patterns.

Adoptions

There is a taboo connected with adoption that multi-genera-tional psychotraumatology touches on. The general view is that children who are given away for adoption by their mothers should be happy and grateful for being given new parents. The mother who gave them away is frequently referred to as an uncaring mother. The adoptive parents are seen as doing a good deed and taking on social responsibility when they adopt an orphaned child. But adopting couples can have a variety of different motives.

I have experienced cases in my therapy practice where the background to the adoption was that the adoptive parents had lost their own child, or children, and the adopted child was seen as a replacement for the loss. Or a childless couple think that the woman's or man's depression would vanish if there was a child in the house. Having had a miscarriage was another reason for some people looking to adopt. These kinds of circumstances are likely to result in symbiotic entanglement of the adopted child in the traumas of his adoptive parents.

In addition, the literature on adoption rarely mentions the fact that adopted children will suffer a trauma by the loss of connection with their mother. Eric Breitinger has published a very commendable book written from the perspective of adopted children (Breitinger, 2012), in which he says that if the child is given by the mother to adoptive or foster parents immediately after birth, the psychosomatic bonds between mother and child that have formed during pregnancy and the birth process are abruptly torn apart. The child is powerless because his signals to his mother achieve nothing, and he has to split in order to survive this situation. He can then only use a part of his vitality to develop a new relationship with his adoptive parents. Basically, he starts his new adoptive life psychologically split, thereby more easily becoming entangled with the traumas of his adoptive parents.

If the mother already rejects her child during pregnancy, the child is in a symbiotic trauma situation right from the beginning, and he will be born as a trauma survivor.

Case study 33

Pointless anger (Lorenz)

Lorenz had been coming to me for psychotherapeutic treatment for two months. This time he arrived furious. "They're total idiots on the road! I'm so angry!" His intention for today's session is to get rid of the anger within him.

Lorenz was adopted as soon as he was born. He was the result of his mother's holiday romance with a waiter. When she came home, her mother (her father had died some time previously) pressured her to have an abortion or to give the child up for adoption. Lorenz was given to adoptive parents who looked after him well. He said he had a reasonably good relationship with his adoptive mother but he often had fights with his adoptive father. He had no chance against the latter's loud and forceful manner.

In the course of his life Lorenz had many physical complaints: overactive thyroid, slipped disc, high blood pressure. In adulthood, when he discovered that he was adopted, he started looking for his parents. He found both of them. His mother had married and had a daughter. He didn't get on with her. He found his father in dire financial straits. He supported him for a while until he realised that he was just being exploited financially by him. His father died in miserable conditions.

A colleague was assisting my therapy sessions that day, and Lorenz chose him to represent his intention. When Lorenz had positioned him, his 'intention' said: 'I don't feel any anger, if anything I feel gratitude.' Lorenz confirmed this feeling. Of course he felt gratitude towards his adoptive parents for bringing him up.

I suggested to Lorenz that he put cushions on the floor to represent his adoptive and his natural parents, which he did, laying them on the floor in couples next to each other on the right of his 'intention'. His 'intention' then turned towards the adoptive parents.

I offered to be a representative for his anger. He placed me in front of the cushions that represented his natural parents. I felt that I wanted to lean over towards them. Opposite the 'natural father' I had felt that he was an idiot, and at the same time the thought occurred to me that I wouldn't be there if he hadn't been an idiot. I felt like an inflated balloon that keeps losing air. Finally I found myself simply struggling to stay on my feet and not fall to the floor. I was afraid that once I was lying down I wouldn't be able to get up again. Lorenz confirmed that he has these feelings. He said that he knew all of them.

The whole time his 'intention' had been standing with his back to me and was not prepared to turn around. On the contrary, the representative of Lorenz's 'intention' now felt he wanted to distance himself further from me. As I had come to a standstill in my role as 'anger', I told Lorenz that I would leave the representative role and return to being the therapist.

Lorenz tried to talk to his 'intention' but the 'intention' turned away from him, saying that he didn't want to have anything to do with Lorenz and his 'anger'. For the 'intention' the past was finished. Suddenly Lorenz lay down on the floor next to the cushions representing his natural parents and curled up like a small child, and started crying.

After a while I explained to him that when he was crying on the floor, he was probably connected with the baby part of him who had been separated from his mother shortly after birth, and that a psychological split took place inside him at this time. One part had stayed connected with his natural mother and a surviving part had been pleased to have found a new mother.

Eventually Lorenz got up from the floor and stood next to his 'intention'. Both agreed that in the future they would not work as separate parts, but together they would look for a way out of the dilemma of Lorenz's adoption. We ended the constellation at this point.

Lorenz's anger at other people, particularly the drivers who annoyed him on his way to his therapy session, originated from an old source. He was angry with his natural parents, particularly his father who got his mother pregnant and wasn't concerned about the consequences. However, the anger at his father displayed an inconsistency. It was only because his father was an 'idiot' who wasn't in the least interested in the consequences of his sexual adventures that Lorenz existed in the first place. Lorenz later found out that there had been another woman whom his father had made pregnant and left on her own to have his child. So Lorenz actually owed his life to the behaviour of a 'lust-driven idiot' as he once put it himself. And with this, the energy of his accusations evaporated as soon as it formed. His anger doesn't lead to any constructive outcome; it stays pent up within him and occasionally erupts. Behind his anger is his desire to be loved by his mother and his father, and he confirmed this by giving his father generous financial support for years after he had found him.

Lorenz's intention for the constellation came in the first instance from an inner survival part: he wanted to get rid of the anger that formed a considerable part of his psychological structure without giving it a more specific context and addressing the issue behind it. The constellation and the behaviour of his 'intention' showed him clearly that this cannot work, and it made his psychological split very obvious. This was shown by the part of him that lay next to his natural mother crying while the other part attempted to get on with his adoptive parents. It became clear that he has to overcome this split caused by his adoption.

Case study 34

Feelings of guilt creating further entanglements (Simone)

Simone is plagued by feelings of guilt. She was in prison for repeatedly making purchases on account or using a credit card without the necessary funds, and had the opportunity to leave prison in order to attend therapy sessions.

I stood for her 'intention', which was to free herself from these feelings of guilt. First of all I experienced unbearable feelings. I felt as if I was going to fall down, having nothing to hold onto and no stability. Simone did her best to stop me falling down, and this seemed to reflect the situation of her earlier childhood. I closed my eyes and felt like I withdrew into darkness. Simone wanted to prevent that. As her 'intention' I found her support very helpful.

When she started to talk about her feelings of guilt, that she doesn't do enough for her children, that she's a bad mother, as her 'intention' I couldn't bear it. I felt really annoyed with her, and I felt like withdrawing further into myself. So it seemed that the guilt feelings actually strengthened her inner tension, leading to another split. One part of her then withdraws further and further and becomes aggressive towards her. The only way out then it seemed was distraction through music, television, reading or making the next purchase with no backup funds.

The feelings of guilt create the illusion of being able to do something, being responsible for something, and that was the situation after Simone's birth. After giving birth to Simone, her mother left her in hospital, and she was then taken to a care home and adopted by a couple one year later. On top of all of this, her adoptive father sexually abused her.

In my role as 'intention' I insistently urged Simone to put a stop to all the talk of feelings of guilt once and for all. We have a brief talk and conclude that feelings of guilt don't help anyone but only make everything worse.

Then we saw that Simone's feelings of guilt were made worse when she was in prison, as it was expected that she acknowledge her guilt for what she had done. When all this became clearer we faced each other openly and were easily able to look the other in the eye. We were now ready to take further steps.

Feelings of guilt are useful if they motivate someone to take responsibility for something they have actually done to another person. Someone who openly admits his guilt becomes psychologically stronger and more mature. However, in many cases the true perpetrators evade their responsibilities, and the victims feel guilty instead. This is often the case with children whose parents did not want to have them; the children then think it is their fault that their parents reject them. However, such feelings of guilt weaken the individual and create the illusion of being able to do something about the rejection. But, tragically, it is particularly such endeavours and later attempts at compensation that lead to the repetition of the original trauma in the individual's own children. In Simone's case one of her daughters had already given up a child for adoption.

Traumas before, during and after birth

A baby needs to feel wanted and loved, but only about half of all children seem to have been planned by their parents: "According to experts' conservative estimates, even today about one in three children comes into the world unwanted" (Häsing and Janus, 1994, p. 9). Children whose mothers have considered abortion or who have attempted an abortion can have unconscious vague feelings of anxiety, of being in danger, and that they have to be on their guard and protect themselves their whole lives. If a child is unwanted, he is more at risk of becoming addicted to drugs and committing a crime, more likely to have troubles and problems in his life and be unhappy in relationships (Matejcek and Dytrych, 1994, p. 196).

Case study 35

Loss of self-esteem (Rosemarie)

Rosemarie's mother had sex with a labourer on a farm and became pregnant with Rosemarie. She rejected the child and felt disgusted by her. Rosemarie identified with these feelings. It was only when she decided not to accept this lack of self-esteem any longer that she achieved better contact with herself. She was finally able to lovingly accept the child part of herself that was still looking for good contact with the mother. It seems that as an unborn child Rosemarie had already sensed her mother's rejection.

With some clients, the process of psychological splitting may already have started before birth, or during or shortly after birth. For those people whose mothers were pregnant during a war for example, the womb does not represent the secure vessel it should. If guns are thundering and bombs are falling, and the mother has to seek shelter in a bunker, if she is hungry and terrified, then these feelings are transferred to the child within her. One consequence can be chronic sleepiness as an avoidance of these early experiences.

Childbirth complications

Common complications of childbirth are:

- the child not being in the correct position to pass through the birth canal
- extended labour without the birth reflex setting in,
- the child becoming stuck in the birth canal,
- forceps delivery, or
- Caesarean section

If we look at these issues across the generations it becomes clear that a mother with a high-risk birth is frequently already traumatised herself, and so does not relate well to her body in the first place, and she also may be ambivalent about having the child. In addition to the psychological stress of the situation, we also have the current practices of obstetrics and paediatric treatment, which often don't take into account the mother and child's psychological needs.

So, for example, Edeltraud was kept in a children's hospital for seven weeks without her mother, even though she was physically healthy and was developing normally, simply because she had been born before her calculated due birth date.

Symbiotic entanglements with the mother or grandmother often overlay and confuse the individual's awareness of their own traumatisation. It is only when the person is ready, and a way has been found to escape from the entanglements that the access to their own traumatisation and their birth trauma opens. Clients can then come into real contact with themselves and their body for the first time.

Even if a symbiotic trauma exists and further traumas come into existence later in life, it is still important for patients to access their birth trauma. In some cases it is the first existential trauma of their life and the rest of the individual's life is defined by this primal fear, originating from the birth trauma.

Case study 36

Operation on an infant (Ursula)

Ursula was given emergency medical treatment directly after birth. In her therapy session she suddenly has physical sensations of being held by her ear and having needles stuck into her body. She gets into a complete panic and becomes disoriented. In her constellation her intention is to emerge from this inner split, and it becomes clear that the little traumatised child directly after her birth is still within her, and that another part of her wants to protect this child from the doctors. However, this part cannot touch the traumatised 'child' part because every touch causes fear and pain.

With the help of her 'intention' in the constellation, she is able to access this 'child'. She then feels that the 'child' is cold and does not dare to live. She imagines holding this child to her breast and having skin contact. Following the therapy session, Ursula wrote to me:

"Everything is running riot inside me. Every cell in my body is trembling. Panic attacks again and again. Seven on a scale of 10! I took a cuddly toy as representative for me as the child in hospital. I now carry it under my T-shirt so that it's bearable. My heart is beating wildly. I rock backwards and forwards with the infant. Give me time, I'm there. I have to throw up, and all the time there is the sense that I'm going to collapse any minute. In my body I feel extreme stress. A part wants to flee. I keep concentrating on my intention. I want to emerge from my split as an infant in hospital and I want my split parts to merge together. I'm there. I'm back in myself.

I realise what stress I experienced as an infant, when the doctors were trying to keep me alive. Of course they wanted to help me. Again and again I feel physical sense of wanting to take tubes out of my body. It's so cold, so very cold. Pain in my breast. A repeated sense of my lungs, my whole respiratory system going into collapse. I talk to myself as my intention. I'm there and I'm stable, in contact with myself. My intention encourages me. Be brave, we can do it. They're physical memories, but today we're safe. As an infant I feel so much unrest in my body, I'm close to madness. I speak to the infant I once was. We have to accept that the fear, the pain and the cold, the examinations and treatment caused us all this stress."

Case study 37

Panic in the incubator (Sonja)

The next example comes from Sonja. She writes about her constellation and shows how her therapeutic work over several years has helped her to understand her life and her history better. She sees the connections more clearly between her situation as a premature baby in an incubator, her entanglement in the traumas of her mother and grandmother and the sexual abuse by her mother's brother.

"A week before the constellation I had the following experience: Panic in the night with the completely absurd and unrealistic idea that G. (my partner) is going to kill me. When he gets out of bed and goes into the bathroom the panic deepens with the idea that he's now getting the murder weapon (nail scissors, tweezers, knife). I'm in shock and can't move or say anything. I freeze in my fear.

"The next day I try to become clear, to sort out what the trigger was; what was G.'s part in this, what was mine. What might there be in my family? At any rate, it all feels totally mad.

"I can identify the following as the trigger: I'd arranged an intimate date for a nice evening with G. But G. didn't turn up. That had never happened before. Then the trigger started working. Old patterns of behaviour made me feel abandoned; thoughts and feelings such as 'I'm not worth loving' released separation anxieties within me. I wasn't able to talk to G. about it. The behaviour pattern, keeping silent, was in force again. And then it came to the chain reaction I described above.

"My intention for the constellation was: I want to be able to differentiate between my panic and what doesn't belong to me! To begin with, we work only with the intention. It's in a state of alert and says it's always one step ahead, always faster than the others. It can understand me but it can't feel what I'm saying. It feels as if it's wearing a heavy-duty weapon belt and is taking care that nothing happens.

"I constellate the panic. It immediately feels panic, feels unwell and thinks: 'Everyone, but not G.! If he were to do anything to me, who or what should I believe in? Who could I trust?' It's puzzled by these thoughts.

"My intention can understand it, but not feel it. I am facing my intention and I tell it that I know how the panic feels.

"I constellate my mother and her mother (both died 22 years previously) but stay with my intention and the panic and turn my back towards my mother and grandmother. I have the feeling that I have nothing to do with either of them; don't even want to know what's going on with them. For a moment the panic has the feeling it belongs with them. It's confused. My intention, on the other hand, immediately stands between the two of them, wants to protect my mother from her mother. I tell her that that's not our task and that I don't want her to do that. She then comes back to me.

"Now I set up the part of me that had a near-death experience as a small child. We know each other and immediately establish a good rapport. The child is very afraid and sad. The panic is suddenly relieved and no longer confused. It says it can go and leaves the circle. It goes back to its place amongst the seminar participants.

"The intention looks at me and at the small child. We embrace. The child says: 'Get me out of here' and means the incubator.

"The intention now has an idea of how she can feel if she no longer has to fight for survival. I tell her: 'I'm standing up for myself now' (the constellation facilitator suggested I say this). She gets calmer and I can establish contact with myself.

"The constellation is then ended and it feels good to me. I had formulated a good intention, one from the healthy part, one that allowed me to come closer to myself, that taught me the difference between my own traumatic experiences and those belonging to my mother. That is the result of a long process in which I kept working on my history and on myself. The benefit is that before the constellation I am already clear in my head about what I want, what's good for me. Years ago that wasn't possible at all. Because of symbiotic entanglements with the traumas of my parents, I wasn't able to feel myself and my own needs.

"On the evening after the constellation I had the following thoughts (and they were verified in their awfulness by further constellations): 'Who knows what they did to me in the incubator? Perhaps people were working on me with tweezers and knives. Children used to be operated on with no anaesthetic in those days; they were thought to be without feeling. No human warmth or bonding, only hands and medical instruments.' These thoughts felt so real that everything in me calmed down. No survival part tried to badmouth this statement or to negate it. At that moment I stood up for myself completely and with no doubts. It was a good feeling, and having the certainty that it was the only right way to continue, constellating my intentions and going on, accompanied by people who are good for me. The therapeutic process begins with the formulation of the intention. This is an assertion made by Franz Ruppert that I can now feel."

Twins and triplets

Twins and those who are of multiple births are psychologically connected with one another in a particular way. They are in close contact with each other during the time before they are born, as well as after. They are symbiotically attached to their mother and to the other siblings in the womb. Ultrasound scans show how multiple-birth children develop relationships. Sometimes they play with one another (Janus, 1993).

It is sometimes assumed that a person's psychological difficulties may originate from the death of other children in a multiple-child pregnancy where only the client survived. The surviving twin is thought to experience this loss almost as the loss of one half of himself, and continually yearns for a reunion with the lost twin.

If it is true that another child had developed for a while in the uterus and then died – in most cases this question cannot be settled completely – and if there has really been an experience of an early loss trauma, then the question arises as to how this loss trauma can be resolved. In my opinion, imagining a reunion with a deceased person is not a sensible solution, since it only reinforces the symbiotic entanglement. In order to end this it is essential to recognise the finality of death, and unravel the feelings of attachment towards the deceased. Otherwise this unresolved issue feelings will continually influence the individual's feelings making it impossible to develop his own identity.

To believe that we can gain energy and vitality from deceased relatives, our 'ancestors', is a widely held illusion. When people say they have to look after the deceased in a family, they do it because no one is looking after them; they have no one with whom they can have a healthy bonding contact. They believe that the deceased feel as lonely and abandoned as they do, and they hope that if they look after the deceased, then someone will look after them. This explains why many people will work to discover those deceased members of the family who have been suppressed or ostracised by the others, and attempt to bring them back to life psychologically. That is the basic pattern of symbiotic entanglements in families and it should not be given additional reinforcement in therapy.

Case study 38

Vanishing triplets (Mrs. R.)

Mrs. R. was convinced that her emotional problems and stagnation in her life could be traced back to the fact that she had originally been one of triplets. She did not know for a fact whether her mother had had a multiple pregnancy, but she had picked up the phrase 'vanishing twin/triplet syndrome' in a lecture. The concept touched her deeply. Her intention for the constellation, was to clarify whether 'vanishing triplets' had any meaning for her.

The representative for her 'intention' immediately fell to the floor and curled up in a foetal position that could be interpreted as a child in the uterus. The 'intention' said she didn't want any contact with the outside world. I asked Mrs. R. to set up a representative for her mother. This representative immediately went into a frozen state and said: "My life is over now!"

Mrs. R.'s mother had become pregnant when she was 18. It was an unwanted pregnancy, and although she didn't love the father, her family forced her to marry him. The marriage was not good. Mrs. R. felt that both her mother and her father had abandoned her.

I asked Mrs. R. to put down two cushions for the two 'vanished' triplets she suspected there had been. She put one in front and one behind the representative of her 'intention', who was still lying on the floor, complaining that it was so cold there. The 'intention' immediately took hold of the cushion lying in front of her and held it tightly to her breast. She tried to warm herself with it. She also pulled the cushion behind her close to her. She was still resisting the client's attempts to make contact with her. Mrs. R. said she was very familiar with this behaviour in herself. She would often not leave the house for days on end and avoid any contact with other people.

I offered her the following explanation for the scenario: The unwanted pregnancy had been a traumatic event for her mother, who as a result had split from any relationship to her body. This had caused a life-threatening situation in the uterus for her (the client) and any other possible children. If there were other children, they did not survive this situation. Only she, the client, had found a way to stay alive despite the cold and lack of emotional contact in her mother's uterus.

As the representative of her 'intention' had shown, it was possible that the contact with other once-living organisms in the mother's womb had given her enough strength to survive until birth. However, she had split off her mortal fear at this point. She also split later from this part of herself in order to be able to actively live after her birth.

However, for the part represented by her 'intention', time had not moved on. This part felt that this was the only way to survive the mother's coldness and inability to offer any contact.

My explanation made sense to Mrs. R. It filled her with a certain pride that she had survived despite her mother's rejection. She thought her will to live must be very strong. For the first time, she moved her gaze away from her 'intention' on the floor to the window of the therapy room and looked out at the countryside.

In the follow-up conversation, the representative of the 'intention' said that she had only started to feel interest in Mrs. R. when she was no longer focused on her (the representative), but on herself.

Trauma and physical symptoms of illness

It is a theoretical error and a practical mistake to separate the physical body from the psyche when working with clients. Body and psyche are an inseparable entity that we can, for analytical reasons, think of as independent, but cannot practically treat as being separate.

The medicine of the 19th and 20th centuries, which was based on materialistic thinking and which originally, for good reason, tried to distance itself from metaphysical ideas about the causes of illnesses, is in a way throwing the baby out with the bathwater. It regarded the inner psychological workings as irrelevant, and clung to the conviction that the physical body was nothing other than a collection of bones, tissue, blood vessels, organs and cells.

This scientific reductionism in medicine paved the way for the treatment of living human bodies as just matter or machines, cutting them open, extracting organs or inserting new ones, filling them with chemicals, etc. All this brought an immense development in the disciplines of surgery, organ transplants, emergency operations, and saved the lives of many people. However, this view of medicine restricted solely to the physical body brings with it other dangers such as:

- psychological damage by physical treatment,
- traumatising the patient,
- activating old traumas and causing the patient to be re-traumatised.

In my opinion we have to question this concept of illness that assumes it can go on without taking the individual's psyche into consideration. To what extent does it help by saying, if someone's head hurts, that it's a 'migraine'? Or if some cells in a person's body are persistently dividing and multiplying, that it's 'cancer'? Equating symptoms with the illness is a tautology, which clouds the real issues, rather than clarifying them. This sort of diagnosis equates things that are visible and measurable with the real problem, but in many cases symptoms (e.g. high temperature, cough, inflammation) are a transitional phase in a self-healing process.

So if physical symptoms are defined as 'illnesses', this is a false abstraction. The signals are deprived of their meaning in the individual's life history, and their integration into an appropriate context. Seeing symptoms such as fear, pain or stress as the actual problem is the same as thinking the warning signals on a technical appliance are the problem. Warning signals are there to point to a dysfunction in order to get to the bottom of it. By treating symptoms we are at risk of removing the warning signals. It is as if we were taking out the red warning lights in, for example, a car, and replacing them with green lights, supposing that the problem would then be fixed. With a technical appliance we realise this is absurd, but in relation to our bodies it is still seen by many as a rational approach.

Something that appears as a lasting pain, inflammation, growth or cell destruction, is initially nothing more than a signal that:

- something in this body is going wrong;
- the body can no longer regulate and regenerate itself;
- the immune system has to fight something;
- regulatory circuits are no longer functioning properly.

We should therefore regard physical symptoms initially as a signal that the person either needs more time, peace and relaxation, or that he cannot cope on his own without external support. The logical diagnostic questions should therefore be: What can this person no longer cope with? What has caused this?

With all symptoms that are expressed by the inner organs, the muscles or joints or through the skin, there is a high risk that the symptoms will re-appear in other parts of the body if they are removed by purely medical, surgical or orthopaedic means, because their causes have not been understood.

In general we can say that physical signs of illness are the consequence of an experience that a person has had and that he has not yet been able to process. He is still occupied with this unprocessed experience, or is still in the middle of dealing with whatever it was that is too much for him and is damaging him. The purpose of the physical signals can therefore only really be properly understood within their complete context, and in relation to their causes. A real recovery can only be made if the somatic phenomena are understood in connection with the pathogenic experience and psychological coping strategies.

In my experience, and from a psychotraumatology perspective, physical symptoms have a dual purpose. On the one hand they are the expression of the split off traumatised parts that cannot get attention any other way, and at the same time they are the result of overloading the body with the efforts of the survival self to keep the traumatised parts under control. Symptoms of illness reveal something, and at the same time there is the counterpart that wants to prevent its discovery. In other words, they are the expression of the traumatised part that is covered up by the survival strategies. They are a compromise in the conflict between the traumatised parts that want to be seen, and the survival strategies that suppress them. The longer the internal conflict continues between the traumatised parts and the survival strategies that are trying to keep them in check, the more physical resources are used and the more damage is caused to the organism. In the end, medicine becomes emergency treatment that has to prevent the patient from dying. It will not, however, stop the trauma emergency reactions and the surviving strategies in the individual.

It also seems to be a strategy often used by the survival parts to cause physical pain as a way of preventing the healthy parts from delving more deeply into the trauma. Someone who is full of fear only feels his fear; someone who is permanently in pain can think of nothing else. As a result, physical symptoms can occasionally increase in therapy when the client comes closer to his trauma. The survival parts become noisy to distract attention.

It must therefore be the job of the doctor or psychotherapist to help the patients and clients to decipher the language of their symptoms. For example asking such questions as:

- What sort of traumatic experience might be hidden within the symptoms?
- What survival strategies are being expressed by the symptoms?
- What sort of symbiotic entanglement are they registering?

Symptoms that have already shown themselves in physical damage can, in my experience, transform into a healing process if the specific trauma they are related to is looked at in therapy. The physical damage then at least does not progress any further, and sometimes disappears altogether.

In the following case studies I have sketched out some of my experiences with physical symptoms in therapy.

Case study 39

Headaches (Marianne)

Marianne was sexually abused as a child. This came to light in several constellations and she accepted it as probable based on the number of symptoms she had. Amongst other things, she had suffered all her life from severe headaches. With the help of dreams she came into contact with the state of shock into which she had fallen when suffering the abuse.

"After the last few nights I had the impression in the morning that I had dreamt something important but I couldn't remember any details. Today that was different. I woke up several times in the night and felt a headache developing, moving upwards from my neck, and half asleep I thought 'I have to move my head. Movement makes it better.' In the morning the headache was almost unbearable and I wanted to get up and take a pain killer. Suddenly I remembered my 'nightmare': I am lying snuggled in a blanket in bed and I feel how someone is standing next to the bed and pulls the blanket away from my face. I have a feeling of horror and fear. I want to scream, but I can't make a sound. I try harder. I open my eyes wide, want to show my fear, want to scream and at the same time I'm scared at the gurgling sounds which are the only ones I can make. My feeling is that I'm only little in this scene.

"Then there were more scenes with men, when I'm grown up, I feel myself threatened but manage to get away. The memory of this part of the dream isn't so intense.

"I know that I used to have similar nightmares. This morning I was at last able to understand more. Yesterday I went to see a non-medical practitioner who has known me for 15 years and does very gentle physical work with me. He works on the tension in my muscles and the pain in my joints.

For a few weeks I've had a pain in my left leg when I move, which prevents me walking far. As well as going through the treatment, we talked about the function of the leg muscles, that they're important for support when I'm walking and that they can get cramp or stay hard if they don't relax in the night.

"At the end of the treatment, his idea was: 'Perhaps you'll find a way to know when you have to hold onto yourself or onto something inside you and when you should relax the tension.'

"And this morning I think that this dream has shown me part of the answer about my inner retention. It's about a state of shock when no movement is possible.

"After I've written everything down the headache has gone (without taking any tablets!) and this also shows me how important it is to understand my dream as a retained memory, to take myself seriously and not just try to push it aside because I'm terrified, and try to forget it, like I used to do."

Many non-medical practitioners, fitness trainers, masseurs, chiropractors, or craniosacral practitioners work through the body on the symptoms that are the consequences of traumas, possibly without knowing it. They are frequently unaware of the original trauma from which their client is suffering. The following description of a client's stay in a clinic might give an impression of the way in which supposedly pleasant and relaxing activities, such as massage, can trigger the trauma of traumatised individuals, and even deepen already existing psychological splits, thereby bringing about the opposite of the hoped-for relaxing effect of the treatment:

Case study 40

No escape (Hanna)

"Here in the clinic I often have the feeling I am being touched in an unpleasant way, even if it's just the normal corrections in the gymnastic exercises. The presence of another patient in whom I see my father and another person makes me anxious to the point of physical pain on one side of my body because I feel I cannot leave my place.

"In the first few days of my stay, the situation at the buffet was very hard to take because I felt I was being subjected to contact that I didn't want. I was anxious, wanted to run away and felt aggression, all brought on by elderly men of a certain size and stature. When I'm subjected to proximity that I don't like, my breathing is almost always very shallow. I don't want to have the other person's breath inside me. Disgust starts building inside me.

"Repeated knocking sounds from the neighbouring cubicle while I'm having a 'fango' mud treatment trigger unpleasant physical feelings in me. The feeling of not being able to leave, but wanting to, means that I endure massages, rather than getting the enjoyment I used to get from them."

It is also important to understand that muscle tension and muscle hardness, misaligned joints or energy blocks can represent a compromise between the traumatised self and the survival strategies, and it is hopeless to fight against the symptoms, which the client actually needs as long as he does not remember his trauma. For a short time, the human body can be made to relax by external means, such as massages or medication, but as soon as the effect of these external influences fades, the survival strategies are quick to reappear and regain control of joints and muscles. These strategies of survival actually retain a vestige of control even while being externally influenced, and do not allow the muscles to relax completely, or the tension in the muscles, tendons and joints to dissipate. As long as there is the risk of the trauma overwhelming the person, the survival strategies can occasionally be softened, but they can never be completely disempowered.

Case study 41

High blood pressure (Sigrid)

Sigrid wanted to do something about her high blood pressure. In her constellation it became apparent that in doing so she was trying to cut off a part of herself; she was trying to remove a traumatised child part within her that contained the memory of her brother's abuse of her. However, in the constellation this traumatised child part fought hard against being 'got rid of'. This shows that no symptom-oriented attempts, not even the 'beta-blockers' she took, would succeed in eliminating the symptoms.

After she began to consciously accept her trauma and integrate it psychologically, her high blood pressure disappeared.

Case study 42

Stomach cramps (Simon)

Simon suffers from strong stomach cramps. In his constellation it became clear that as a child he had been permanently under stress through his contact with his traumatised mother, and his autonomic nervous system was in turmoil. His mother's existential fear, with which he was symbiotically entangled, is present in his stomach. His symptoms diminished the more he realised his symbiotic trauma.

Case study 43

Teeth grinding (Viola)

Viola's teeth are almost ground down to nothing through the tension she holds in her jaw. She has already had countless courses of orthopaedic dental treatment and orthodontic treatment. Whilst undergoing these she lost more teeth, dental bridges were broken and dental braces couldn't be fitted properly. When Viola decided to look into the causes of the tension in her jaw in a constellation, it transpired that her mother's treatment of her was totally unloving. She was supposed to endure patiently what her mother expected of her, which was to wait alone at home from a very young age while her mother was out.

As a little child, Viola wanted to try and make her mother understand her, wanted to show her what she needed, but she couldn't. It was as if her lips were sealed shut. She wasn't able to express herself. This led to the first level of splitting in Viola. One part couldn't stand the internal pressure and split off. This part withdrew into isolation. Another part was furious with the part within Viola that was so needy. It felt very tense physically and was absolutely furious with anyone who dared to come close. It had an almost murderous anger inside. It twisted its arms into grotesque shapes and ground its teeth in fury.

In this constellation, Viola's internal perpetrator/victim split became apparent. The part of her that cried a lot and didn't know what to do got absolutely no sympathy from the other, angry part and was scared that this part would get completely out of control. In this constellation Viola realised how quickly she lost contact with herself, thereby losing contact with her 'intention' again and again. Her injuries and her psychological splits were so entrenched that she was unable to develop a loving relationship with herself. Until now she was only able to react from her victim part or from her perpetrator part.

In later constellations it turned out that Viola was sexually abused by her father as a baby.

Case study 44

Rotten tooth (Mrs. P.)

Teeth are often the object of much abuse by the survival parts. An individual can go to a dentist and get a tooth pulled out if it causes pain. The fact that the infection of the rotten tooth might be the expression of a life situation that is rotten is something I experienced in the work with Mrs. P.

Mrs. P. was abused most horribly as a child by her parents and friends of her parents. In her helplessness and inability to voice her pain, she sacrificed teeth, parts of her skin and finally she almost allowed her reproductive organs to be taken out in the hope of being able to protect at least the 'essence' of her psychological self. In a constellation she was able to put a stop to this madness inside her, and use her anger to distance herself from the perpetrators. She realised that in contact with the perpetrators she could no longer dissociate psychologically, leaving them her body to abuse.

Case study 45

Chronic pain (Sybille)

For seven years Sybille had been going from pillar to post seeking treatment for the pain in her lower back, and those treating her had tried all their respective healing methods to alleviate her pain. Most recently she had been in a specialist pain clinic for several weeks, but just a few days after returning home, the pain was back again, as strong as ever.

Her pain had started when she was writing a biography about her father who was killed in the Second World War. She had been rejected by her mother all her life, and had always nurtured the hope that at least her father would have loved her. In the constellation, however, the representative of her father showed no interest in her. He was involved in a conflict with his wife, who also rejected him.

271

For Sybille this was the first time she had had a starting point for making sense of her chronic pain. She was very happy about the disillusioning result of the constellation, which opened up the possibility of getting more in contact with the child within her who had been rejected by both her parents.

8
How can we become psychologically healthy?

Starting your journey

There are different ideas about what leads to the healing of illnesses:

- healing comes from outside and from above (from the gods, through healers, shamans...),
- it is brought about by rituals (through prayer, incantations, sacrificial offerings...),
- it can be physically, chemically, technically and industrially produced (through medication, radiation, operations, massages...),
- it is the result of the relationship of the ill person to himself and to the people supporting him, who encourage his self-healing ability.

The latter path appears to me to be the most promising way in the long term. It is the most likely to lead to lasting physical and psychological health. I therefore encourage people to set out on this path to find themselves, and to seek out helpful companions who will support them on the way to finding good health.

However, many people are not able to admit that they are psychologically ill, and insist that their difficulties are external and not grounded in their own psyche. It is therefore naïve to imagine that everyone who seeks psychotherapeutic help is committed to regaining psychological health. As long as we are under the control of our survival strategies, we may think that we are normal, and that what we do and experience is normal. The extent of the physical and psychological disturbance usually only becomes clearer to people in the course of psychotherapy, when they gradually become aware of what it means to feel physically and psychologically healthy.

As the case studies have shown, it is not the fault of the person concerned if they are unable to regulate their psychological condition, but if there is a psychological split, the person will probably make decisions more from their survival self than their healthy self. That only makes their situation worse, and may cause harm to other people. To start the ball rolling in the direction of better health, the person needs to make a clear and definite decision to go for it, and maintain the will to continue. The survival strategies will always cast doubt on these decisions, and will work against the person's perseverance with all the tricks that the survival self employs. Beginning the process of withdrawal from the survival state is often laborious, and sometimes progresses very slowly.

So the therapist needs to be very experienced in order to anticipate this internal struggle between the healthy and the survival parts in their clients, and to support the healthy parts in not being diverted from the goal. Good therapists are also patient and watchful, identifying and naming the survival programs they see, which often appear as normal activities to the client.

It is also important for the therapist to have a suitable method in order to understand the complexity of the psychological processes, and not just be concerned with one single aspect of the whole process. I believe the constellation method is of enormous benefit here. It is not just the lone therapist who is trying to understand the patterns that are often confusing in a person's psyche, but in the representatives in the constellation he has excellent and often very competent assistants.

A supportive social environment for clients is also helpful in the process of escaping from their splits and entanglements.

If, for example, only one person in a couple is trying to access his split off emotions, then there might be no future for the couple together.

Constellations groups that have been together for some time are not necessarily free from conflict, because there can be destructive symbiotic entanglements here too, but in my experience the goodwill the participants have for one another can prevail. The use of the constellations method in groups will very quickly kindle a strong feeling of solidarity amongst group members. The participants know that each of them needs the others to be representatives in their own constellation, and they help each other. In this way many experiences are shared and touching interpersonal relationships created.

A significant part of trauma therapy is to do with memory and consciousness work. Memory barriers have to be pushed aside so that things can be revealed as they really were. Constellations can help to create access to memories that are stored non-verbally.

Four steps in the healing process

I have noticed that the tempo and rhythm of the process of change is different in each client. In principle there are four steps that are beneficial:

- the growth of healthy structures,
- letting go of survival strategies and recognising illusions,
- encountering the split off traumatised parts, and
- filling the autonomy achieved with self-determined life goals.

I have put these four steps into an image: figure 16. With the healthy parts growing, an individual can pass through three gates:

- the gate of illusions,
- the gate of fear and pain, and
- the gate to freedom.

It is only when one has passed through the first gate, the gate of illusions, that the second gate, the gate of fear and pain, becomes more clearly visible, and this leads to the encounter with the traumatised parts. This gate, which previously triggered dissociation and an immediate impulse to flee, can only be approached purposefully and consciously if the individual has freed himself from the illusion that establishing contact with his traumatised parts should be avoided at all costs. Encountering the split trauma feelings can be attempted with the clear awareness that the only way to achieve health is by resolving the psychological split.

Once this dark and dreaded space is entered and crossed, the third gate opens, the gate into freedom. But this freedom also has to be accepted and filled. If a person has spent his whole life being concerned with keeping the trauma feelings at bay, he will know the feelings intimately, but he will not know what he can do to live free of the anxiety. New goals and desires have to be found, and feelings and energies have to be channelled in directions other than those previously chosen.

Only the individual's own intention enables progress

In my experience, the method of the 'constellation of the intention' initiates an incremental process of change, whereby an individual's current stage of development, what he has achieved and what is missing, gradually becomes clearer. Therapy takes place in achievable steps and at the tempo set by the patient. It can, for example, be an important step for the patient to formulate his intention himself, rather than having it dictated to him by others, as was originally the case with the man, whose constellation I have documented on the next page.

Integration of splits following a trauma

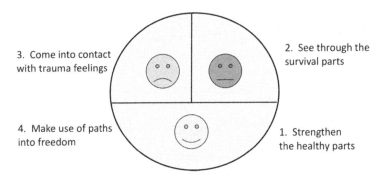

3. Come into contact with trauma feelings

2. See through the survival parts

4. Make use of paths into freedom

1. Strengthen the healthy parts

Figure 16: The path to psychological health

Case study 46

'We can do it!' (Achim)

Achim has come to therapy for the first time at the suggestion of his wife, who had had a therapy session with me a few weeks previously. He is very distressed because nothing is going right professionally at the moment and his wife is threatening to leave him if he doesn't make some changes soon. She accuses him of being unapproachable. His intention therefore is to learn to allow closeness.

Achim's parents divorced when he was nine years old. His parents swapped partners with another couple and his mother moved in with her new husband. He and his older brother went with her. By this time he had withdrawn internally from his mother. He is still caught up in arguments with her today. She thinks she has to look after him, but she is not present emotionally for him. He does not feel that she takes any notice of him.

We are a small group in my therapy room for Achim's constellation: there are just two women there as well as him and me. For his 'intention' Achim chooses one of the women. He positions her with her back to a wall and stands immediately next to her, so that both are looking into the room. Both Achim and the 'intention' feel that a wall is rising up between them. The 'intention' feels as if she is being pushed sideways. Achim meanwhile withdraws more and more into his shell.

I suggest to Achim that he set up a representative for his mother. He chooses the other woman and positions her to the left of himself and the 'intention'. This increases his tendency to withdraw.

I tell him that this constellation cannot lead to anything as it is, and ask him what he really wants. He admits that this 'intention', "to allow closeness", is not his main problem at the moment. His professional situation concerns him far more. He wants to get back on his feet professionally and be successful. I suggest that he set me up as this 'intention'.

He has scarcely positioned me when the sentence comes up in me: "We can do it!" I hold both of Achim's hands and then I feel a deep sadness. I begin to weep and Achim does too. We hug each other tightly, with each of us resting our head on the other's shoulder and tears flowing down. After a while I say to him that we don't have a problem with closeness: our embrace shows that. When the closeness is appropriate, it isn't a problem. Achim confirms this.

Meanwhile, the 'mother', who has been standing next to us, comes up and embraces us both and says "We'll do it". Neither Achim nor I like that and we ask her to stop; it's none of her business any more. Then we end the constellation.

So Achim came to the session out of fear that his wife could leave him. For that reason he originally made his wife's intention his own, which was demonstrated by his choosing a woman as the representative for his intention, who probably actually represented his wife. It quickly became apparent in the constellation that this would not lead to anything. When, instead, he formulated his own intention, he immediately came into his feelings and thereby into contact with himself. He was then able to distance himself from his mother, with whom he is still very entangled.

If Achim is not in contact with his own feelings, with his sadness and his optimism, he can only distance himself from his mother and his wife by making accusations or by withdrawing internally. He then gets into a blocked state and is also unable to look after himself professionally.

Perceiving and feeling instead of acting out

As a therapist, you get a feeling in the course of time for the quality of a stated intention. With intentions that are formulated to a great extent from survival parts of the person, the attempt is often made to pack everything in at once. These kinds of intentions are usually formulated from the head.

Even so, it does not help to tell the client that the illusions in his intention are clearly visible and that he should choose a less illusory intention. That would only confuse him and bring him even more into his split. So it is important, as the therapist, to be able to rely on the fact that the constellation of the client's intention that is currently uppermost in his mind, will have the best possible therapeutic effect. And one good result of a constellation can be, for example, to understand that not everything is achievable at once.

During a constellation it is important to recognise when a client moves into acting out, trying to use behaviours and rituals to 'solve' a situation that is almost unbearable for him, rather than genuinely seeing and feeling the truth. Unfortunately many therapists tend to direct and encourage such acting out, thereby further solidifying the splits. I have come to a place now where I am not overly keen on the concept of finding 'solutions' through the constellation. As a rule it is enough to see the situation more clearly and explicitly, and to take a further step into the real feelings.

Case study 47

The therapist as an auxiliary ego

A psychosomatic clinic had invited me to demonstrate my work with constellations. This clinic has worked for some time with family constellations. Clients and therapists were assembled together. The client whose constellation this was going to be chose a man for her 'intention' who was her therapist.

The client came from a family where there was a great deal of violence. The father was an alcoholic and therefore unpredictable. The mother didn't know her father; the grandmother had kept his identity a secret. Her stepfather and half-brother had both sexually abused the mother.

To begin with, the client was completely disoriented in the constellation, while her 'intention' immediately started to organise things. He wanted to protect the mother and the grandmother from the evil men. The more the 'intention' was pre-occupied with this, the more the client withdrew into a state of high anxiety and helplessness. Her 'intention' tried to soothe her: "You're a big girl now, the past is behind you. You can move forward! Look, your mother and grandmother are also broken women," etc. But this didn't help the client because the 'intention' who was behaving like a therapist (therefore, one could say, her internal therapist-ego self), in his eagerness to help her didn't notice her distress and helplessness, nor her symbiotic entanglement. Another representative who was depicting the client's inner burden was standing close to the mother and the grandmother.

So the client's 'therapist self', as portrayed by her 'intention', was a survival strategy, and my intervention then was to encourage the client to make it clear to the 'intention' how she had really felt as a child. I also drew her attention to the fact that she had chosen a man for her 'intention', which is a part of herself, even though she is a woman. The more the client was able to express herself through her tears and body language, the more relief the representative for her inner burden felt, and the more her 'intention' became aware of how bad the patient's childhood had really been.

When thinking about relational therapy, where the client-therapist relationship is figural, the therapist is in danger of the following:

- playing down the clients' traumas,
- not taking them seriously,
- persistently referring the client to the immediate here and now situation rather than the past,
- wanting to comfort them too quickly, and
- overlooking their symbiotic entanglements.

In this way the therapist is acting with the intention of helping and protecting the client, instead of:

- supporting the process of self-discovery and feeling,
- putting the client's experience into the right words for them, and
- thereby supporting the client's self-awareness.

The therapist's own unrecognised traumatic entanglements and psychological splits are often behind their attempts to help others with psychotherapy. In my view, the therapist's entanglement with his client begins if he only sees his client's symptoms, and doesn't see him within the context of his family of origin. The therapist unconsciously positions himself at a place in the client's bonding system that is not appropriate for his level of significance, for example by trying to be the better mother or father. He therefore becomes a projective screen for the client's symbiotically entangled survival parts. The perpetrator-victim dynamic in the client, as well as in the therapist, then frequently gains momentum – a dynamic that will probably lead to disappointment, frustration and aggression in both. I have arrived at this conclusion based on many supervision sessions for therapists that I have done.

Recognising illusions and relinquishing them

Illusions that have been created as survival strategies as a result of trauma are longer lasting than the real conditions. Reality changes continually, while illusions stay as they are as long as the trauma behind them is not recognised as a reality. Traumas cannot be consciously overcome as long as the survival strategies continue to hang onto the illusion that it is not necessary to deal with the traumatised past.

It is senseless pointing out their illusions to people until they feel the need to question their views and their actions. Even if someone is confronted with the best arguments, if he still needs his illusions to avoid becoming conscious of the pain and entangled inner process, it will only lead to more denial. People will defend their survival strategies all the more tenaciously if they feel these strategies under threat, because they are afraid they will end up in the chaotic depths of their trauma feelings and lose control over their lives if they don't.

At the beginning of therapy, the clients' intentions usually lead to an improvement in their ability to recognise and understand the illusions of their survival strategies. Only when clients recognise that what they perceive, feel, think or remember when in their survival mode shields them from contact with reality, can the survival strategies start to lose their power. Then the healthy parts of the self have more space to develop.

In the end, illusions can only be demystified by recognising the reality of a trauma. Only then can the psyche regain its original purpose, to enable absolute clear access to actual reality and not just to a fictional world. Recognising the fact of a trauma deprives the survival strategies of their previously unopposed and absolute authority. They then become increasingly irrelevant. Their function is to exclude the real trauma from the person's consciousness as long as the healthy parts are insufficient to deal with the trauma. Once freed of the illusions that obscure reality, the psyche can work on understanding reality in its many and diverse forms, and deal with it constructively.

When I lead constellations, I try to find out, amongst other things, which survival strategies a client shows in the foreground. In the following example it is the strategy of controlling another person – in this case, the client's mother.

Case study 48

Futile attempts at control (Alexander)

Alexander experiences a lot of external resistance in his professional and private life, at least that's the way it seems to him. He asks himself where it comes from. His spinal column is damaged, and he has no access to his emotions. He asks himself what stops him from experiencing feelings.

His intention for the constellation is: He wants to have a look at this 'control circuit' so that he can get out of it.

Alexander comes from a family in which, in his view, there is not a single psychologically healthy person. He is an only child. His grandmother on his father's side had been schizophrenic; she had been raped by his grandfather, and she died in a psychiatric clinic from TB. His grandfather had also suffered from mania. His father had grown up in a home and later became an alcoholic. On his mother's side there had also been a lot of violence; the children had frequently been beaten by their grandfather and grandmother. The mother's sister suffered from phobias; and Alexander said his mother was an extremely controlled woman.

When I asked Alexander to set up a representative for his 'intention', he chose a woman, although there were also several men in the group whom he could have chosen. The following dialogue developed between the 'intention' and Alexander:

Intention: "I feel angry and aggressive; I also feel fear, I'm having palpitations and I'm trembling."

Alexander: "I have to concentrate so that I don't fall down on the floor."

Intention: "We can sit on the floor and you can lean against me." They sit on the floor and Alexander sits between the intention's legs and leans his back against the 'intention's' upper body. But he only partly relaxes. The 'intention' feels the same.

I suggested that Alexander say to his 'intention': "With my mum I was always afraid that when I needed support she wouldn't be able to bear it."

Alexander: "I couldn't lean on anything as a child because the others were all too weak, particularly my mother. I always thought I'd break something. As a child I learnt that leaning on anything was dangerous. This mistrust is deep within me. And now I notice how I am in my head and how I have split."

I suggested that Alexander set up a representative for his mother. Once in position, the representative walked up and down, her confused gaze directed at the ceiling. The 'intention' and Alexander were alarmed by the 'mother's' appearance. Both stood up, and then Alexander sat down again with his back to the wall so that his 'mother' couldn't be behind him. He was again very tense and fixated on her.

I pointed out to Alexander that there was this split inside him: one part of him was afraid of his mother and tried to get away from her to be safe, while the other part dearly wanted to be able to lean against her, which explained why he chose a woman for his 'intention'.

A: 'I know I'm entangled. I know I want to let go of my mother but I'm afraid to let her go.'

I suggested that Alexander set up the little child Alexander within him. Alexander chose a representative for the child.

Child to Alexander: "My legs are heavy, my feet are heavy, my whole body hurts and I'm surprised that you've sustained this for so long. I'd really like to slam my mother against the wall." The 'child' moves away from Alexander. Alexander tried without success to establish contact with this 'child', but the 'child' wouldn't listen to him because he was trying to get away from the mother. Alexander wanted to help the 'child', but his 'intention' says to him "It's not about helping, but about accepting this situation, as it is now, as the reality and seeing your entanglement with you mother, which is still present."

I confirmed this, and pointed out to Alexander that he could only give up his attempts to control when he is prepared to disengage himself from his mother completely. It is not possible for him to control his mother's behaviour, or to bring his feelings relating to his mother under control, and this then leads to the split that had become apparent. Alexander was surprised at how clearly the constellation had brought his unresolved symbiotic entanglement with his mother to light. He now knew that the resistance and his problems are not external to him, but are within him.

As a child, Alexander did not get any support from his mother. She could hardly manage with her own feelings, and transferred her anxieties and anger onto her child. So when Alexander is in contact with his mother, he has to suppress his feelings and split them off. One part of him wants to trust his mother and lean on her for support, and another part is unable to trust her at all. He tries to shield himself from her by controlling her in order to be able to run away if it becomes too dangerous again.

This constellation can help Alexander to understand that the resistance he encounters in his present life is caused by this entanglement with his mother. This resistance is the expression of his split into the part seeking closeness and support and the part that is under pressure and is afraid of his mother. His survival strategy of wanting closeness and contact with other people, but at the same time being afraid of them and therefore having continually to control his own feelings, leads to a permanent experience of overload and stress. The tension in his body is so high that it has led to damage of his spinal column, and this creates further rejection and resistance in those people Alexander wants to establish contact with.

He therefore has to recognise that this survival strategy of controlling his feelings and those of others is an illusion. It is not achievable and originates in his relationship with his traumatised mother. When he acknowledges the reality that the bond with his mother was traumatising for him, he will be able to overcome his internal split. Then he is more likely to achieve his private and professional goals.

Case study 49

'Continual overload' (Annette)

Annette spent her childhood trying to please her parents, who had both been badly traumatised in the war. She continually pushed herself to the limit without realising it. She wrote me a letter following a constellation in which she had clearly recognised this overload:

"This constellation continued to affect me strongly after it had finished. I established sympathetic contact with this completely overloaded part of me and was able, for the first time, to establish physical contact with the overload.

"I have now realised why, in my imagination, my mother always appeared to me as a nine-year-old child during my Somatic Experiencing Training. There simply is no adult mother in my spiritual landscape. What really shocked me is the fact that I am still at the whim of this traumatised girl/mother, and, so to speak, carry her about on my shoulders. This morning I woke up shattered. All the muscles in my shoulders and back were hurting.

"And what promptly happened? My mother rang up and wanted to invite herself over for Christmas! What should I do? Palpitations, shortness of breath, shaky legs and absolute fear, yes, real fear – unbelievable! I always used to try to invite my parents over for Christmas (harmony under the Christmas tree – finally united, etc.) and they always thanked me and refused – and now? As if they'd foreseen it, they want to come and visit me this year at Christmas! For two years I've managed to wangle my way out of it with dozens of excuses – really mean, but true – and now this frontal attack!

All my healthy parts have joined together and fended off this request. This time I stood my ground and told them that I don't want to have any contact with them any more! I was absolutely frantic and was afraid of turning them down – the old feelings of guilt, of being abandoned, etc. But they finally swallowed the bitter pill! And after being so frantic, that was absolutely unbelievable for me, I felt really good. I feel as if I'm free! I was finally able to say plainly that this is the end of excuses and diversions! The children and I are no longer at their disposal and they have to accept that. I will only get in touch with them again when they have started to work on themselves – and of course that's not going to happen.

"This step is really important and necessary for myself and my inner lucidity and I now understand that we can't escape from our entanglements if we don't take the necessary steps on the outside! You're quite right – we have to take a stand and put into practice what we've realised and understood and make it our reality!"

Childish illusions of love, something the symbiotically entangled survival parts maintain so as to stay in contact with the traumatised parents, are often strengthened by traditional family constellations. These illusions of love can even lead to spiritual attitudes where someone believes:

- that they are above it all,
- that they are able to forgive everyone everything,
- that they do not see any contradictions any more, and
- that they accept everything as it is, they are helping to establish peace in the world.

However, by doing this spiritual believers avoid confronting reality as it in fact is; they avoid any encounter with their own trauma. I experienced this in a constellation when a client had set up not only her traumatised child part, but also her survival part that was interested and engaged in spiritual pursuits. This latter part believed it was connected to everything – except the furious, crying traumatised child within her that was screaming for help. The survival part simply felt annoyed by the helpless child.

Case study 50

Illusions of love (Doris)

Doris suffers a lot from gastroenteritis, and she wanted to find out the cause of it. Her memories of childhood are of having a war-traumatised and alcoholic father who bullied, tormented and terrorised her mother, her older brother and her. Amongst other things, he threatened to blow up the family house with dynamite.

When Doris set up representatives for her 'intention', her 'symptoms in her abdomen', her 'father' and 'mother', the 'intention' turned immediately to the 'father', beamed at him and said she felt a lot of love for him. Doris confirmed this. She said she loved her father very much, and often tried to calm him down with her love. The 'intention' felt as if it were above everything, and said that it also believed it loved Doris, and even the 'stomach aches'. However, Doris and the 'stomach aches' are very mistrustful of the 'intention' and refuse to be touched. Only when Doris talked more about all the things her father did to her, was more contact established between her and the 'stomach aches', which actually was her traumatised child part. The 'intention', which portrayed a survival part caught in symbiotically entangled illusions of love, withdrew suddenly. Doris could now, while in contact with her traumatised child part (the 'stomach ache') come into better contact within her body, and thence with reality.

Understanding the meaning of symptoms

It is an important step towards growing self-awareness when we understand that it is not a case of getting the symptoms to disappear, but rather of understanding their deeper meaning. In the case of anorexia, for example, the issue is to gain control over the individual's body, usually connected with sexual abuse. Those concerned try to prevent their body's reactions, and most of all, experiencing any form of physical pleasure, using food to practise an extreme form of self-denial and rejection of physical pleasure, because such experiences put them in touch with the sexual abuses that were forced upon them.

Case study 51

'Anorexia is only a symptom' (Jutta)

Jutta became anorexic because of the terrible situation she was in during her childhood. Today she understands how this symptom helped her for a while. "I don't see myself as being 'cured' of anorexia – even if the symptom 'anorexia' is gone. After the session with you I realised that the way I dealt with 'I can eat when I'm pregnant because it's for the child' was not facing up to it. I didn't realise that then – in fact I didn't realise it until yesterday. I've got rid of the symptom, but what I unconsciously communicated to my son M. (my first pregnancy) was 'I need you so that I can eat'. I used him to satisfy my needs, thereby entangling him very early in my unresolved issues. That has really affected me and made me very sad. I realise that it was only last year, with you, that I found the path to allowing myself to have needs for my own sake. Viewed in this light, I'd say that, even though the anorexia symptom itself is a thing of the past and no longer a symptom of mine, I'm now working on the background to my anorexia with my current symptoms and intentions."

Case study 52

'My inner child' (Beatrice)

The following text might give an impression of how split child parts react when the survival self has regained the upper hand. Beatrice wrote this when I asked her to describe how her inner traumatised child feels when she makes a professional decision out of a survival strategy.

"Perhaps my inner child hoped that I would soon lead her to green pastures filled with light and life. She's disappointed now that my survival parts seem once again to have gained the upper hand. In the constellation she was just pleased to have her grievances recognised and enjoy loving attention. She didn't want to have anything to do with all the issues that I have to deal with professionally. She didn't want to have anything to do with the suffering of other people. She didn't want to have to look after other people any more. She wanted to go into a new space beyond hopelessness.

"My problem was that I had no idea what space that is. The disappointment of the inner child has to do with her not having any chance of being loved, however hard she tries. The feelings of disappointment were there in moments when she realised all this, as soon as the filters of illusion vanished."

Work with the inner child, which is popular in some psychotherapies (Chopich und Paul 1996; Bradshaw 2000) must understand the complexity of traumatic splits and symbiotic entanglements, otherwise change appears too simple and one thinks it enough to embrace the 'poor' inner child. The first thing to do is to decide which inner child is the focus:

- The traumatised one?
- The symbiotically entangled one?
- The one busy with survival strategies?
- Or the child that has identified with a perpetrator?

There is also no sense in thinking that we can simply go and pick up the inner child from the past. This idea thrives on the illusion that we can undo the past. If anything, it is more a matter of being sympathetic towards oneself, and opening up to the feelings and suppressed needs. How much anxiety, suffering and mental overload were involved in the childhood situation? We can learn to recognise, understand and accept our own past, and our powerlessness as a child. Wanting to change it retrospectively is illusory. Change can only take place in the present.

Letting go of transferred feelings and symbiotic illusions

In order to overcome a split it is always necessary to differentiate between the person's own experiences and feelings and those experiences and feelings that have been transferred from the mother, grandmother, etc. A person will feel hypnotically drawn towards such feelings when they are transferred. A person's own feelings, however, are a resource, they come and go depending on the situation and are appropriate for the situation. Letting go of transferred feelings means giving up those feelings that have previously, unconsciously, connected the person with their mother. This frightens people because then feelings of loneliness and abandonment will surface. A conscious decision therefore has to be made, to confront transferred feelings.

Case study 53

'Similar fate, but totally different' (Mrs. L.)

The following account was written by Mrs. L. on the day of her therapy session.

"Today I had an appointment with Professor Ruppert. I went there with the intention of finding out where my immense mistrust of everything and everyone comes from. I described to him what happened during my long-distance walk from Lyon to Toulouse. I told him that, because of my poor knowledge of French, I hadn't thought I'd have much company in those three weeks. As a result, I was more than surprised that I met lots of really nice, friendly people who were patient enough to talk to me despite my bad French. And their friendship didn't end with the end of my journey, but they have emailed me and sent me photos and postcards since then. They are obviously interested in staying in contact with me.

"The holiday was an extremely relaxed and happy time for me. But during this time I noticed a growing mistrust towards the people who had treated me so kindly and self-lessly and looked after me. Looked at rationally, this mistrust was completely groundless and unfounded. But I couldn't stop myself from feeling this mistrust. This meant that at the end of my holiday one part of me immediately fled, while another part didn't want to go home, and led to a very difficult and tense situation for me.

"First of all, Professor Ruppert asked whether I tended to mistrust women or men. I said I mistrusted men more, but definitely women as well. He then asked me whether there had been any situations in my childhood when I mistrusted my parents. The first thing that occurred to me was the rela-tionship with my mother. It was always difficult for me to gauge my mother's intentions and actions.

"Symptomatic of that is a situation from my childhood which I can remember very clearly and which defines our relationship. We were on holiday in the mountains together with my father's siblings. Our family had rented an old shepherd's cottage where we always spent our holidays. I'd done something naughty, I can't remember what; I think I'd been cheeky to my aunt. That morning my mother called me to her bed. I remember clearly that I deeply mistrusted her because of the punishment due to me for my bad behaviour, and I didn't want to go to her. But she lured and cajoled me and finally I decided that she didn't mean it nastily and hopped into her bed.

Once I was there she took hold of me, shook me, slapped my face and hissed angrily at me: 'What did you think you were doing?' I froze in fear and disappointment. This feeling of 'always being on the alert' is deeply embedded within me.

"The experiences with my father were different: He was a very loving father who always looked after us and did lots with us. But he was always strangely absent when it was a question of upbringing or when I needed support because I felt my mother hadn't treated me fairly in a dispute.

"Prof. Ruppert asked if I have any brothers or sisters. I've got a sister who is three years younger than me and before me there were two miscarriages, one late in the pregnancy and one early on. I don't know when they were in relation to my birth, nor do I know anything about my own birth. My mother just told my sister about the miscarriages, she never spoke to me about them. When I had a miscarriage she reacted with consternation, tears and sympathy and told me to 'lay everything in God's hands and never speak about it again'. We've never mentioned it again.

"'Well exactly! You wouldn't have wanted to thrust your mother into unhappiness by talking about the distress your miscarriage caused you, would you?' was Prof. Ruppert's comment. This sentence really got to me and shook me up; it made me stop and listen. Then he asked me more about my mother's life history. My mother was born in 1948 and was the illegitimate child of my grandmother and a soldier who had returned from the front in Africa. At the same time my natural grandfather had another affair, which also produced a daughter, my mother's half-sister. Both girls are only six weeks apart in age. My mother's half-sister died as a small child. My grandfather didn't marry either of the two women.

"My grandmother married my step-grandfather, a very reliable, decent man, whom we all loved dearly. My mother's half-brother comes from this relationship. My grandmother and my step-grandfather were great friends and had a long and harmonious marriage. But deep down I'm not sure whether they loved each other.

"Even so, my mother and we grandchildren regularly saw my natural grandfather and his family. We met frequently, although my grandmother and my grandfather didn't meet again until I received my doctorate, over 50 years later.

"In answer to the question about my father I said: My father comes from a family with many children: he has ten siblings. According to him, he regarded his mother as a saint because she had to look after the farm and all the children on her own. The grandfather was away a lot with the music club and other clubs and occasionally had a bit too much to drink. He left my grandmother to do all the work. She died very young, apparently completely exhausted, when my father was 14. My father never accused my grandfather and always kept himself from bearing a grudge. But he was, and is, definitely on his mother's side, whom he saw as the victim of the situation.

"Prof. Ruppert then asked: 'Who was actually the father of your child?'

"I hesitated a bit and wasn't sure how to begin, because the story is very embarrassing and difficult for me. Richard is a very gifted scientist. During a field trip to Africa he was kidnapped by Islamic fundamentalists and held for three months. I think he was badly traumatised by that. He told me I was the love of his life and he wanted a child. For me, that was like the fulfilment of my dreams. But when I look back today, it was all much too quick. And when I was pregnant he left me and I had the miscarriage. I don't think I bear him a grudge any more. Although I was extremely resentful to begin with, because he infected me with chlamydia, which can often be a cause of a miscarriage.

"He actually left in the nick of time. When I found out that I was pregnant, he'd already gone. I never told him that I was pregnant. I was afraid from the outset that something could happen and I really wanted the child. I didn't want to expose myself to him. When I think back today, it seems absurd to me that I didn't say anything to him, but at that time it was the right reaction for me.

"'I think you're living a part of your grandmother's history', Prof. Ruppert said. I replied: 'Yes, I've considered that and it scared me that it was Africa again.' 'Yes', he said, 'a severely traumatised man who comes from Africa, fathers a child and runs off.'

"Then he asked: 'And today, what's your relationship with men like today? Are you in a relationship?' I replied: 'No, I've been on my own since then, a bit more than three years (which isn't true, it's a bit less than two years, in this situation it was as if I wanted to create more distance). When I meet men nowadays I always ask myself what they want from me. And I always find men who have difficult histories. It's as if I couldn't expect someone who isn't stressed to accept me with my life history, as if I needed someone who understands me on some level with all the stuff I carry around with me, because he's also carrying a lot round with him. A little while ago I met a very nice colleague, Richard. He's so open and positive and happy. It's as if there's no way we could get together, as if I live on a different planet. There's no access on an emotional level, only friendship, and I ask myself whether I'm perhaps just not able to meet a normal person.

"Professor Ruppert was silent for a while and then said: 'Yes, if you would like to, we can try to constellate that. Could you formulate your intention again?' I said: 'I would like to know where this mistrust in my life comes from; this mistrust that influences every relationship with a person.' He said: 'Good, then please set me up as this intention.'

"I pushed him in front of me a little way and positioned him opposite me and slightly offset, perhaps an arm's length away; in doing so it was difficult for me to pull my arm back, I didn't want to let go of him. As soon as I took my hands away from his arms he turned away and began to jump about, wave his arms and generally cause great disquiet. He said: 'I can't stay there; I have to go away. I could slip behind the curtain and simply disappear. I don't trust anyone, not even myself; I just want to get away. The only thing I can trust is nature. No human being at all. Just nature. But there are birds there. And they flutter about and make me very uneasy again.' He rubs his arms and appears furtive and sunken. He says: 'I believe I'm very confused and really stupid; no, I'm making myself stupid; I don't want to remember anything, remember nothing. Only plants. Plants are the only things that are bearable. But there's a butterfly! And it's fluttering! And I can't be doing with that either. Only plants and no one else.' (I remember that, as a child, I used to grow plants like mad, all sorts of plants.) After some running to and fro he stands still on the right, in the corner of the room, where he now stands, turned away from me, his arms wrapped round himself. He says: 'I can trust no one. No human being. I just want to get away. And myself, I can't trust myself either! Not at all! I can't trust myself!'

And me? I feel – nothing. Absolutely nothing. I watch this hysterical running about and am simply glad that all the disquiet is in him and I don't have to feel it. 'Yes', I say slowly, 'that's actually fine by me. I want to hang it all on you and then sink you somewhere!' We stand like that for a while. I try to get closer to him, which he notices and which leads to further irritation on his part, but doesn't cause any emotion in me. I am confused.

"Finally he says: 'I am now going to leave the role and we'll look at the whole thing from the outside. We're not getting any further like this.'

"We both leave the constellation and he explains to me: 'This is all about split parts that don't want to remember anything. Both are survival parts. One that doesn't feel anything any more, and the other that is escaping into nature. If you want, we can set them all up now.'

"So I set them all up. Professor Ruppert has left his shoes in the corner for the part that doesn't want to remember anything and is fleeing. I position my grandmother to his left and my natural grandfather on my mother's side next to her; a colourful cushion for her that stands up against the wall, a dark cushion for him. They stand back to back. I position my mother on their right, also a colourful cushion, but not as colourful as the one for my grandmother. She looks away from them all. Behind her I lay two black cushions, one large and one small, for the dead children. I stand between them and put down a green cushion with an oriental pattern for Richard and, slightly offset, a large orange cushion for my lost child.

"I stand in the middle and immediately feel dreadful. Totally tense, in between all of them; I can't move, can't go anywhere. I can't look anywhere either. The only place I can bear to look, at least out of the corner of my eye, is towards my dead siblings. I feel a lot of pain that makes me raise my shoulders and put my hands in front of my mouth. I feel immense powers behind and in front of me that drag on me. I sway to and fro and can't avoid them or move.

"Professor Ruppert again positions himself in the role of the intention and begins to speak: 'I can only be abstract. Everything has to dissolve into the abstractions otherwise I can't stand it. It has to go into shapes and abstractions.' (I think of the fact that for a long time I avidly collected minerals and crystals. I feel very uncomfortable.) 'Yes, and in colours. Blue! Yes. Blue is a good colour.' (As a child I lay for hours in the summer in the long grass of the meadow behind the house and gazed up into the sky to watch the swallows in flight.) Professor Ruppert continues: 'Yes, with this blue, this abstract and these plants I feel fine. The only thing that's bothering me is this naked woman at the back there, in the picture.' (I think at first that I've misheard him. It hits me totally unprepared and like a shock.) 'Yes', he repeats, 'this naked woman lying relaxed behind the plants!' I go hot and cold. A burning feeling of shame and anger overcomes me. I can't go anywhere. It doubles me up and I stare grimly at the ceiling, I gag and tears run down my face; I stay like that because I don't know what else to do.

Professor Ruppert continues: ' And it's true, everywhere in this nature I see penises and sperm. It's all sexuality. I think my head's going to burst.' Bang! A door bangs shut inside me – in the truest sense of the word. It's as if I've inwardly gone off somewhere. At this moment I am completely clear in my head, completely cold and completely devoid of feeling. (Even now, thinking about it, I can't actually see the situation in all its depth; it's as if there's a shadow or a blanket of confusion over the memory at this point.) I turn round and look at him. He comes out of the role again.

We both move out of the constellation and look at it from a little way away. He says: 'That is an absolute distraction, withdrawal, flight into nature – but all nature is sexuality, is becoming, nurturing, reproducing.' I add: 'Yes, that's nature.' I am overwhelmed but don't want to give up. It's as if everything is in a fog. He then tells me that my constellation has shown me where this mistrust comes from. It comes from what happened in your family in relation to sexuality.

"I have an idea and ask: 'How can I go on? I can't live like this!' He asks me: 'Do you really want to go on with this?' I say: 'Yes! I can't go home like this.' He says: 'Please formulate your intention again.' I say: 'I want to stand up to my fear!' He says: 'But that's a different intention to the previous one.' I say: 'Yes, I know, but the other one is no longer there. I don't even know the sentence any more.' He replies: 'OK, you wanted to understand where your mistrust comes from. That has now become clear. Have a look at it, this is where it comes from!' I look at it and say: 'I want to go on.' He says: 'Good, then set me up for the new intention.'

"I am suddenly confused again and ask: 'And what are we going to do with all them? Clear them all away?' And even while I'm saying it I realise how absurd that is and he mirrors that back to me by saying: 'You have to decide what you want! A new constellation and clear all those away, that's absurd!' I nod and have to laugh. I position him in his former place, but turned towards me this time and a bit more wedged in between mother and grandfather. He looks at the floor and comments: 'I feel exactly the same as before, just turned round. And those, the others, what are they looking at exactly?' He looks at me. 'They're all looking away', I say, while I feel tears pricking my eyes. 'They're all looking away. All of them, all of them!' And I'm all alone I think, but I don't say it. He says: 'If they're all looking away and you decide to look in the other direction, then you don't belong to them any more. Then you don't belong to them any more, to this lot.' A violent pain overcomes me and I begin to cry in complete despair. 'You lost your home!' he says. 'Yes' I say, 'that's why I went away. I couldn't stay there any more.' 'But only externally' he adds. 'Never inwardly!' 'Yes', I confirm.

He looks at me with a great deal of sympathy. Suddenly he holds his arms out and I fall into them, hold onto him and sob pitifully. And something inside me relaxes. Opens. I feel again. More than before. Very gingerly, because it's very new, but I feel. And all of a sudden I realise that in all my encounters I have sought precisely this situation, an encounter with this, my running away part. And always waited for it to turn round and accept me as I am.

"At some point I calmed down and eased myself out of the embrace. And I suddenly find it extremely embarrassing that I've left a huge tearstain on Prof. Ruppert's shoulder. I recover myself and we look at the situation. He says, still in the role of my intention: 'This is how I like you. Now I can trust you a little bit. And with that we can at some point leave this circle together.' I look around me. Then I move cautiously out of the circle towards Richard and the child and look at the situation. I say: 'I don't have to do it like them!' 'Of course not', says Professor Ruppert, he almost sounds a bit amazed, 'it's not the same situation!' I'm confused. He explains it to me and says: 'The one child was born anyway. The other children died. It's different. Similar, but different.' Only now do I realise that it's really like that. I'd never grasped that the situations are really different.

"While I stand in front of it, undecided and somehow uncertain, Professor Ruppert mirrors to me: 'The cushion for your own dead child is too big, too exaggerated, too idealised, too embroidered.' I nod. It feels much too big, this child. I start looking for something to replace the huge orange-red cushion: something small, something pretty. At last I find a little shell. 'Yes, that fits now, that's appropriate. It's also good as a symbol: something that hasn't opened', is Professor Ruppert's comment.

"I put the shell down in the place of the cushion. It has a similar colour to the carpet. Suddenly it seems to me that I'm on the beach and the sea is washing over the little shell and letting it sink gradually into the sand until I can no longer see it. And for the first time I'm really sad. It's like the pain of parting. What was previously just wild rebellion and quarrelling, has now become silent sadness. And at the same time it's as if Richard is getting further away. As if he's becoming paler and insignificant. 'I haven't got anything to do with his things!' I say. 'Yes, and perhaps this green, this green of past hope, can pale at some point', Professor Ruppert adds. I nod.

"'And the man you've met recently is called Richard as well?' he asks me out of the blue. And again I'm confused, start to say: No, that's not true, then remember that I had told him about Richard, my colleague, right at the beginning, sort of as an example of a 'normal' man as a potential partner, and I realise that they actually do have the same name. I nod. 'Yes, they have the same name.'

"We look at the constellation again from the side. He says: 'It's good like this. I'm calmer now; I felt very strongly that it was continually pulling at me. As it is now I can trust you and your actions. And I can perceive you as a whole. When I held you, I felt you as a woman. I think the two previous generations were not allowed to freely exercise sexuality, it was taboo.' I notice that this is very new for me and very unsettling. I ask myself for the first time how I've seen myself up till now. As a neuter? I look at him and say: 'Yes, I've always left, in my previous relationships.' He nods. 'But it's good like this now, a better feeling. You can trust yourself better now.' 'And rely on my instincts', I add and say: 'Yes, good, let's leave it like that.' 'Yes', he says. 'Do you now release me from my role?' I have to laugh because I'd forgotten. I take his arms, dust him down, release him and thank him.'

This account impressed me for several reasons:

- It showed me how many internal processes take place in a client that I, as therapist, only catch glimpses of, and how easily clients dissociate in a constellation.
- Children who cannot trust their own parents do not learn to trust themselves. It is therefore a good indication of the healing process if a person begins to trust himself again, his perceptions, feelings, thoughts and memories. If he no longer runs away from himself, but can accept himself as he is, with all he has experienced in his life.
- Trust in a therapist, in his knowledge, his ability, his methods and above all in his goodwill, is a significant catalyst to be able to gain self-trust again. We therapists therefore have to be prepared for clients to keep testing us to make sure we are trustworthy.
- The coincidental appearance of the therapy room (here it was the picture on the wall with a naked woman hidden in the background of the picture, the carpet hanging on the wall with the birds of paradise, the luxuriant plants) can be included in the context of a constellation in a startling way.
- Altering an intention is nearly impossible because the client has to take this step first before he can move on.

This example also shows clearly that an intention is not accidentally chosen. It marks the client's current horizon. If she wants to go beyond this, she first has to overcome an inner barrier, usually involving the letting go of a further illusion. Just wanting to know about something generally means that the person is not yet prepared to feel the trauma or remove the split between what he or she knows and the feelings. Knowing and feeling only come together in the whole context of the traumatising situation, and the person's own trauma situation can have a similar pattern as the trauma in the generations before.

So if someone has realised that he has traumatised parents, and he was and is not able to establish loving, supportive contact with them, then the question remains as to how he should handle his childlike need for loving parents. What should be done with the inner emptiness and disorientation of a child for whom his parents mean everything?

For a child, the realisation that there is no mother who can provide an orientation is like the loss of all hope and all reason for living, because the child cannot exist on its own. This leads to a loss of energy and motivation. The mother is the child's world, and therefore the inner emptiness is, for the child, the space without the mother. Life is a mountain that cannot be conquered without the mother.

Therefore the child part that surfaces has to be able to orientate itself according to the adult part that has become more mature through therapy. He can now name his life goals and the motives that make his life worth living. He knows that he can cope with many of life's tasks on his own, without help from outside. He can also ask for advice and help from people other than his own mother. He therefore needs

- to recognise that what he originally needed as a child – contact with the mother and being able to orientate himself according to her – are completely normal and appropriate needs,
- to be supported in his autonomy and ability to cope with his own fear of abandonment,
- the motivation to lead his life as an independent and adult person, and
- the orientation towards other people with whom constructive relationships are possible.

In addition, he has to allow himself to be happy even when he sees that other people are unhappy. As a symbiotically entangled child he was used to being unable to feel happy if his mother or father were suffering; his unhappiness was inseparably connected to their unhappiness. They were all caught up in their own victim roles. The person has to achieve the risky disentangling of this connection, which had been normality for him: "I can be happy even if my parents are still struggling with their traumas."

Some therapeutic approaches have developed the technique of offering the client an 'ideal substitute mother' – whether in the form of the therapist, or an abstract image – which I am sceptical about. I think that this technique continues to encourage symbiotic illusions, and actually obstructs the client from becoming an adult. I see disillusionment as a necessary phase of the transition to establishing real contact with one's self. It is important for the individual to recognise his own victim role and to name it.

Case study 54

Empty space (Ingrid)

Ingrid describes her internal process that occurs when, as a result of therapy, she recognises her symbiotic survival strategies as no longer useful:

"Dealing with my life up until now has taken a lot of space and time. Now this space inside me is empty and I don't know how to fill it. It's like a chasm opening up in me. I have the feeling that I haven't got an inner voice any more telling me what to do.

"I used to know how to deal with myself; I knew what I needed. But now there doesn't seem to be any clear line any more. How does one learn to live, when something like that has happened and has been overcome? When sadness overwhelms me and I so want to have someone who can show me how life works? Ok, I'm breathing, I'm eating, but what's the essence of why I actually am?

"First of all this morning I thought I would like to have a mother who shows me how to do things, like a mother does for her daughter. Then I started to cry because I just long to have a mother. I didn't think of my own mother at that moment, more along the lines of: I can be my own mother. But there's more that I have to do.

"At the moment there's nothing much that interests me. I go to work and try to fit in. I stay at home and don't go out. No one can force me anyway. I'm alone a lot. I have every opportunity in the world, but I'm just sad and angry, also at myself a bit, because I sound like a wet rag. I'm not though. I just want to know what direction is my life taking now?"

Healing pain

If someone does not feel anything, it is as if they are psychologically dead. It is therefore a definite sign of healing in patients if, during and following therapy sessions in which they have been able to access their split traumas, they experience pain and unpleasant psychological feelings such as despair, loneliness, resentment or anger for a while.

Many traumatised people fear that they will have to go through the pain of their psychological injuries again, and so they avoid dealing with their traumas. They would rather stick to the illusion of being able to lead, if not a pleasant, then at least a bearable life.

In my opinion it is not possible for someone to find his way out of his split psyche without coming into contact with the fear, anger and pain that he split off within himself. If someone wants to find his way out of the labyrinth and prison of his survival mechanisms, he first has to pass through the gate of his illusions, see through his own survival strategies, and recognise how much effort and energy he has spent pushing aside his traumatic experiences. Then he will see the next gate more clearly, behind which lie his fear, anger and pain. If he dares, with much more clarity and decisiveness than before, to go through this gate, he will meet his split-off traumatised parts and for a while he will be immersed in his feelings. He will not only experience his previous feelings, but he will realise that

- he is no longer as helpless as he once was because his healthy parts are now able to support him with their clarity and decisiveness,
- there is now hope for continued improvement,
- he can once more venture to feel with all his energy and express himself fully in his gestures, his voice, his words, and with his whole body.

Confronting the old trauma is a stressful thing for everyone. It lasts for a longer or a shorter while, depending on the trauma; sometimes it can be days, sometimes weeks. If the person does not interrupt this process, but gives it the space and time needed to remove the existing blockades and melt away the layers of ice accumulated by his survival strategies, he will escape from his previous state of permanent stress. Slowly he will arrive at the next gate, the gate to freedom, which can point him back into the realm of a healthy psyche.

Loving encounter with oneself

So what does it really mean to escape from a psychological split caused by a trauma? How can something that has been split be re-integrated into the whole psychological system? It is certainly not helpful to imagine that healing only happens when one relives the trauma, feeling once again the pain, the fear or the anger. Here I agree with Peter Levine that this simply represents blind abreaction: "The process of emotional abreaction can become a self-perpetuating mechanism by which patients crave further 'emotional release'." (Levine, 2011, p. 376).

My version of 'trauma confrontation' consists of joining together the split psychological structures enduringly into one stable and homogeneous unit that can stand up to reality. Seeing, feeling, thinking, remembering and self-awareness have to come together again and be able to deal with past and present reality. Part of this is being able to give up all forms of blanking out reality that were previously necessary to guarantee survival, and that repeatedly led to new damage and injury.

This can be done primarily by

- movement of the healthy psychological parts of the self towards the traumatised parts,
- a willingness to establish contact, and
- the understanding of how to achieve it.

In essence, therefore, I believe that a client who has gained the necessary courage by his persistent work on his life issues, and who decides from his healthy self to encounter with love and empathy his split-off and long-suppressed traumatised parts can resolve that trauma. The traumatised parts are picked up at the point where their development came to a standstill. They can then be given the chance to develop usefully and catch up on the growth opportunities they have missed up until now. The traumatised parts that have been kept out of the person's life, unable to evolve further, can then complement the psychological potential that the client has been missing in his healthy part.

Being able to feel and to express oneself again

In my view the crucial thing is that the blockage that came into being during the original trauma, that prevented the person from feeling, moving and expressing himself in his total vitality, can be removed, and the survival parts then lose their dominance. The purpose of establishing contact with the split off traumatised part is to allow the expression of feelings that were frozen by the trauma to flow freely again. Only then does the person exist in his true form, and not as a façade or a role that is expressed through the survival strategies.

Stability, confrontation and resources?

In trauma work there are different ideas about how to resolve trauma. There is the idea of the need for security and stability to be established before confrontation of the trauma can be attempted. However, methods of doing this that use breathing exercises, tapping or visualisation are, in my view, survival techniques, and I would add medication and the use of Bach flower or homeopathic remedies to this. All these techniques and tools do help keep the flood of trauma feelings at bay, but only temporarily.

However, the question then arises: how can the trauma be confronted while the survival strategies are active, even supported and strengthened by therapeutic intervention? When is the right moment for a trauma confrontation then?

In my view resources for working with trauma must not support survival strategies because, by definition, the task of such strategies is the prevention of contact with the reality of the trauma. Resources can only come from the healthy parts of the person that are in contact with reality without illusions.

Rituals?

Sometimes participants ask why a ritual cannot be used to give the transferred burdens back to the parents, as a means of resolving the trauma. The practice of handing the trauma burden back to the parents by handing over an object (a heavy stone), or by ritualised phrases (e.g. 'I've carried it a long time for you, now I'm giving it back to you.') is a well-intentioned idea, but in my view does not work. Children are entangled with their parents' traumas because they hope to establish contact with the parents through connection with the parents' trauma, and resolve their feelings of abandonment and loneliness. So it is not the parents who are at the centre of the trauma therapy I am describing here, but the person's own psychological splits. In addition, many traumatised parents who steer well clear of any form of psychotherapy would react with a total lack of understanding if their child were to say to them that they had carried their trauma burden. They like to think that their children have had a good life, had everything they wanted and are simply being ungrateful.

Doing things in psychotherapy that are unrealistic leads to the client's further disorientation and feeds their survival parts.

Reconciliation?

Many people with symbiotic traumas want to be reconciled with their parents. However, because the parents are traumatised it is an illusion to think that they can have any other relationship with them unless the parents address their trauma themselves. If the parents really do work on their own traumas, then there will be a basis for a new relationship. If they do not, the symbiotic entanglements will continue in the relationship with the parents.

The symbiotically-entangled survival parts fear the prospect of becoming autonomous and separate from the parents. They believe that they will then have to give up any form of contact with their parents. However, a person can only determine the kind of parental contact that is useful after he has understood and separated himself from his original childhood needs. It is usually easier for a person to imagine being reconciled with his traumatised parents than to feel his own symbiotic trauma.

Something that is realistic and can be pursued by everyone is reconciliation with oneself. We can overcome the perpetrator/victim splits within us that have developed from our own traumatisation. As long as we remain separated from our self, split in other words, any attempt at reconciliation with other people will be fruitless. The idea that we can reconcile with our parents is a nice illusion to hold onto for a while; such attempts will dissolve into thin air in the daily course of events. Only a person who has resolved the split inside himself can be at peace with his fellow man. Then he can see his parents as they are, without expectation or dependency on them being any other way. He will then meet them where a constructive relationship is possible. He is more able to see whether he still has to split and be under an illusion in order to establish contact with them, and so he is able to realistically assess what contact with his traumatised parents is still possible and what is not.

Being, and remaining oneself

A path can be found to escape from even the most severe traumas and entanglements. Martina has worked on her trauma for many years and now experiences times of happiness: "I want to tell you how happy I am at the moment. Even being happy is easy, not connected to anything or anyone, it just is, and that's unbelievably good and a big deal. I don't have to think for a long time: is that nice now, is that appropriate – but there's a clarity there, that it's right at the moment and I can decide whether I want it that way or not. That's a very liberating feeling. Autonomy! I can describe it another way: I'm living from inside myself, I'm not so dependent on other people, on the outside world, on my mama, on my papa, on my husband, on my clients who are all supposed to ensure my existence, but I can do it on my own, whenever I want and whenever I do anything! Simply brilliant, simply right, simply easy!"

Case study 55

A start in a new life (Karin)

Karin was able to experience what it's like to be at one with herself and feel a new relationship with her mother: "I set up my constellation yesterday, with the intention of being allowed to finally start my own life. In the three constellations before, that had always been the subject, but somehow it had got stuck. Yesterday I was standing in front of a representative for my mother with shaky legs, my whole body was really trembling, full of warmth; that was the amazing thing, but I absolutely decided that I was going to leave. For the first time I got an inkling, I think, of what you mean by love without entanglement – I was able to love her and at the same time I wasn't for her use any more.

And again I heard that she might not survive if I do that. It became obvious once more how much she needs me. I think that my experience with my own son helped me to go away from her – the fact that I love him and at the same time can use him as a projection screen for my own fears, that I love him and even so I can burden him. That helped me understand and feel that my mother is not bad, that she loves me, but that in this love there is a dark element from which I am allowed to free myself. And now it feels as if I've dared to take a giant leap, one I've been running up to in the last few months. As if I really can make a start in a new life, my own life. At the age of 43! It's about time. It wouldn't have happened without your support. I'm so grateful to you for that!"

A little while later this patient found a new job a long distance away from her mother.

9
A social and cultural framework for psychological health

Stop traumatising each other

The general findings of multi-generational psychotraumatology are clear-cut:

- Wars, which as a rule are mainly waged by men against men, traumatise the armed forces and the civilian population: men, women and children.
- People traumatised by war have traumatising relationships and entangle people (as yet untraumatised) in their trauma.
- Traumatised parents are the source of the traumatisation of their children, causing symbiotic traumas, neglecting them and even sexually abusing them.
- Mothers are the central link, transmitting the traumas of one generation down to the next.
- Children who suffer from a symbiotic trauma become in turn traumatised parents who traumatise their children.
- Traumatised people have no feeling for their healthy needs, and lose themselves in the endless twists and spirals of their survival strategies.
- Psychological and physical symptoms are the consequence of trauma.

311

- Assistance offered by people acting from their survival strategies is of no help; on the contrary, it leads to an increase in damage and entanglement.

The quality of our social and societal relationships is in my opinion very dependent on the extent of the traumatisation of the people involved. If we want to improve the circumstances of our society, we first of all have to stop traumatising one another.

For us men in particular, it ought to be clear that our potential for violence, the unconsidered way in which we can live out our sexuality, our strange concept of what makes a 'real man', can be a huge source of traumatisation for other men, women and children. The more the old role models prove themselves to be a source of destruction, clearly leading to a dead end, the more men are challenged to define themselves anew and develop a healthy form of autonomy. Gerald Hüther describes this in his book *Männer: Das schwache Geschlecht und sein Gehirn* (Men: The weak sex and their brain) with the memorable words: "Others cannot make you into a man, only you can – through a process of maturity and differentiation that every male goes through, and that takes place not so much externally as internally, within himself." (Hüther, 2009, p. 89).

For women this means that if they submit to societal relationships shaped by male violence and sexual craziness, if they only see themselves as dependent and reliant on men, then they will always stay the victims of trauma; they cannot be good and healthy mothers to their children, but will themselves instead be a source of traumatisation for their children.

So if we see clearly and distinctly

- how much human suffering is caused by traumatisation,
- what huge consequences traumatisation has,
- how much time and energy are wasted by the survival strategies on suppressing and compensating for the consequences of trauma,
- how laborious and protracted the healing process can be

we will receive the message: As human beings we must stop traumatising each other!

Everyone must therefore ask themselves:

- What societal structures cause trauma and increase the probability that people are traumatised?
- How might I let myself be traumatised by another person?
- When do I play a part myself in traumatising other people?
- To what extent do I offload my unaddressed trauma onto others?
- To what extent do I inflict fear, insecurity and strain onto others with my survival strategies?
- How do I get involved in relationships and systems that are shaped by the survival strategies of others?

Create a safe space for children to develop

The best way to interrupt the vicious cycle of traumatisation is to protect children from being drawn into them. According to the pioneer of psycho-history, Lloyd deMause: "The history of childhood is a nightmare from which we have only recently begun to awaken" (deMause, 1980). For centuries children were first and foremost the projective screen for the psychological damage of adults, who had themselves suffered terribly as children, carrying the victim/perpetrator spiral over from one generation to the next.

What children need above all is loving attention, security and a protected space in order to develop healthily. If the original (symbiotic) traumatisation of most children happens before, during or shortly after birth, a significant task for society must be to provide pregnant women and mothers of small children with a societal environment in which they are not traumatised. Pregnancy and birth should not be the domain of highly technical medical practitioners who do not understand the importance of the psychological bonding process between mother and child.

- Birth should take place in places of warmth and security, rather than cold and soulless delivery rooms.
- Babies should be left to determine the timing of their birth, when they are prepared to come into the world. Birth should not be dictated by the gynaecologists' time schedules, or a date chosen by the parents. The fact that 30–50% of births are Caesarean sections can surely not be attributed to medical emergencies.
- Women who have experienced pregnancy and birth are best suited to help other women give birth with as little use of epidurals, anaesthetics, episiotomies or Caesarean sections as possible.

Positive experiences of childbirth enhance the mother-child bonding (Kennell, 2007). Psychotherapy during pregnancy could help the expectant mother see physical and psychological symptoms of her own life history, and process her own traumatic childhood experiences so that they are not immediately transferred to the child within her (Klaus, 2007; Harms, 2008).

The younger children are, the less they are able to cope with any separation from their mother. Mothers therefore need sufficient support to be able to devote themselves without stress to the task of being as close as possible to their child for as much of the time as possible, particularly in the first years of the child's life. Mothers should not have to leave their child in the care of a nursery or a nanny, or give the child up for adoption, for career or financial reasons.

Mothers must have the opportunity to stay with their children in the case of illness too. Hospitals and clinics must be prepared for this and should make it possible for mothers and children to stay together. Any financial expenditure that enables mothers and small children to live together with as little stress as possible is a worthwhile investment in society. The cost involved in healing bonding disorders and traumatisations that have been brought about by ignorance and incorrect medical focus are far higher, and this is quite apart from the fact that the psychological damage may not be able to be remedied.

The whole medicinal and psycho-social health system should therefore be informed about bonding and trauma processes, and should orientate support programs accordingly. There is no point in focusing solely on the symptoms of hyperactive children for example, or children with learning difficulties and other psychological and physical disorders, trying to 'get rid of' these symptoms with medication or behavioural therapy treatment. Usually bonding disorders and symbiotic traumas are behind these symptoms, and these have to be understood and given appropriate therapeutic and pedagogic attention. And in my view all seemingly pointless medical examinations or operations on babies and small children, such as the removal of tonsils, nasal polyps, circumcision etc. should cease, since they are all likely to be the cause of trauma.

Children also need their fathers. They need them as a source of emotional support, for the playful investigation of the world around them, and as a role model. If a boy, they have to learn from their father how men are and how they can become a man. How to behave sensibly towards men also applies to daughters; from their father they should be able to learn to develop into a self-confident woman.

Developing a culture of healthy autonomy

Even if we humans have mitigated our vulnerability to the forces of nature in some regions of the earth, and have created an excess of goods, our economic system still does not allow our fears and cares to disappear. In our capitalist economy we are dependent on a dominating financial system and competition. Even large companies are dependent on what their competitors are doing and the current consumer mood. 'Consumers' on the other hand are completely dependent on the amount of money granted to them in a capitalist economic framework. 'More and more' is no guarantee for a happy life (Diefenbacher und Zieschank 2011; Pinzler 2011).

In politics too, more and more military power and forces do not lead to a greater feeling of security and independence. Every person in power watches others' strategies and intrigues with anxiety, afraid of losing his position.

Far too many people are caught up in watching others instead of looking at their own needs and abilities. Their existential and abandonment fears drive them, and vague hopes and visions draw them forward into an uncertain future.

What would happen if more and more people were at peace within themselves? If they were to focus more on themselves than on others? If they were to do what they think is sensible? What they really enjoy? If they no longer made themselves dependent on others? If they were to avoid people who spread fear and seek only power? If they were to take their life into their own hands and not wait for others to tell them what is right and where they should be going?

Everyone can ask himself in his partnership, his marriage, family, firm, party, or society, how much dependence is really necessary, and at what point he starts to conform with something he regards as wrong out of fear. I believe we humans have lived much too long in cultures of fear and dependence. What we cannot yet do well is live together with others in autonomy. We are only just starting to develop ideas for cultures of healthy autonomy. It seems to me to be a worthwhile project for the future.

References

Allen, J.G., **Fonagy**, P. & **Bateman** A.W. (2008). *Mentalizing in Clinical Practice*. American Psychiatric Publishing, Washington DC, USA.

Antonovsky, A. (1987). *Unraveling the Mystery of Health – How People Manage Stress and Stay Well*. Jossey-Bass Publishers, San Francisco, USA

Baecker, D., **Krieg**, P. & **Simon**, F. (2002). *Terror im System*. Der 11. September und seine Folgen. Carl-Auer-Systeme, Heidelberg, Germany.

Baer, U. & **Frick-Baer**, G. (2010). *Wie Traumata in die nächste Generation wirken*. Affenkönig Verlag, Germany.

Bäuml, J. (1994). *Psychosen aus dem schizophrenen Formenkreis*. Springer, Berlin, Germany.

Bauer, J. (2002). *Das Gedächtnis des Körpers. Wie Beziehungen und Lebensstile unsere Gene steuern*. Eichborn, Frankfurt/M., Germany.

Bauer, J. (2005): *Warum ich fühle, was du fühlst. Intuitive Kommunikation und das Geheimnis der Spiegelneurone*. Hoffmann und Campe, Hamburg, Germany.

Bentall, R. (2003). *Madness Explained: Psychosis and Human Nature*. Penguin, London, UK.

Bentall, R. (2009). *Doctoring the Mind: Why Psychiatric Treatments Fail*. Penguin, London, UK.

Bode, S. (2004). *Die vergessene Generation: Die Kriegskinder brechen ihr Schweigen*. Klett-Cotta, Stuttgart, Germany.

Bode, S. (2009). *Kriegsenkel: Die Erben der vergessenen*

Generation. Klett-Cotta, Stuttgart, Germany.

Bossard, M., **Ebert**, U. & **Lazarus**, H. (2007). *Soziale Arbeit in der Psychiatrie.* Psychiatrie-Verlag, Bonn, Germany.

Bowlby, J. (1969). *Attachment.* The Tavistock Institute of Human Relations, London, UK.

Bowlby, J. (1973). *Separation – Anxiety and Anger.* The Tavistock Institute of Human Relations, London, UK.

Bowlby, J. (1980). *Loss – Sadness and Depression.* The Tavistock Institute of Human Relations, London, UK.

Blasius, D. (2001). *Deutsche Erinnerungen – Wegstrecken der Psychiatriegeschichte.* In: M. Wollschläger (Hrsg.). Sozialpsychiatrie (S. 29–42). dgvt-Verlag, Tübingen, Germany.

Bradshaw, J. (1990). *Homecoming.* Bantam Books, New York, USA.

Breggin, P. (1991). *Toxic Psychiatry.* St. Martin's Press, New York, USA.

Chalmers, A. (1999). *What is This Thing Called Science?* University of Queensland Press, St. Lucia, Brisbane, Australia.

Chopich, E. & **Paul**, M. (1996). *Aussöhnung mit dem inneren Kind.* Bauer, Freiburg, Germany.

Colbert, T.C. (1996). *Broken Brains or Wounded Hearts.* Kevco Publishing, Santa Ana, USA.

Damasio, A.R. (1994). *Descartes' Error: Emotions, Reason and the Human Brain.* G.P. Putnam's Son, New York, USA.

deMause, L. (1974). *The History of Childhood.* The Psychohistory Press, New York, USA.

deMause, L. (2002). *Die Ursprünge des Terrorismus in der Kindheit.* In F. Simon (Hrsg.). *Terror im System.* Der 11. September und die Folgen. (S. 51–60). Carl-Auer-Systeme, Heidelberg, Germany.

Diefenbacher, H. & **Zieschank**, R. (2011). *Woran sich Wohlstand wirklich messen lässt. Alternativen zum Bruttoinlandsprodukt.* oekom Munich, Germany.

Dörner, K. & **Plog**, U. (1992). *Irren ist menschlich. Lehrbuch der Psychiatrie/Psychotherapie.* Psychiatrie Verlag, Bonn, Germany.

Drechsel-Schlund, C., **Feddern**, K., **Klinkert**, M. & **Ludwig**, C. (2010). *Reha-Management bei Traumatisierung nach Arbeitsunfällen.* Zeitschrift für Psychotraumatologie, Psychotherapiewissenschaft, Psychologische Medizin, 3, S. 33–48.

Eckart, W. U. (2012). *"Entgegen der Stimmung im Land ..." Deutsche Diskurse um Gewalttraumatisierung im Nationalsozialismus und die ›Entschädigung‹ der Opfer.* Trauma & Gewalt

1, S. 6–15.

Eschenbach, U. (1994). *Die Spiegelung frühen Leids im Bild.* In H. Häsing und L. Janus (Hrsg.). Ungewollte Kinder (S. 28–37). Rowohlt, Frankfurt/M, Germany.

Fest, J. (2000). *Hitler. Eine Biographie.* Propyläen, Munich, Germany.

Finkelhor, D. (2006). *Decline of Child Abuse in US: What can be learned?* Zeitschrift für Psychotraumatologie und Psychologische Medizin. 4, S. 9–16.

Fischer, G. (2011). *Minima Pathologica: Auszug aus der Logik der Psychotherapie – philosophische Grundlagen der Psychotherapiewissenschaft.* Zeitschrift für Psychotraumatologie, Psychotherapiewissenschaft und Psychologische Medizin, 2, S. 55–70.

Fischer, G. & **Riedesser**, P. (1998). *Lehrbuch der Psychotraumatologie.* Ernst Reinhardt, Munich, Germany.

Flatten, G. (2011a). *150 Jahre Psychotraumatologie.* Trauma & Gewalt, 3, S. 190–199.

Flatten, G. (2011b). *Neuropsychotherapie der Posttraumatischen Belastungsstörung.* Trauma und Gewalt, 3, S. 264–275.

Fröhling, U. (1996). *Vater unser in der Hölle. Ein Tatsachenbericht.* Seelze-Velber: Kallmeyer'sche Verlagsbuchhandlung.

Fuchs, T. (2012). *Das Gehirn – ein Beziehungsorgan: Eine phänomenologisch-ökologische Konzeption.* Stuttgart: Kohlhammer.

Goldner, C. (2003). *Der Wille zum Schicksal. Die Heilslehre des Bert Hellinger.* Ueberreuter, Vienna, Austria.

Gruen, A. (2002). *Der Fremde in uns.* Dtv, Munich, Germany.

Haas, W. (2005). *Familienstellen – Therapie oder Okkultismus? Das Familienstellen nach Hellinger kritisch beleuchtet.* Asanger, Kröningen, Germany.

Harms, T. (2008). *Emotionelle Erste Hilfe. Bindungsförderung, Krisenintervention, Eltern-Baby-Therapie.* Ulrich Leutner Verlag, Berlin, Germany.

Häsing, H. & **Janus**, L. (1994). *Ungewollte Kinder. Annäherungen, Beispiele, Hilfen.* Rowohlt, Frankfurt/M, Germany.

Hellinger, B. (2008). *Alles ist weit. Wegweiser.* Hellinger Publications, Bischofwiesen, Germany.

Herman, J. L. (2001). *Trauma and Recovery: From Domestic Abuse to Political Terror.* Pandora, London, UK.

Hinterhuber, H. (2001). *Die Seele. Natur- und Kulturgeschichte von*

Psyche, Geist und Bewusstsein. Springer, Vienna, Austria.

Huber, M. (1998). *Multiple Personen. Überlebende extremer Gewalt.* Fischer, Frankfurt/M, Germany.

Huber, M. (2003). *Trauma und die Folgen. Trauma und Traumabehandlung.* Junfermann, Paderborn, Germany.

Huber, M. (Hrsg.) (2011). *Viele sein. Ein Handbuch. Komplextrauma und dissoziative Identität verstehen, verändern, behandeln.* Junfermann, Paderborn, Germany.

Hüther, G. (2009). *Männer. Das schwache Geschlecht und sein Gehirn.* Vandenhoeck & Ruprecht, Göttingen, Germany.

Hüther, G., **Korittko**, A., **Wolfrum**, G. & **Besser**, L. (2011). *Neurobiologische Grundlagen der Herausbildung Psychotraumabedingter Symptomatiken.* Trauma & Gewalt, 4, S. 18–31.

Janus, L. (1993). *Wie die Seele entsteht.* Dtv, Munich, Germany.

Junge, T. & **Müller**, M. (2004). *Bis zur letzten Stunde. Hitlers Sekretärin erzählt ihr Leben.* List, Munich, Germany.

Kennell, J.H. (2007). *Kontinuierliche Unterstützung während der Geburt: Einflüsse auf Wehen, Entbindung und Mutter-Kind-Interaktion.* In K.H. Brisch und T. Hellbrügge (Hrsg.). Die Anfänge der Eltern-Kind-Bindung (S. 157–169). Klett-Cotta, Stuttgart, Germany.

Klaus, M.H. & **Klaus**, P.H. (1998). *Your Amazing Newborn.* Perseus Books, Reading, UK.

Klaus, P.H. (2007). *Kurzzeitpsychotherapie in der perinatalen Zeit zur Verringerung von psychischen und körperlichen Symptomen und zur Erleichterung der Mutter-Kind-Bindung.* In K.H. Brisch und T. Hellbrügge (Hrsg.). Die Anfänge der Eltern-Kind-Bindung (S. 237–252). Klett-Cotta, Stuttgart, Germany.

Klee, E. (2001). *Euthanasie im NS-Staat. Die Vernichtung lebensunwerten Lebens.* Fischer, Frankfurt/M, Germany.

Kloiber, A. (2002). *Sexueller Missbrauch an Jungen.* Asanger, Kröningen, Germany.

König, O. (2004). *Familienwelten. Theorie und Praxis von Familienaufstellungen.* Klett-Cotta, Stuttgart, Germany.

Lahore, I. (2009). *Spiegelneuronen, Quantenphysik, morphische Felder und Familienstellen.* Praxis der Systemaufstellung, 1, S. 60–63, Germany.

Lehmann, P. (2001). *Blinde Flecken in der psychiatrischen Wahrnehmung.* In M. Wollschläger (Hrsg.). Sozialpsychiatrie. Entwicklungen, Kontroversen, Perspektiven (S. 273–289). Dgvt-

Verlag, Tübingen, Germany.

Levine, P. (2010). *In an Unspoken Voice. How the Body Releases Trauma and Restores Goodness*. Berkeley: North Atlantic Books, USA.

Lewis, T., **Amini**, F. & **Lannon**, R. (2001). *A General Theory of Love*. Vintage Books, New York, USA.

Lütz, M. (2009). *Irre! Wir behandeln die Falschen. Unser Problem sind die Normalen*. Gütersloher Verlagshaus, Gütersloh, Germany.

Mahler, M. (1968), in collaboration with Manuel Furer. *On Human Symbiosis and the Vicissitues of the Individual, Vol 1: Infantile Psychosis*. International Universities Press Inc. New York, USA.

Matejcek, Z. & **Dytrych**, Z. (1994). *Abgelehnte Schwangerschaften und ihre Folgen*. In H. Häsing & L. Janus (Hrsg.). Ungewollte Kinder (S. 194–199). Rowohlt Verlag, Frankfurt/M, Germany.

Neitzel, S. & **Welzer**, H. (2011). *Soldaten. Protokolle vom Kämpfen, Töten und Sterben*. S. Fischer, Frankfurt/M, Germany.

Nonne, M. (1922). *Therapeutische Erfahrungen an den Kriegs-neurosen in den Jahren 1914 bis 1918*. In K. Bonhoeffer (Hrsg). Handbuch der ärztlichen Erfahrungen im Weltkrieg 1914/18 (BD. 4, S. 102–121). Leipzig, Germany.

Orwell, George (2004) Nineteen Eighty Four. Penguin Books, London, UK.

Pinzler, P. (2011). *Immer mehr ist nicht genug*. Pantheon, Munich, Germany.

Porter, R. (2002). *Madness. A Brief History*. Oxford University Press, Oxford, UK.

Preiter, M. (2010). *Die Logik des Verrücktseins. Einblicke in die geheimen Räume unserer Psyche*. Kösel, Munich, Germany.

Rahn, E. & **Mahnkopf**, A. (2000). *Lehrbuch Psychiatrie für Studium und Beruf*. Psychiatrie-Verlag, Bonn, Germany.

Rampe, M. (2012). *Resilienz – der Stehaufmännchen-Effekt*. Deutsche Angst-Zeitschrift 1, S. 16–17, Germany.

Reddemann, L. (2001). *Imagination als heilsame Kraft: Zur Behandlung von Traumafolgen mit ressourcenorientierten Verfahren*. Klett-Cotta, Stuttgart, Germany.

Riedesser, P. (1994). *Traumatisierung bei Kindern – Entwicklungslinien der Diagnostik und Therapie*. Zeitschrift für Psychotraumatologie und Psychologische Medizin 4, S. 5–6, Germany.

Roth, G. (2001). *Fühlen, Denken, Handeln. Wie das Gehirn unser*

Verhalten steuert. Suhrkamp, Frankfurt/M, Germany.

Ruppert, F. (2002). *Verwirrte Seelen. Der verborgene Sinn von Psychosen.* Kösel, Munich, Germany.

Ruppert, F. (2008). *Trauma, Bonding and Family Constellations: Understanding and Healing Injuries of the Soul.* Green Balloon Publishing, Frome, UK.

Ruppert, F. (2011). *Splits in the Soul: Integrating Traumatic Experiences.* Green Balloon Publishing, Steyning, UK.

Ruppert, F. (2012). *Symbiosis & Autonomy: Symbiotic Trauma and Love Beyond Entanglements.* Green Balloon Publishing, Steyning, UK.

Saß, H., **Wittchen** H.U. & **Zaudig**, M. (1998). *Diagnostisches und statistisches Manual Psychischer Störungen.* Hogrefe, Göttingen, Germany.

Schmidbauer, W. (2008). *Psychologie des Terrors. Warum junge Männer zu Attentätern werden.* Gütersloher Verlagshaus, Gütersloh, Germany.

Schneider, K. (1992). *Klinische Psychopathologie.* Georg Thieme, Stuttgart, Germany.

Seidler, G. H., **Wagner**, F. & **Feldmann**, R. (2008). *Die Genese der Psychotraumatologie. Eine neue Disziplin im Kanon der medizinischen Fächer.*Trauma & Gewalt 3, S. 178–191, Germany.

Index

Green Balloon Publishing

Other Publications

By Franz Ruppert:

Trauma, Bonding & Family Constellations: *Understanding and healing injuries of the soul* (2008)
Splits in the Soul: *Integrating traumatic experiences* (2011)
Symbiosis & Autonomy: *Symbiotic trauma and love beyond entanglement* (2012)

By Vivian Broughton:

In the Presence of Many: *Reflections on Constellations emphasising the individual context* (2010)
The Heart of Things: *Understanding trauma – working with constellations* (2013)
becoming your true self: *a handbook for the journey from trauma to healthy autonomy* (2014)

www.greenballoonbooks.co.uk
info@greenballoonbooks.co.uk

42 Goring Road, Steyning, West Sussex, BN44 3GF, UK.
Tel: +44 (0) 1903 814489 – info@greenballoonbooks.co.uk

Lightning Source UK Ltd.
Milton Keynes UK
UKOW04f115070817

306830UK00001B/41/P